The ROSE EXPERT

Dr. D.G. Hessayon

| 1st Impression | 300,000 |
| 2nd Impression | 50,000 |

Previous Editions:
12 Impressions   2,675,000

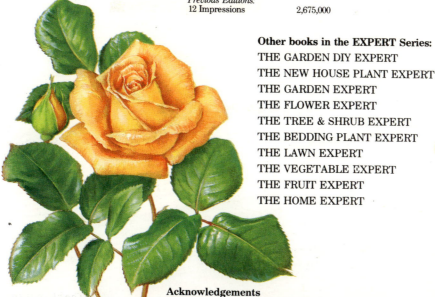

Other books in the EXPERT Series:
THE GARDEN DIY EXPERT
THE NEW HOUSE PLANT EXPERT
THE GARDEN EXPERT
THE FLOWER EXPERT
THE TREE & SHRUB EXPERT
THE BEDDING PLANT EXPERT
THE LAWN EXPERT
THE VEGETABLE EXPERT
THE FRUIT EXPERT
THE HOME EXPERT

Acknowledgements
The author wishes to acknowledge the painstaking work of Gill Jackson,
Jane Llewelyn, Jane Roche and Peggy Easterling. Grateful acknowledgement
is also made to Angela Pawsey, Len Turner, Lt.Col Ken Grapes, Carolyn Lathrope,
Joan Hessayon, Constance Barry, Linda Fensom and Angelina Gibbs.
John Woodbridge provided both artistry and design work;
Henry Barnett and Norman Barber prepared the paintings for this book.

A rose book without full-colour illustrations is like a beautiful bloom without perfume. Many people and
organizations have provided photographs, with Dick Balfour heading the list. Thanks are also due to
Cants of Colchester, James Cocker & Sons, Dickson Nurseries Ltd., Fryer's Nurseries Ltd.,
Gandy's (Roses) Ltd., C. Gregory & Son Ltd., R. Harkness & Co. Ltd., C. & K. Jones, E.B. LeGrice (Roses) Ltd.,
John Mattock Ltd., Meilland Star Roses Ltd., Sealand Nurseries Ltd., Brian J. Tysterman, Wheatcroft Roses Ltd.,
A-Z Botanical Collection, Bernard Alfieri, Pat Brindley, Floracolour, Robert Harding Picture Library,
Photos Horticultural, Rose Growers Association, Royal National Rose Society, Kenneth Scowen and
Harry Smith Horticultural Photographic Collection.

pbi PUBLICATIONS · BRITANNICA HOUSE · WALTHAM CROSS · HERTS · ENGLAND

Contents

Printed and bound in Great Britain by Jarrold & Sons Ltd., Norwich

ISBN 0 903505 25 8

CHAPTER 1
LOOKING AT YOUR ROSES

The first edition of The Rose Expert was for the 1980s — this one is for the 1990s. In the years between, much has happened in the rose world. Ground cover and Patio Roses have moved into the spotlight, and new varieties have appeared. About a third of the roses in the first edition have been replaced by more recent varieties.

Our national love of roses remains undiminished and they seem to have been with us for ever. But this plant came to us late as a popular bush for the garden. The first National Rose Show met with little interest from the general public. It was not until 1900 that the National Rose Society managed to increase its membership to 500. The simple truth is that Victorian gardeners regarded it as a plant for the shrubbery or the house wall but not for the flower bed.

And they were right. In the first half of the 19th century roses were large shrubs, or climbers which bloomed for only a few weeks. But everything changed during Queen Victoria's reign. Before she died the old roses of Europe, tough and hardy with red, white and pink flowers had been bred with the repeat flowering beauties from China. The blood of the Persian roses had been added, bringing bright yellow and orange to the beauty of our roses. All the ingredients were there for breeders to produce the ideal bedding plant.

Repeat flowering is linked with winter hardiness. A breathtaking array of colours is linked with vigorous growth, and it has been Britain's favourite flower since the First World War. Eight out of 10 gardens have one, and each year in this country about 35 million new ones are bought.

The choice is vast — there are thousands of varieties on sale. Nearly all are grown for the beauty or fragrance of their flowers, but there are also roses which bear decorative hips, leaves and even beautiful thorns. The plant may reach a height of 4 or 5 in., or it may tower 40 ft into the sky. This book shows you how to choose, plant and care for the fairest of all flowers.

Using rose catalogues

More roses are purchased over the counter than are ordered by post from growers, but for countless rose lovers one of the joys of the gardening year is studying the new catalogues.

New varieties get the largest photographs and the most alluring descriptions, but this does not always make them the best choice. For the ordinary gardener who just wants a few reliable bushes it is sometimes better to wait a year or two to see how the new ones succeed.

Many reliable favourites will, of course, be listed and they are the grower's own selection from the world's top roses. Read the descriptions carefully, but do not expect to find all the faults listed. Don't pay too much attention to the photographs — they give little idea of size or appearance in the garden, and printing cannot capture all flower colours. Yellows and oranges are usually quite accurate, but reds can be distinctly poor. Never reject a rose just because there is no photograph.

More than 80 per cent of rose sales are H.T.s or Floribundas. The Shrub, Miniature and Climbing Rose descriptions are therefore usually briefer and the photographs smaller, but do not neglect them on that account.

Using this book

For most readers, the main purpose of this book will be to learn more about the roses in their garden and about other varieties they may wish to buy.

For them the A–Z section (pages 7–72) provides information on the important properties of each rose, together with an overall assessment of its value for garden or exhibition use. There are two important features of these 332 descriptions — first of all, there has been no attempt to choose the "best" roses. The chosen ones have been included solely on the basis of their popularity and the probability of finding them in garden centres, stores, catalogues and the Royal National Rose Society Analysis of reliable varieties.

Secondly, catalogue-type descriptions have been avoided. Bad points have been listed as well as good ones, and in some cases the drawbacks outweigh the advantages.

Apart from information on varieties, the general reader will need guidance on planting (Chapter 5), upkeep (Chapter 6) and troubles (Chapter 7). For some, however, roses are more than just a flower — they are an absorbing hobby. For them Chapter 8 provides more specialised information on such topics as propagation, exhibiting, famous rose gardens, rose history and rose classification.

PLANT PARTS

BLIND SHOOT

TRUSS (FLOWER CLUSTER)

PEDICEL (FLOWER STALK)

STIPULE

LEAF STALK

LEAFLET

LATERAL BRANCH

HIPS (HEPS) produced after flowering

MAIN STEM (BASAL SHOOT or CANE)

NEW WOOD stem of current year's growth

LEAF

NODE

BREAKING BUD

DORMANT GROWTH BUD (EYE)

OLD WOOD stem of a previous year's growth

SNAG

SUCKER

NECK

BUD UNION

ROOTSTOCK

FLOWER PARTS

FILAMENT

PETAL

ANTHER

STYLE

STIGMA

OVARY

SEPAL

RECEPTACLE matures into a HIP

BRACT

ROOTSTOCKS

Modern roses are not usually grown on their own roots. They are budded on to the roots of wild roses or their close relatives. Rootstocks used by nurserymen include:

Rosa 'Laxa' Now the most popular of all. Reliable, transplants well and rarely suckers. Almost thornless for easy budding.

Rosa canina Produces the hardiest plants. Selected varieties used — a good choice for heavy soils. Suckers freely — popularity has declined.

Rosa multiflora Produces vigorous plants. Popular in the U.S. but not the U.K. Hard to bud and can be short-lived.

Rosa rugosa Sometimes used for standards. Not recommended for bushes — suckers freely and is not suitable for heavy soils.

GROWTH TYPES

The four basic growth types are ground cover, bush, standard and climbing (see chart below). A bush may be a Hybrid Tea, Floribunda or Shrub Rose (see page 7).

| 1 ft or less | 1¼ ft or less | stem 1 ft | 2 ft or less | over 2 ft | stem 2½ ft | stem 3½ ft | stem 5 ft | approx 8 ft | |
| PROSTRATE ROSE | MINIATURE BUSH | MINIATURE STANDARD | DWARF BUSH | BUSH | HALF STANDARD | FULL STANDARD | WEEPING STANDARD | PILLAR ROSE | CLIMBING ROSE |

FLOWER TYPES

Number of Petals

SINGLE	SEMI-DOUBLE	DOUBLE		
less than 8 petals Examples: Ballerina Dortmund Fred Loads Mermaid	8-20 petals Examples: Frensham Joseph's Coat Masquerade Topsi	MODERATELY FULL 21-29 petals Example: Pascali	FULL 30-39 petals Example: Dearest	VERY FULL 40 petals and over Example: Peace

Flower Colours

SINGLE COLOUR Petals similarly coloured throughout, although some changes may occur as blooms get older. Example: Iceberg	**BI-COLOUR** Colour of the outside of each petal distinctly different from the inside hue. Example: Piccadilly	**MULTI-COLOUR** Colour of the petals changes distinctly with age. Flower trusses have several colours at the same time. Example: Masquerade	**BLEND** Two or more distinct colours merge on the inside of each petal. Example: Peace	**STRIPED** Two or more different colours on each petal, one of which is in the form of distinct bands. Example: Rosa Mundi	**HAND PAINTED** Silvery petals with red blotched and feathered over the surface, leaving a white eye at the base. Example: Picasso

Petal Shapes

The petals of many roses are **plain**, but those of Hybrid Teas and some Floribundas are **reflexed**. A feature of a few roses is a wavy or **ruffled** edge to the petals, and in the *Grootendorst* varieties the petals have a carnation-like **frilled** edge.

PLAIN
Example: Nevada

REFLEXED
Example: Alec's Red

RUFFLED
Example: Just Joey

FRILLED
Example: F. J. Grootendorst

Flower Shapes

HIGH-CENTRED Classical shape of the Hybrid Tea – long inner petals forming a regular central cone.	**SPLIT-CENTRED** Inner petals confused, forming an irregular central area.	**BLOWN** Normally well-shaped bloom past its best – opened wide to reveal stamens.
GLOBULAR Bloom possessing many petals forming a ball-like arrangement with a closed centre.	**OPEN-CUPPED** Bloom possessing many petals forming a cup-like arrangement with an open centre.	**QUARTERED** Inner petals folded into 4 distinct sections rather than forming a cone.
FLAT Flat, low-centred bloom with a small number of petals.	**ROSETTE** Flat, low-centred bloom with many short petals regularly arranged.	**POMPON** Rounded bloom with many short petals regularly arranged.

FOLIAGE TYPES

Leaf Surfaces

The typical rose leaf has a smooth surface and is made up of five or seven leaflets. This standard pattern applies to nearly all garden varieties, but the shininess of the surface varies greatly. Some are highly polished as if they have been recently treated with oil — others are distinctly dull. Many varieties have leaves between these two extremes, so the three basic groups are **glossy**, **semi-glossy** and **matt**.

Not all roses have five or seven leaflets — a few such as *Rosa willmottiae* have attractive ferny foliage composed of many small leaflets. Also the surface of the foliage is not always smooth — the Rugosa group of Shrubs have leaves which are deeply ribbed (**rugose**), giving them a characteristically wrinkled effect.

GLOSSY
Example: Peace

SEMI-GLOSSY
Example: Red Gold

MATT
Example: Tip Top

RUGOSE
Example: Rosa rugosa alba

Leaf Colours

Nearly all mature rose leaves are green, varying from the insipid pale green of *Fred Loads* to the very dark green of *Cornelia*. As illustrated below, the three basic groups of rose leaf colours are **light green**, **medium green** and **dark green**. Some varieties have green foliage which is **bronze-tinted**, giving the leaves a coppery sheen.

There are exceptions to this general picture, especially amongst the Shrub Roses. Young foliage is sometimes distinctly purplish or crimson, and in some varieties such as *Rosa rubrifolia* and *Buff Beauty* this red coloration persists in the mature leaves. At the other end of the colour spectrum, the leaves of the Alba group are grey-green with a bluish tinge. Several varieties have attractive autumn tints — the Rugosa group is outstanding.

LIGHT GREEN
Example: Escapade

MEDIUM GREEN
Example: Blessings

DARK GREEN
Example: Korona

BRONZE-TINTED
Example: Bettina

HIPS

After the flowers have gone, the coloured and fleshy fruit cases of some Shrub Roses are an extra bonus in the autumn garden. The bottle-shaped red hips of *Rosa moyesii* and the large tomato-like fruits of *Frau Dagmar Hartopp* are well-known but there are many other varieties to choose from.

ROUND: LARGE & RED
Example: Rosa rugosa scabrosa

ROUND: SMALL & RED
Example: Rosa virginiana

ROUND: SMALL & BLACK
Example: Rosa spinosissima

ELONGATED
Example: Rosa moyesii Geranium

PRICKLY
Example: Rosa roxburghii

FLOWERING PERIOD

Repeat flowering Roses produce two or more flushes of blooms during the flowering season. Modern roses generally produce blooms at intervals throughout the summer months and into the autumn — one of the main reasons for the unrivalled popularity of Hybrid Teas and Floribundas. Repeat flowering varieties, also known as recurrent and remontant varieties, may produce some flowers between the main flushes. When this feature is strongly marked the descriptions perpetual and continuous flowering are sometimes used, but they are not strictly correct.

Once flowering Roses produce a single flush of blooms which usually last for several weeks. Occasionally a few flowers may appear in autumn, but this flowering is far too sporadic to be considered a second flush. The once flowering varieties most frequently bloom in June/July (**summer flowering**), but there are varieties of Shrubs and Ramblers which bloom in late spring, early summer or late summer.

FRAGRANCE

People will always smell an open bloom if they are trying to decide on its merits. Because of the importance of this feature, the descriptions in the A–Z Guide (pages 7–72) include an indication of the strength of the perfume of each variety — **no fragrance**, **slightly fragrant**, **fragrant** or **very fragrant**.

These statements, however, cannot be taken as a universally agreed assessment. Fragrance depends on many factors —
- **Personal taste**: Some people like heavy sickly smells, others prefer spicy or fruity aromas.
- **Personal sensitivity**: Some people have a deficient sense of smell, which unlike poor eyesight or deafness may go unnoticed.
- **Stage of growth**: Some roses are most fragrant in early flower, others when fully open.
- **Weather**: Warmth and high air humidity enhance fragrance.

Fragrance is, of course, associated with flowers but there are a few varieties with fragrant foliage — see *Lady Penzance* (page 67).

CHAPTER 2

ROSES A~Z

Each rose can be placed in one or other of the five classes listed below. In most cases placing a rose into its proper class is a simple matter, but in recent years the dividing lines have become increasingly blurred. The result is that the classification of some roses depends on which book or catalogue you are reading — you can find *Joseph's Coat* listed under Shrub, Large-flowered Climber or Floribunda!

A new method of classification (see page 108) has been adopted and is expected to replace the present simple system during the next few years. It has the advantage of removing the blurred boundaries, but it has the disadvantages of complexity and the abandonment of household words such as Hybrid Tea and Floribunda.

HYBRID TEA ROSES

see pages 8—29

The most popular class, available in both bush and standard form. The flower stems are long and the blooms are shapely. The typical Hybrid Tea bears blooms which are medium-sized or large, with many petals forming a distinct central cone. The blooms are borne singly or with several side buds.

FLORIBUNDA ROSES

see pages 30—46

Second only to Hybrid Teas in popularity. The Floribunda bears its flowers in clusters or trusses, and several blooms open at one time in each truss. This class is un-rivalled for providing a colourful, reliable and long-lasting bedding display, but in general the flower form is inferior to that of the Hybrid Tea.

MINIATURE ROSES

see pages 47—50

A class which is increasing in popularity due to its novelty and versatility. Miniatures can be used for edging beds, growing in tubs and rockeries or taking indoors as temporary pot plants. Both leaves and flowers are small, and under normal conditions the maximum height does not exceed 15 in. Many varieties are considerably shorter.

CLIMBERS & RAMBLERS

see pages 51—60

A class of roses which if tied to a support can be made to climb. There are two groups: Ramblers with long pliable stems, bearing large trusses of small flowers as a single summer flush, and Climbers with stiff stems, bearing flowers which are larger than Rambler blooms and may be repeat flowering.

SHRUB ROSES

see pages 61—72

A large class of bush roses with only one feature in common — they are neither Hybrid Teas nor Floribundas. The typical Shrub is taller than a bedding rose, and is a Species variety (related to a wild rose), an Old-Fashioned variety (dating back to pre-Hybrid Tea days) or a Modern Shrub Rose.

HYBRID TEA ROSES
(Large Flowered Bushes)

There are five classes of roses, as described on page 7, but when planting time comes around the average gardener looks no further than the Floribundas and the Hybrid Teas. And it is the Hybrid Tea which usually wins the day, because it is the aristocrat of roses.

Each flower on the bush or standard is a thing of beauty in itself. Here is the "classic" rose — a long, pointed bud which opens to reveal many velvety or satin-like petals, neatly reflexed and regularly arranged to form a high central cone. The range of colours is bewildering, the fragrance is usually moderate or strong. It is the prime choice for the show-bench and the flower vase. It is the flower which brings forth the comment "Now that's what I call a rose!"

But it was not always so. When Florence Nightingale tended her sick, the "classic" rose was unknown. It was a chance cross, a hybrid between a delicate Tea Rose and a Hybrid Perpetual, which gave rise to the first Hybrid Tea — *La France*. This event in 1867 is well-known to the keen rose grower — less well known is the lack of interest aroused by the discovery.

Nearly 20 years passed before the first lists appeared in catalogues, but then the popularity of the Hybrid Tea began. In 1900 the first yellow (*Soleil d'Or*) appeared and a steady stream of innovations, noted on page 111, has led to the thousands of different varieties which grace the gardens of the world.

The glowing descriptions in catalogues and the features of the H.T. bloom outlined above sometimes give the impression that this class represents the **ideal** rose. This is certainly not true — many H.T. bushes are upright and rigid and many H.T. blooms are ruined by wet weather. In general, Hybrid Teas bloom less frequently and provide less garden colour than Floribundas. They will not put up with bad conditions like many Shrubs and Floribundas, and the number of blooms produced by some Exhibition H.T.s is disappointing.

So choose carefully. As you will see in the following pages, not all Hybrid Teas are suitable for garden display — some are designed to be cossetted for appealing to show judges rather than the neighbours. The Hybrid Tea is quite rightly regarded as the Queen of Roses — shapely blooms on long stems appearing in flushes throughout the summer and autumn . . . but it is not always divine.

KEY TO THE ROSE GUIDES

Number of Petals
See page 5

Size of Bloom
Large = over 4 in.
Medium = 2 – 4 in.

Foliage
Leaf colour and surface quality
(see page 6)

Colour
See page 74

Fragrance
See page 6

Height in ft
Bush height under average growing conditions

Blooms: 45 petals
Dark crimson
Medium-sized
Very fragrant

Foliage: Medium green
Semi-glossy

Health: Average disease resistance

Growth: Moderately vigorous
Spreading

Awards:

Awards
Major awards from Britain and overseas
(see page 105)

Growth
Vigour (= robustness) and growth habit (spreading, upright, bushy, etc.)

Health
Resistance to mildew and black spot

Blooms:	30 petals Rosy red Medium-sized Slightly fragrant
Foliage:	Medium green Semi-glossy
Health:	Good disease resistance
Growth:	Vigorous Bushy
Awards:	

ABBEYFIELD ROSE
Other Name: COCBROSE

A rose of the mid 1980s, noted for the warm colour of its flowers. It is not a variety to choose if you delight in exhibiting or flower arranging — *Abbeyfield Rose* is a compact bush for bedding. It doesn't take up a great deal of space, so it is a good selection for the smaller plot. The blooms have high centres, but they are neither very large nor packed with petals — their claim to fame is that they appear in large numbers on leafy stems. Widely recommended as a standard.

Blooms:	30 petals Dark red Large Fragrant
Foliage:	Dark green Glossy
Health:	Good disease resistance
Growth:	Vigorous Upright
Awards:	

ACE OF HEARTS
Other Names: KORRED, ASSO DI CUORI

The large buds open slowly into velvety blooms which are cup-shaped when mature. Cut flowers last for a remarkably long time in water — according to at least one grower this variety is the best cut-flower bedding rose available today. The fragrance is noticeable but not very strong, and the large leaves are plentiful. The parentage of this Kordes variety is unknown and it has received no awards. Still, it has become a reasonably popular choice for flower arrangers.

Blooms:	45 petals Pale rose pink; pink reverse Large Very fragrant
Foliage:	Light green Glossy
Health:	Good disease resistance
Growth:	Vigorous Upright
Awards:	

ADMIRAL RODNEY

Not popular, but many experts believe that *Admiral Rodney* is one of the best roses you can buy for exhibition purposes. The pink blooms with their pale pink centres are exceptionally large and well-shaped — a frequent sight amongst the prize winners at major rose shows. The flowers are strongly scented and the rather tall bushes bear large, healthy leaves. However, it is not free-flowering enough for ordinary garden display — this variety is best left to the exhibitor.

Blooms:	45 petals Crimson Large, globular Very fragrant
Foliage:	Medium green Glossy
Health:	Good disease resistance
Growth:	Vigorous Upright
Awards:	

ALEC'S RED

Some experts still consider this to be the best red rose you can buy — choose it for bedding, cutting or exhibition. You will have no difficulty in finding this best-seller. Fragrance is an outstanding quality — very rich and sweet. It has an impressive list of virtues — vigorous healthy growth, strong flower stalks and abundant large blooms throughout the season. The flowers have good rain resistance and hold their colour well with age, but the rather pale crimson petals do not appeal to everyone.

Blooms:	22 petals Orange vermilion Medium-sized Slightly fragrant
Foliage:	Dark green Semi-glossy
Health:	Good disease resistance
Growth:	Very vigorous Upright
Awards:	

ALEXANDER
Other Name: ALEXANDRA

Brilliant flower colour is the outstanding feature — the vermilion is much more luminous than in its famous parent *Super Star* and the blooms have good rain-resisting properties. This tall bush is ideal for a large bed or for hedging, but it is not a good choice if you like large, full blooms with lots of petals or if space is limited. Young flowers have pointed centres and the long stalks make them excellent for cutting.

HYBRID TEA ROSES

Height in feet

ALPINE SUNSET

An English-bred rose which bears large, fragrant blooms suitable for general garden display and exhibition. It is a sturdy, tolerant variety which reaches the average height for Hybrid Teas, and the flowers are recommended for cutting. It comes from a good family (*Grandpa Dickson* is one of its parents), the bush is free-flowering and the colour is attractive. A minor drawback is its tendency to produce blooms in distinct flushes rather than continually.

Blooms:	30 petals Creamy yellow, flushed peach pink Large, globular Very fragrant
Foliage:	Medium green Glossy
Health:	Good disease resistance
Growth:	Vigorous Upright
Awards:	

APRICOT SILK

A well-named rose — the petals are an unusual shade of apricot with a surface which has a silky sheen. It is a must for the keen flower arranger — the elegant buds are borne on long stems and have excellent keeping qualities in water. In the garden it is a tall-growing bush with bronzy leaves which are purple when young. It will require spraying to protect it from mildew and black spot, and it needs careful pruning — hard pruning will spoil the display.

Blooms:	20 petals Apricot; reddish orange reverse Large Slightly fragrant
Foliage:	Bronze-tinted Glossy
Health:	Prone to disease
Growth:	Moderately vigorous Upright
Awards:	

BEAUTE

A rather low bedding rose with an abundance of dark green foliage. This variety is best known for its buds — long and shapely, beautifully coloured in orange-yellow and freely produced. Not surprisingly, this variety is popular with flower arrangers. The buds open into golden apricot blooms which have good rain resistance. The drawbacks are a lack of strong fragrance, rather loose flowers and the need for regular spraying against mildew.

Blooms:	25 petals Golden apricot Medium-sized Slightly fragrant
Foliage:	Dark green Semi-glossy
Health:	Prone to disease
Growth:	Moderately vigorous Branching
Awards:	

BELLE BLONDE

For many years this variety was regarded as one of the finest yellow Hybrid Teas for bedding, but its popularity is now declining. The colour of its blooms is a rich golden yellow which does not fade as the petals age. The bush is compact and free-flowering, with fragrant blooms which are rather larger than average. Unfortunately it is particularly susceptible to black spot, and is not really suitable for areas where this disease is a serious problem.

Blooms:	35 petals Golden yellow Medium-sized Fragrant
Foliage:	Dark green Glossy
Health:	Prone to disease
Growth:	Vigorous Upright
Awards:	

BETTINA

This variety is one of several yellow and orange Hybrid Teas bred in France during the 1950s with *Peace* as one of the parents. *Bettina* is quite distinct from the others because of the dark bronze veins which cover the orange petals. It has long been a favourite for use as a cut flower, and the bush is a good choice if your garden is in an area which does not suffer from black spot. It is vigorous and free-flowering, with blooms which are resistant to rain.

Blooms:	35 petals Orange, veined red or bronze Medium-sized Fragrant
Foliage:	Bronze-tinted Glossy
Health:	Prone to disease
Growth:	Vigorous Branching
Awards:	

HYBRID TEA ROSES

Blooms:	30 petals Coral pink Medium-sized Fragrant
Foliage:	Medium green Glossy
Health:	Good disease resistance
Growth:	Vigorous Upright
Awards:	

BLESSINGS

Blessings has been described as the ideal bedding variety, and yet it is neither exceptionally fragrant nor are the blooms exceptional in size or shape. The colour is attractive, but it is the sheer number of blooms on the bush which makes this rose so outstanding. From very early in the season until late in the autumn the pink flowers appear in great numbers, borne either singly or in clusters, maintaining their attraction even in rainy weather.

Blooms:	35 petals Silvery lilac Medium-sized Very fragrant
Foliage:	Medium green Glossy
Health:	Average disease resistance
Growth:	Moderately vigorous Upright
Awards:	

BLUE MOON
Other Names: MAINZER FASTNACHT, SISSI

Although it is generally agreed to be the best of the so-called 'blue' roses, this variety is distinctly pale lilac and not blue. Many people dislike the washed-out appearance of the petals in the garden, but indoors the blooms make excellent cut flowers. The buds are tall and pointed, the stems long and the fragrance exceptionally strong. *Blue Moon* used to have a good reputation for disease resistance, but nowadays spraying is often necessary. Die-back is a serious problem.

Blooms:	35 petals Deep pink; silver reverse Large Fragrant
Foliage:	Dark green Semi-glossy
Health:	Prone to disease
Growth:	Vigorous Upright
Awards:	

BOBBY CHARLTON

A popular choice for gardeners who dream of winning a prize at the flower show. It is an excellent exhibition variety — large, high-centred blooms of classic shape and with good keeping qualities on the show-bench. For garden display it forms a strong-growing and somewhat disease-prone bush with blooms which have a spicy fragrance. Unfortunately the flowers appear later than with many other varieties and the number of blooms can be disappointing.

Blooms:	20 petals Deep orange scarlet Large Fragrant
Foliage:	Dark green Glossy
Health:	Average disease resistance
Growth:	Vigorous Bushy
Awards:	

CAN CAN
Other Name: LEGGLOW

A short and compact bush for the front of the border. Despite its lack of inches, *Can Can* bears large flowers very freely — 'eye-catching' according to the breeder. The scent is sweet and quite strong — the colour a blend of orange, red and salmon. The blooms are borne singly or in clusters and the form of each one is nothing special. The real attraction is that they appear unusually early in the season — a good choice if you like to beat your neighbours.

Blooms:	50 petals Creamy gold, flushed pink and red Large Very fragrant
Foliage:	Light green Glossy
Health:	Prone to disease
Growth:	Moderately vigorous Bushy
Awards:	

CHAMPION

A good multi-purpose variety which has lost some of its popularity. For the exhibitor it has extra large, well-shaped blooms, although there are better varieties to choose from if showing is your main interest (see page 75). For the flower arranger there are long, pointed buds and for the gardener the compact bushes are sufficiently free-flowering to provide a good display of colourful blooms with a pronounced fragrance. Poor resistance to disease has become a problem these days.

HYBRID TEA ROSES

Height in feet

CHESHIRE LIFE

The outstanding feature of this rose is its ability to withstand cold and rainy conditions. The vermilion colour of its blooms will appeal to lovers of *Super Star*, but this new variety has the great advantage of outstanding resistance to disease. The bush is short or medium in height, bearing thick leathery leaves and an abundance of blooms which are brightly coloured. The main drawback of *Cheshire Life* is the absence of a strong fragrance.

Blooms:	35 petals Vermilion orange Large Slightly fragrant
Foliage:	Dark green Semi-glossy
Health:	Good disease resistance
Growth:	Vigorous Upright
Awards:	

CHICAGO PEACE

A colourful sport of *Peace*, discovered by chance in a Chicago garden. It has the great qualities of its famous parent plus the virtue of more attractive blooms. Copper and pink dominate the petal surface and the reverse is tinged with coppery yellow. An excellent general purpose rose reaching 3½–5 ft, depending on pruning. It can be used for bedding, hedging and exhibiting. Lack of strong scent is its only vice, and it is now less resistant to black spot than it used to be.

Blooms:	45 petals Pink, copper and yellow Large Slightly fragrant
Foliage:	Dark green Glossy
Health:	Average disease resistance
Growth:	Very vigorous Bushy
Awards:	

CONGRATULATIONS
Other Name: KORLIFT

This rose is often described as elegant. The bush is slender and rather tall — the buds are long and pointed. The clear pink flowers are beautifully formed and are borne in small clusters — you may find it listed with the Floribundas. *Congratulations* has never become really popular. One drawback is that the blooms pale as they age, but there are several good points — abundant autumn flowering, excellent hedging properties and blooms which last well in water.

Blooms:	40 petals Rose pink Medium-sized Slightly fragrant
Foliage:	Medium green Semi-glossy
Health:	Good disease resistance
Growth:	Vigorous Upright
Awards:	

DEEP SECRET

You will find this one in most catalogues because it has two outstanding features. First of all the colour — it is reputed to be the darkest of all red roses, darker even than *Josephine Bruce* or *Papa Meilland*. Secondly there is the fragrance — as rich and strong as you are likely to find these days. The bushes are medium-sized and the flowers are often borne in small trusses rather than singly. The buds are almost black — an unusual bedding rose for those who like dark colours.

Blooms:	40 petals Deep crimson Large Very fragrant
Foliage:	Dark green Glossy
Health:	Good disease resistance
Growth:	Vigorous Upright
Awards:	

DIORAMA

One of the best yellow roses for the bed or border. The flowers appear early in the season and you can expect an attractive display throughout the summer even if the weather is rainy. The free-flowering nature of *Diorama* in the autumn is one of its most outstanding features. The blooms are high-centred, which makes them popular with flower arrangers, but even recommended varieties have drawbacks — the blooms blow quickly and the leaves need black spot protection.

Blooms:	30 petals Deep yellow, outer petals flushed red Large Fragrant
Foliage:	Medium green Semi-glossy
Health:	Average disease resistance
Growth:	Vigorous Branching
Awards:	RNRS

HYBRID TEA ROSES

Height in feet

Blooms:	30 petals Tangerine, darker at edges Medium-sized Slightly fragrant
Foliage:	Bronze-tinted Glossy
Health:	Prone to disease
Growth:	Vigorous Upright
Awards:	

DORIS TYSTERMAN

An English-bred rose which was introduced in 1975 and soon became popular as a bedding variety. Its free-flowering nature and good performance in autumn ensure a pleasing display throughout the season, and the well-shaped, orange-red blooms on long, straight stems are excellent for cutting. There are few major drawbacks, although the blooms are only average in size, the leaves need mildew protection and the fragrance is not strong.

Blooms:	40 petals Creamy white, rimmed red Large Very fragrant
Foliage:	Medium green Semi-glossy
Health:	Prone to disease
Growth:	Vigorous Upright
Awards:	

DOUBLE DELIGHT

This American-bred rose aroused a great deal of interest when it was introduced in 1976 and its popularity spread to Europe. The main attractions are its strong fragrance and the novel colour of its petals — "like a vanilla ice dipped in strawberry juice" according to one of the catalogues. The ratio of cream to red on the petals is highly variable. The bush grows strongly, and the blooms are of exhibition size. They are freely produced and last a long time.

Blooms:	30 petals Deep pink Large Very fragrant
Foliage:	Dark green Semi-glossy
Health:	Average disease resistance
Growth:	Vigorous Spreading
Awards:	

DR MACALPINE
Other Name: PEAFIRST

A small, low-growing bush. It is usually found in the Hybrid Tea section of the catalogues — the large blooms have the classic shape you would expect in this group. The flowers, however, are borne in trusses with up to 10 blooms in each cluster, so some growers include this variety with the Floribundas. It is a rose of the 1980s and the parentage is unknown. The flower colour is not exceptional but the fragrance is — a good choice for the front of the border.

Blooms:	30 petals Orange vermilion Medium-sized Very fragrant
Foliage:	Dark green Semi-glossy
Health:	Prone to disease
Growth:	Moderately vigorous Branching
Awards:	

DUKE OF WINDSOR
Other Name: HERZOG VON WINDSOR

For many years a favourite with gardeners who have wanted blooms possessing the same luminous vermilion as *Super Star* but on a bush with a more compact growth habit. *Duke of Windsor* has very thorny stems which are densely clothed with large, leathery leaves and the flowers are borne in small clusters throughout the season. These blooms open rather quickly. The major problem is mildew — regular spraying with carbendazim is essential.

Blooms:	35 petals Golden yellow Large Very fragrant
Foliage:	Medium green Glossy
Health:	Good disease resistance
Growth:	Vigorous Upright
Awards:	

DUTCH GOLD

Within a year or two of its introduction in 1978 this outstanding variety was listed in many catalogues. Obviously a new yellow rose which was strongly perfumed and large enough for the show-bench was bound to be a success. The blooms are well-shaped and freely produced. The colour does not fade as the flowers age. Both its parents, *Peer Gynt* and *Whisky Mac*, are more compact in growth habit and the flowers they produce are smaller with a tendency to be open-cupped.

HYBRID TEA ROSES

ELIZABETH HARKNESS

One of the best cream-coloured Hybrid Teas you can buy. The colour of the large, high-centred flowers is hard to describe — the pale, creamy buff shades deepen in autumn. It is an early-blooming variety, continuing to flower freely throughout the season. The blooms are sweet smelling, although the perfume is not particularly strong, and they are excellent for cutting. *Elizabeth Harkness* does well in a good season, but like so many pale-coloured varieties it does not like rain.

Blooms:	35 petals Creamy white, shaded buff and pink Large Fragrant
Foliage:	Medium green Semi-glossy
Health:	Average disease resistance
Growth:	Upright Bushy
Awards:	

ENA HARKNESS

A great old favourite — the most popular red rose planted in Britain for many years. These days its faults are often highlighted — the need for good cultivation, the lack of vigour which is found in modern varieties and above all the weak necks which cause the blooms to hang their heads. But it is still widely grown because the beauty of its form and the richness of its colour have few rivals. It is free-flowering, especially in autumn, and there is little or no fading of colour.

Blooms:	30 petals Crimson scarlet Large Very fragrant
Foliage:	Medium green Semi-glossy
Health:	Average disease resistance
Growth:	Moderately vigorous Branching
Awards:	

ERNEST H. MORSE

Red roses may come and go, but *Ernest H. Morse* was introduced in 1964 and is still in the best-seller lists. It has proved to be thoroughly reliable, but it now needs some protection from mildew in a bad season. It is almost ideal as a bedding rose — large, fragrant flowers in glowing red which stand up to rain. They are borne prolifically throughout the season and the best of them can be used for exhibition and floral decoration. Grow this variety if you want a red-flowering standard.

Blooms:	30 petals Rich turkey red Large Very fragrant
Foliage:	Dark green Semi-glossy
Health:	Average disease resistance
Growth:	Vigorous Upright
Awards:	

FORGOTTEN DREAMS

Forgotten Dreams is perhaps an appropriate name for this rose of the 1980s. It has the large flowers and the exceptional fragrance you would expect from an offspring of *Fragrant Cloud*, but it has been overlooked. It is offered by comparatively few growers, and appears in none of the best-seller lists. The buds are pointed and the flowers are borne singly or in small trusses. Good as a cut flower — often recommended as a specimen bush or standard rather than as a bedding rose.

Blooms:	25 petals Cardinal red Large Very fragrant
Foliage:	Medium green Semi-glossy
Health:	Average disease resistance
Growth:	Vigorous Bushy
Awards:	

FRAGRANT CLOUD

Other Names: DUFTWOLKE, NUAGE PARFUME

One of the all-time greats which needs little description. Its crowning glory has remained untarnished since its introduction in 1964 — an intense perfume which some believe is unsurpassed by any other modern variety. The blooms appear very early and are well dispersed on the bush, making it an excellent bedding as well as an exhibition variety. But its reputation has declined — mildew as well as black spot can now be a problem and the colour soon fades with age.

Blooms:	30 petals Geranium red Large Very fragrant
Foliage:	Dark green Glossy
Health:	Average disease resistance
Growth:	Vigorous Upright
Awards:	

HYBRID TEA ROSES

Blooms:	15 petals Deep yellow Medium-sized Very fragrant
Foliage:	Dark green Glossy
Health:	Average disease resistance
Growth:	Vigorous Upright
Awards:	

FRAGRANT GOLD
Other Name: TANDUGOFT

This Tantau rose appeared in 1982 and is now to be found in the Royal National Rose Society's list of recommended fragrant roses. It has not really caught the public's fancy, despite its good bedding habit and strong fragrance. The colour of the frilled petals is attractive, but there are not many of them. These days a rose has to be outstanding to get to the top — amongst the newer yellow Hybrid Teas it is *Freedom* and *Pot o' Gold*, not *Fragrant Gold*, which have star quality.

Blooms:	30 petals Deep yellow Medium-sized Fragrant
Foliage:	Medium green Glossy
Health:	Good disease resistance
Growth:	Vigorous Bushy
Awards:	RNRS

FREEDOM
Other Name: DICJEM

Yet another yellow rose, this one introduced by Dickson in 1984. *Freedom* is expected to become one of the great names of the 1990s, because it has outstanding bedding as well as show-bench qualities. The yellow petals do not fade with age and they fall cleanly. The scent is pleasant and the leaves are abundant. Colourful, healthy, vigorous — a good choice for mass planting or as a standard. Quite widely available, but you will not find it in all the catalogues.

Blooms:	25 petals Orange-yellow and red Medium-sized Slightly fragrant
Foliage:	Dark green Glossy
Health:	Prone to disease
Growth:	Vigorous Bushy
Awards:	

GAY GORDONS

If you are looking for a compact, low-growing bush with bi-coloured blooms then *Gay Gordons* would be a reasonable choice. The flowers are similar to those of the much more popular *Piccadilly*, but the yellow is much richer. This variety has good rain resistance, the leaves are attractive and the medium-sized blooms are borne with remarkable freedom, but it is becoming increasingly difficult to find. Black spot can be a problem; spray early to control it.

Blooms:	35 petals Very deep yellow Large Slightly fragrant
Foliage:	Dark green Semi-glossy
Health:	Average disease resistance
Growth:	Vigorous Upright
Awards:	RNRS

GOLD CROWN
Other Names: GOLDKRONE, COURONNE D'OR

A tall-growing rose for the large bed or border. It has the good points of its parents — the vigour and large flowers of *Peace* and the colour, high-pointed buds and long stems of *Spek's Yellow*. The blooms are well-formed and suitable for exhibition, but split centres can be a problem. There is a major drawback — the early growth is often blind and so the display at the start of the season can be disappointing. Like other *Peace* children, it has never matched its parent's popularity.

Blooms:	30 petals Deep yellow Medium-sized Slightly fragrant
Foliage:	Pale green Matt
Health:	Good disease resistance
Growth:	Vigorous Upright
Awards:	H

GOLDSTAR
Other Name: CANDIDE

This Cants rose of the 1980s won top honours at the Hague. It has a special appeal for flower arrangers — the blooms are borne on long and straight stems. These flowers are carried singly or in small clusters at the top of the plant. A good garden rose, but the flowerless lower part of the bush is best hidden by planting a low-growing variety in front. The pure yellow blooms appear freely throughout the season, and the colour does not fade with age.

HYBRID TEA ROSES

GRANDPA DICKSON
Other Name: IRISH GOLD

The best pale yellow Hybrid Tea you can buy. It appears in most catalogues and all rose books sing its praises. Superbly formed blooms with long petals — the star of countless shows. In addition, its good rain resistance, freedom of flowering and late-season blooming make it an excellent bedding variety. But even an "ideal" rose can have a drawback or two. The bush sometimes has a gaunt appearance, and good soil plus feeding are necessary.

Blooms:	35 petals Lemon yellow, sometimes edged pink Large Slightly fragrant
Foliage:	Dark green Glossy
Health:	Good disease resistance
Growth:	Vigorous Upright
Awards:	RNRS · RNRS · RHS · B · H

HARRY WHEATCROFT

Fittingly named after one of the great characters of the rose world, you will either love this sport of *Piccadilly* for its flamboyant novelty or you will hate it for its garishness. Each large, pointed bloom is a riot of colour, and this variety is excellent for bedding — compact, free-flowering and rain resistant. Unfortunately it has little perfume and it will need spraying against black spot. The blooms are long-lasting and recommended for flower arranging.

Blooms:	25 petals Scarlet, striped yellow Large Slightly fragrant
Foliage:	Medium green Glossy
Health:	Prone to disease
Growth:	Vigorous Bushy
Awards:	

INGRID BERGMAN
Other Name: POULMAN

A recent addition to the list of red velvety roses. A good one to choose if you like this type of flower — it has started to pick up its share of awards and medals since its introduction by Poulsen of Denmark in the early 1980s. Its dense and leathery foliage makes it a good bedding and hedging rose. The flowers are borne singly on strong stems and they last well in water — a good flower-arranger's rose. It is a free-flowering variety, and is expected to be a popular 1990s rose.

Blooms:	35 petals Deep red Medium-sized Fragrant
Foliage:	Dark green Semi-glossy
Health:	Good disease resistance
Growth:	Vigorous Upright
Awards:	RNRS · B

JOHNNIE WALKER
Other Name: FRYGRAN

The blooms are the colour of whisky, as you would expect from the name. A 1980s rose bred in Scotland by Fryer — perhaps linked with its birthplace is the outstanding ability of *Johnnie Walker* to flourish in cold and wet conditions. The flowers are large and have a fine classic shape — they appear reasonably freely throughout the season. This is a strong-growing and rather tall variety — make sure that you provide enough room for the bushes.

Blooms:	20 petals Apricot Large Very fragrant
Foliage:	Medium green Matt
Health:	Good disease resistance
Growth:	Very vigorous Bushy
Awards:	RNRS

JOSEPHINE BRUCE

Several dark red, velvety roses have recently appeared but this old favourite still keeps its place in the catalogues. The average-sized bushes have a sprawling growth habit which can be controlled by pruning to inward-pointing buds. This variety is particularly good when grown as a standard. The early-season display is best — well-shaped blooms which are good enough for the show-bench. In late summer the petals tend to be ragged and there is a constant fight against mildew.

Blooms:	25 petals Deep velvety crimson Medium-sized or large Very fragrant
Foliage:	Dark green Semi-glossy
Health:	Prone to disease
Growth:	Vigorous Spreading
Awards:	RNRS

HYBRID TEA ROSES

JULIA'S ROSE

Blooms:	25 petals Copper-tinged parchment Medium-sized No fragrance
Foliage:	Reddish green Semi-glossy
Health:	Average disease resistance
Growth:	Moderately vigorous Upright
Awards:	

Named after famous flower arranger Julia Clements, this rose is grown as a source of cut flowers. The elongated buds open slowly to produce porcelain-like flowers. The colour is hard to describe — "parchment-like" is the most frequent description. Excellent indoors, but a poor bedding variety. Growth is upright, and the long straight stems give a spindly appearance in the garden. Provide good conditions and shelter against wind. Prune lightly.

JUST JOEY

Blooms:	30 petals Coppery orange, paler at edges Medium-sized Fragrant
Foliage:	Dark green Matt
Health:	Good disease resistance
Growth:	Moderately vigorous Bushy
Awards:	

This English rose, bred by Cants, is quite unmistakeable with its unique colouring and ruffled petals. It has become one of the most popular of all the bedding roses introduced in the 1970s, combining novelty with beauty and reliability. The buds are attractive and excellent for cutting, appearing with great freedom throughout the season. Not one for the show-bench, but the open blooms are colourful and rain-resistant. It blooms well into the autumn.

KING'S RANSOM

Blooms:	40 petals Rich pure yellow Medium-sized Fragrant
Foliage:	Dark green Glossy
Health:	Good disease resistance
Growth:	Vigorous Branching
Awards:	

Many roses come and go, but this American-bred variety first appeared in 1961 and is still in the catalogues, even though there are better yellow varieties these days. Growth is straggly but it has its good points — non-fading blooms which are high-centred and rain-resistant, bushes which produce stems, flowers and leaves abundantly, and buds which are beautifully shaped and excellent for cutting. It is not completely reliable in all soils — choose another rose if your soil is sandy or chalky.

KRONENBOURG
Other Name: FLAMING PEACE

Blooms:	45 petals Crimson; old gold reverse Large Slightly fragrant
Foliage:	Dark green Glossy
Health:	Average disease resistance
Growth:	Very vigorous Bushy
Awards:	

A sport of *Peace*, with the growth habit and shape of its parent. The blooms are much brighter — even more eye-catching than the colourful *Chicago Peace* (see page 12). It has not become a popular rose because the flowers discolour badly with age. The attractive young blooms soon turn dull and purple, and must be dead-headed regularly. Like other sports of *Peace*, it is no longer resistant to black spot. The big problem is that this sport sometimes reverts back to its parent.

LADY SYLVIA

Blooms:	30 petals Pale pink; yellow at base Medium-sized Very fragrant
Foliage:	Medium green Matt
Health:	Average disease resistance
Growth:	Moderately vigorous Upright
Awards:	

An old favourite, still widely grown for the cut flower trade and as a bedding rose. The blooms are classically shaped, making up in fragrance for what they lack in size. An outstanding feature is the abundance of blooms which appear during late summer and autumn, each flower being borne on a long stem. The bushes are rather tall, but as you might expect from an old variety the stems may be rather sparsely covered. A good choice for the keen flower arranger.

HYBRID TEA ROSES

Height in feet

LINCOLN CATHEDRAL
Other Name: GLANLIN

It is always romantic to hear of an amateur beating the legendary professionals — this rose was raised by G.W.T. Langdale and received the Royal National Rose Society's Gold Medal in 1985. The flower colour is most unusual with a tinge of yellow on the reverse of the pink and orange petals. The well-shaped flowers are borne profusely and some(but not all)experts predict that *Lincoln Cathedral* will become a popular rose in the 1990s.

Blooms:	30 petals Deep pink, gold centre Large Fragrant
Foliage:	Dark green Glossy
Health:	Good disease resistance
Growth:	Vigorous Bushy
Awards:	

L'OREAL TROPHY
Other Name: HARLEXIS

A sport of *Alexander* which is waiting to receive some of the popularity and adulation given to its illustrious parent. Judges in several countries have given it their highest awards, but it is still offered by only a minority of rose growers. *L'Oréal Trophy* has all of the good points of its parent — attractive foliage, luminescent flowers, a vigorous growth habit and a healthy constitution. There are two differences — the flowers are orange and the bushes are not as tall.

Blooms:	25 petals Orange Large Slightly fragrant
Foliage:	Dark green Semi-glossy
Health:	Good disease resistance
Growth:	Very vigorous Upright
Awards:	

LOVELY LADY
Other Name: DICJUBELL

A new pink, which will have to fight against all of the established Hybrid Tea pinks for a place among the best-sellers. Some experts expect it to obtain popular acclaim — there is an impressive list of virtues. The flowers are large and fragrant, the stems are strong and the leaves are large and numerous. It is also a healthy plant, and so it is recommended for bedding. The flowers are shapely and high-centred, which means that *Lovely Lady* may become a popular exhibition variety.

Blooms:	35 petals Rose pink Large Fragrant
Foliage:	Medium green Glossy
Health:	Good disease resistance
Growth:	Vigorous Bushy
Awards:	

LOVERS' MEETING

The powers that be can't agree where to place this orange star of the 1980s. A Cluster flowered (Floribunda) rose according to the Royal National Rose Society — a Hybrid Tea in the view of nearly everyone else. There is no disagreement about its virtues. First of all, the colour — a new one (clear indian orange) according to the breeder. The foliage is bronzy green and is borne on strong stems. The blooms are Hybrid Tea-shaped but are often borne in clusters.

Blooms:	30 petals Tangerine orange Medium-sized Slightly fragrant
Foliage:	Bronze-tinted Semi-glossy
Health:	Good disease resistance
Growth:	Very vigorous Upright
Awards:	

MADAME BUTTERFLY

An old favourite introduced over 70 years ago, but still capable of keeping its place in many catalogues. The charm of *Madame Butterfly* lies in flower colour and form, not size. The flesh pink blooms are not large, but they are perfectly formed with pronounced high centres. They are borne freely, and some disbudding is necessary. This variety has long been a favourite for cutting. Unfortunately, the bushes you buy nowadays have lost much of the beauty and form of *Madame Butterfly* in her early days.

Blooms:	30 petals Pale pink; yellow at base Medium-sized Very fragrant
Foliage:	Medium green Matt
Health:	Average disease resistance
Growth:	Moderately vigorous Upright
Awards:	

HYBRID TEA ROSES

Blooms: 45 petals
Dark crimson
Medium-sized
Very fragrant

Foliage: Medium green
Semi-glossy

Health: Average disease resistance

Growth: Moderately vigorous
Spreading

Awards:

MADAME LOUIS LAPERRIERE

One of the better deep red roses, even though it has declined in quality. It is still a good choice if you want a low-growing bush which will come into flower early and stay in bloom until late autumn. The flowers are strongly scented and shapely, with good rain resistance, but they are not large. The small leaves are reddish when young and healthier than most other dark reds such as *Josephine Bruce*. Another plus point is the good colour stability of the blooms.

Blooms: 40 petals
Salmon pink
Medium-sized
Fragrant

Foliage: Dark green
Glossy

Health: Average disease resistance

Growth: Vigorous
Upright

Awards:

MARY DONALDSON
Other Name: CANANA

Another pink Hybrid Tea, to compete with all the others. The bush is not remarkable — the larger-than-average leaves are dark and the growth habit is upright rather than bushy. The flowers, however, are a cut above the average pink — there are lots of petals and the classic shape is high-centred. *Mary Donaldson* can therefore be considered as an exhibition flower and also an excellent choice for cutting. Flower form and fragrance make it a good variety to grow as a standard.

Blooms: 35 petals
White
Medium-sized
Slightly fragrant

Foliage: Light green
Matt

Health: Prone to disease

Growth: Moderately vigorous
Upright

Awards:

MESSAGE
Other Name: WHITE KNIGHT

The catalogue description of this offspring of *Virgo* makes it sound most desirable — shapely, greenish buds opening into pure white, high-centred blooms which are large for a rose of this colour. The flower stems are long and straight and the bushes are free-flowering. Unfortunately this is not a rose to choose unless you actually like spraying regularly with a fungicide. It is very susceptible to mildew, and the blooms are damaged by rain.

Blooms: 30 petals
Coral salmon
Medium-sized
Slightly fragrant

Foliage: Light green
Semi-glossy

Health: Prone to disease

Growth: Vigorous
Bushy

Awards:

MISCHIEF

Introduced in 1961, *Mischief* remains one of the most popular of bedding roses. Its great appeal lies in the remarkable profusion of beautifully shaped and rain-resistant flowers which appear throughout the season. Flower colour is "cut strawberry" in summer but turns more orange in autumn. Flower size is variable — small blooms may appear, but disbudding can produce large blooms fit for exhibition. Not a good choice for gardens where rust is a problem.

Blooms: 40 petals
Deep bronze yellow
Medium-sized
Fragrant

Foliage: Dark green
Glossy

Health: Average disease resistance

Growth: Vigorous
Bushy

Awards:

MISS HARP

Some professional rose growers expected this variety to become a winner. Its long-lasting, elegant buds make it an excellent choice for the flower arranger. The Royal National Rose Society listed it as a reliable rose for beginners and for unfavourable positions, and its flowers are both long-lasting and reasonably rain-resistant. But despite its favourable features it never really challenged *King's Ransom* for the deep yellow Hybrid Tea crown.

HYBRID TEA ROSES

MISTER LINCOLN

A good choice if you want a velvety, deep red rose for cutting — the flowers are borne on long stems and last well in water. *Mister Lincoln* is also a fine variety for garden display in a large bed — it is less prone to mildew than the old dark reds such as *Chrysler Imperial*, and the blooms are less likely to turn purple with age. There are drawbacks — the attractive buds quickly turn into open-cupped blooms and the tall, unbranched stems make it an unsuitable bush for a small bed.

Blooms:	35 petals Dark red Large Very fragrant
Foliage:	Medium green Matt
Health:	Average disease resistance
Growth:	Very vigorous Upright
Awards:	US

MOJAVE

A strong and hardy rose, which many consider to be the best of the deep orange Hybrid Teas. The blooms are plentiful, and it is easy to see its appeal to the flower arranger — long slim buds, straight stems and practically no thorns. Its appeal as a bedding rose is less easy to justify — the bushes appear gaunt and leggy, the buds quickly open to produce loose blooms in which the stamens can be seen and the scent is insignificant. A rose with a distinguished past but a doubtful future.

Blooms:	25 petals Deep orange, veined red Medium-sized Slightly fragrant
Foliage:	Medium green Glossy
Health:	Average disease resistance
Growth:	Vigorous Upright
Awards:	RNRS US G P

MULLARD JUBILEE
Other Name: ELECTRON

An excellent bedding rose, for expert and beginner alike. It grows strongly and will tolerate poor conditions. When treated properly it produces a profusion of pointed buds, either singly or in small groups, throughout the season. These buds open rather quickly into loose flowers, which are not often suitable for the show-bench. In the garden, however, they can be spectacular — exceptionally large, rain-resistant and reasonably fragrant. Rust is now a problem.

Blooms:	40 petals Deep rose pink Large Fragrant
Foliage:	Dark green Semi-glossy
Health:	Average disease resistance
Growth:	Vigorous Bushy
Awards:	RNRS B US H H

MY CHOICE

This bi-colour was expected to become a best-seller after its Gold Medal award by the Royal National Rose Society. Its list of virtues is indeed impressive — profuse flowering, strong growth, superb scent, large blooms and above-average disease resistance. What went wrong? Nobody can be sure, but the following faults might be the cause — the flowers are rather globular and open quickly, which means they must be cut at a young stage for exhibition. Also, the foliage is rather dull. The number of growers has declined.

Blooms:	35 petals Pink; pale yellow reverse Large Very fragrant
Foliage:	Light green Matt
Health:	Good disease resistance
Growth:	Vigorous Branching
Awards:	RNRS RHS

NATIONAL TRUST
Other Name: BAD NAUHEIM

You will not find it in the list of roses to grow for fragrance nor for exhibiting, yet *National Trust* is one of the outstanding red Hybrid Teas of our time. The bushes lack height and the blooms lack the size of the show varieties, but it is an excellent choice for the front of the bed or border. The blooms are held erect, their shape is impeccable and their colour unfading. The free-flowering bushes are well-clothed with foliage which is coppery red when young.

Blooms:	60 petals Crimson Medium-sized No fragrance
Foliage:	Dark green Matt
Health:	Good disease resistance
Growth:	Vigorous Upright
Awards:	RNRS

HYBRID TEA ROSES

Blooms:	30 petals Pale pink; yellow at base Medium-sized Very fragrant
Foliage:	Medium green Matt
Health:	Average disease resistance
Growth:	Moderately vigorous Upright
Awards:	

OPHELIA

Keen rosarians sometimes grow the very early Hybrid Teas as museum pieces but *Ophelia*, the oldest of all in general cultivation, is still planted by ordinary gardeners for the beauty and fragrance of its flowers. Petals of palest pink, sometimes almost white, are arranged in classic form on blooms which appear in large clusters. Avoid this senior citizen of the rose world if the site is exposed or is subject to late frosts; keep an eye out for thrips in summer.

Blooms:	35 petals Dark crimson Large Very fragrant
Foliage:	Dark green Glossy
Health:	Prone to disease
Growth:	Moderately vigorous Upright
Awards:	

PAPA MEILLAND

This variety demonstrates the need to consider both the flower *and* the plant before deciding to buy. If you were guided by the flower alone then *Papa Meilland* would be one of the finest Hybrid Teas available. Nearly black buds open into large, dark red blooms, velvety-petalled and with a scent which is unsurpassed. Unfortunately the plant does not live up to the blooms — in the garden it is unreliable, it is not a prolific bloomer and it is extremely prone to mildew.

Blooms:	25 petals White, shaded cream Small or medium-sized Slightly fragrant
Foliage:	Medium green Glossy
Health:	Average disease resistance
Growth:	Vigorous Upright
Awards:	

PASCALI

Introduced in 1963, *Pascali* remains an excellent choice. It is less prone to mildew and much more resistant to rain than most other varieties of this colour, and the blooms hold their shape longer than many roses. It is one of the best of all varieties for cutting — the stems are long and straight, and the flowers last well in water. Despite the bouquets it is not the ideal white rose — the bushes are spindly, the blooms are rather small, the petals are not pure white and the scent is faint.

Blooms:	30 petals Salmon pink, peach at base Large Very fragrant
Foliage:	Dark green Semi-glossy
Health:	Average disease resistance
Growth:	Vigorous Bushy
Awards:	

PAUL SHIRVILLE
Other Name: HARQUETERWIFE

This Harkness rose is widely available and has become a popular choice. The unusual flower colouring has caught the public eye — the blend of pink, salmon and peach plus outstanding fragrance are inherited from its parent *Compassion*. Growth is leafy and rather spreading — the young leaves are reddish and the elegantly-shaped blooms are high-centred. Choose it for bedding or cutting, but you have to spray against black spot in disease-prone areas.

Blooms:	45 petals Pale or dark yellow, edged pink Large Slightly fragrant
Foliage:	Dark green Glossy
Health:	Average disease resistance
Growth:	Very vigorous Bushy
Awards:	

PEACE
Other Names: GLORIA DEI

For so long the world's favourite rose. Always vigorous, always reliable, the 5–6 in. blooms remain attractive from bud to the full-blown stage. It is not a rose for every location — it must have adequate space. It will reach 3½–6 ft high and should never be hard pruned. Nowadays it is sometimes susceptible to black spot so spraying is necessary. Its drawbacks are few — the lack of fragrance, the late start to flowering and the occasional blind shoot.

HYBRID TEA ROSES

Height in feet

PEAUDOUCE
Other Names: DICJANA, ELINA

Proof, if proof is needed, that it is outstanding quality rather than an outstanding name which turns a rose into a star. A larger-than-average bush well clothed with large leaves — the flowers are borne singly on strong stems. Pointed buds open to produce porcelain-like flowers — pale primrose at first but mainly ivory when mature. Despite the delicate appearance of the flowers, they stand up well to poor weather. A popular choice for bedding and cutting.

Blooms:	40 petals Ivory, pale yellow at base Large Fragrant
Foliage:	Dark green Glossy
Health:	Good disease resistance
Growth:	Vigorous Bushy
Awards:	(RNRS)

PEER GYNT

Peer Gynt possesses the basic ingredients of a successful bedding rose — attractive blooms which appear early in the season and continue to appear throughout the summer and autumn. The compact bush is taller than average and well-clothed with large leaves. The edges of the petals turn pink with age, providing a colourful garden display, but this variety is not really for the show-bench as the blooms are open-cupped. Weak mildew resistance is the only serious problem.

Blooms:	40 petals Canary yellow, flushed pink Large Slightly fragrant
Foliage:	Light green Matt
Health:	Prone to disease
Growth:	Vigorous Bushy
Awards:	(RNRS) (B)

PERFECTA
Other Name: KORDES' PERFECTA

The name of this rose describes the form of the flower — large and high-centred with a multitude of petals; when skilfully grown under glass it is as near perfection as the rose breeder has yet achieved. A wise and popular choice for the exhibitor but definitely not recommended for general garden display. The buds and early flowers are distinctly unattractive and the large mid-summer blooms can droop or even snap off in windy weather.

Blooms:	65 petals Cream, edged and flushed crimson Large Slightly fragrant
Foliage:	Dark green Glossy
Health:	Average disease resistance
Growth:	Vigorous Upright
Awards:	(RNRS) (RNRS) (RHS)

PICCADILLY

Piccadilly remains the most popular of the bi-colours. To see it at its best, look at young blooms in cool weather; with age and in hot sunshine the vivid reds and yellows merge and fade. It is a splendid bedding variety — very early and remarkably free-flowering bushes which bear attractive coppery foliage. There are a few drawbacks — petals are not numerous and disease resistance, once very good, has decreased in recent years.

Blooms:	25 petals Scarlet; pale yellow reverse Medium-sized Slightly fragrant
Foliage:	Bronze-tinted Glossy
Health:	Prone to disease
Growth:	Vigorous Upright
Awards:	(RNRS) (RHS) (R) (M)

PINK FAVOURITE

This American-bred rose is high on the list of disease-resistant varieties; mildew and black spot are almost unknown. Excellent for bedding — the shiny foliage is attractive and the pink blooms appear throughout the summer on top of sturdy stems. The high-centred flowers, darker on the outside of the petals than on the inside, start to appear rather late but this is its only drawback as a bedding rose. It is also a very popular exhibition variety — disbud to produce a single show bloom.

Blooms:	30 petals Deep pink Large Slightly fragrant
Foliage:	Dark green Glossy
Health:	Good disease resistance
Growth:	Vigorous Branching
Awards:	(RHS)

HYBRID TEA ROSES

Blooms:	55 petals Deep pink Large Fragrant
Foliage:	Bronze-tinted Semi-glossy
Health:	Good disease resistance
Growth:	Vigorous Upright
Awards:	

PINK PEACE

Like its famous parent *Peace*, this rose bears large blooms on vigorous bushes which are taller than average. However, there is no other similarity between the two varieties so the name *Pink Peace* is distinctly misleading. Growth is upright, not bushy; foliage is bronze-tinted, not dark green, and the loose, open-cupped flowers are strongly scented. The bushes do not reach the height of *Peace* and the foliage is susceptible to rust, but this pink offspring is more free-flowering.

Blooms:	35 petals White Medium-sized No fragrance
Foliage:	Medium green Matt
Health:	Good disease resistance
Growth:	Vigorous Upright
Awards:	

POLAR STAR
Other Names: TANLARPOST, POLARSTERN

No awards for this variety from the Royal National Rose Society — the supreme award (Rose of the Year) from the Rose Growers Association. It is generally considered to be the best white Hybrid Tea introduction for years. The high-centred blooms are exhibition quality, and are borne profusely on sturdy stems. The bushes are taller than average — rather upright but branching freely. Give it space, and grow *Polar Star* for cutting, showing and general garden display.

Blooms:	30 petals Old gold Medium-sized Very fragrant
Foliage:	Medium green Semi-glossy
Health:	Good disease resistance
Growth:	Vigorous Bushy
Awards:	

POT O' GOLD
Other Name: DICDIVINE

In several catalogues you will read that *Pot o' Gold* is destined to become the outstanding fragrant yellow Hybrid Tea of the generation. It has a number of good points — there is great freedom of flowering and weather resistance is good. The fragrance is strong and the blooms are borne in large sprays. However, in most gardens the blooms are not large and tend to be flat rather than high-centred. Still, an excellent rose for bedding and cutting.

Blooms:	35 petals Bright crimson Medium-sized Fragrant
Foliage:	Medium green Glossy
Health:	Good disease resistance
Growth:	Vigorous Branching
Awards:	

PRECIOUS PLATINUM
Other Names: RED STAR, OPA POTSCHKE

This rose from N. Ireland has won no awards in Britain, has blooms which are not high-centred classic beauties and its fragrance is sweet but not strong. Yet it has remained popular as a bedding rose since its introduction in 1974. The reason is its colour — dazzling red which can be seen from afar. These blooms are borne very freely in small clusters, and they are resistant to rain. Disease resistance is above average, but watch for mildew.

Blooms:	25 petals Cherry pink Medium-sized Very fragrant
Foliage:	Light green Semi-glossy
Health:	Prone to disease
Growth:	Vigorous Upright
Awards:	

PRIMA BALLERINA
Other Name: PREMIERE BALLERINE

You will find this rose in nearly all the catalogues. The glowing descriptions are justified as far as they go — *Prima Ballerina* is indeed a vigorous bedding variety, taller than average, with beautiful buds and shapely flowers which are outstandingly fragrant. Unfortunately it is now less free-flowering than it used to be and there can be quite long flowerless gaps in late summer. Also it is now susceptible to mildew so that regular spraying may be necessary.

HYBRID TEA ROSES

Height in feet

PRISTINE
Other Name: JACPIO

Not many American Hybrid Teas have success-fully crossed the Atlantic, but *Pristine* is an exception. Bushes are healthy and covered with large leaves, making it an excellent hedging plant. It is also useful for cutting and exhibiting, as the buds are long and the flowers very large. Despite all these points plus its exceptional fragrance, it has not reached the top 20 group. The shape of the bloom is good, but perhaps not as perfect as the catalogues claim.

Blooms:	25 petals Ivory, shaded pink Large Very fragrant
Foliage:	Dark green Glossy
Health:	Good disease resistance
Growth:	Vigorous Upright
Awards:	

REBECCA CLAIRE

Here is a rose with an almost unique claim to fame. It shares with *Alec's Red* the honour of receiving both of the Royal National Rose Society's highest awards. To win these awards it needed all the expected characteristics — health, classic high-centred flowers, vigour, fragrance etc. In addition it required something special, and that perhaps is the unusual colour of the blooms. It should have been a winner for the 1990s, but interest began to decrease quite soon after its introduction.

Blooms:	30 petals Light copper, blended coral pink Large Very fragrant
Foliage:	Medium green Semi-glossy
Health:	Good disease resistance
Growth:	Vigorous Bushy
Awards:	

RED DEVIL
Other Name: COEUR D'AMOUR

One of the most popular and successful exhibition varieties, which deserves all the praise it has received. The form of the blooms is perhaps the closest yet achieved to the perfect Hybrid Tea shape, and by disbudding, even a beginner can produce prize-winning flowers which are extremely large and fragrant. It is also a good bedding rose — the bush is large, vigorous and the flowers are borne freely. There is one serious drawback — the blooms are damaged by rain.

Blooms:	70 petals Scarlet; pale scarlet reverse Large Fragrant
Foliage:	Dark green Glossy
Health:	Good disease resistance
Growth:	Vigorous Upright
Awards:	

REMEMBER ME
Other Name: COCDESTIN

Remember Me has the good health and fine foliage you would expect from an offspring of *Silver Jubilee* and *Alexander*. This rose of the mid 1980s is widely grown and is expected to become increasingly popular. The flowers are well-shaped and are brightly coloured, but the most outstanding feature is their arrangement on the plant. Each flower is borne on a stiff stalk in a wide-spreading truss. Large flowered *and* Cluster flowered — rose classification is difficult!

Blooms:	25 petals Coppery orange, blended yellow Large Fragrant
Foliage:	Dark green Glossy
Health:	Good disease resistance
Growth:	Vigorous Upright
Awards:	

ROSE GAUJARD

It may seem surprising that such a well-known and well-loved rose should have its faults. The purists frown on the garishness of its colour, the tendency of its blooms to split and the absence of any worthwhile fragrance. But for the ordinary gardener it is a good choice for bedding — the bushes are vigorous, hardy, long-lasting and remarkably easy to grow in poor conditions. It stands up to rain and the blooms are borne very freely. The leaves are large and quite healthy.

Blooms:	30 petals Rose red; silvery reverse Large Slightly fragrant
Foliage:	Dark green Glossy
Health:	Good disease resistance
Growth:	Very vigorous Branching
Awards:	

HYBRID TEA ROSES

ROSEMARY HARKNESS
Other Name: HARROWBOND

Blooms: 35 petals
Orange yellow, blended salmon
Medium-sized
Fragrant

Foliage: Dark green
Semi-glossy

Health: Good disease resistance

Growth: Vigorous
Bushy

Awards:

The latest rose to bear the proud Harkness name — one for bedding rather than exhibiting. The shrubby bush is clothed with large leaves, which is just what you want from a garden rose. It also drops its petals cleanly and the flowers are an eye-catching blend of many hues. These blooms are borne singly or in clusters, and they open wide when mature. A good all-rounder but lacking that vital spark which would put it in everybody's catalogue.

ROSY CHEEKS

Blooms: 30 petals
Red; pale yellow reverse
Large
Fragrant

Foliage: Dark green
Glossy

Health: Good disease resistance

Growth: Vigorous
Bushy

Awards:

You would expect a rose with flowers which are fragrant, bi-coloured and as large as *Peace* to be on every gardener's shopping list. This has not proved to be so for this Scottish-bred rose — its failure to reach the big time is hard to explain. It is very free-flowering and the blooms are certainly striking. Growth is strong and it does not seem to have any health problems. The reason must be that the colour combination lacks popular appeal.

ROYAL HIGHNESS
Other Name: KÖNIGLICHE HOHEIT

Blooms: 40 petals
Flesh pink
Large
Fragrant

Foliage: Dark green
Glossy

Health: Prone to disease

Growth: Vigorous
Branching

Awards:

The catalogue description could make you rush out and buy one. Long pointed buds open into large and fragrant classically-shaped blooms with reflexed petals, each one on top of its tall stem like a delicate porcelain flower. Do buy one if you are interested in exhibiting, and if you can provide protection against rain. But it is not a good choice for ordinary garden display, especially if you live in a rainy area. It suffers badly in wet weather and is prone to mildew.

ROYAL ROMANCE
Other Names: RULIS, LISELLE

Blooms: 30 petals
Salmon peach
Medium-sized
Fragrant

Foliage: Dark green
Semi-glossy

Health: Good disease resistance

Growth: Vigorous
Bushy

Awards:

You will find this one in a number of catalogues, and of course in the Fryer's list as they introduced this De Ruiter rose to Britain. It really is a delightfully coloured flower of excellent shape which has many admirers, but there are relatively few suppliers compared with the mass-appeal roses. It has no obvious drawbacks — the flowers are not large and the scent is not particularly strong but many a top-selling rose shares these drawbacks. Perhaps its time will come.

ROYAL WILLIAM
Other Name: KORZUAN

Blooms: 30 petals
Deep red
Medium-sized
Fragrant

Foliage: Dark green
Matt

Health: Good disease resistance

Growth: Vigorous
Upright

Awards:

This deep crimson rose did not set the experts of the Royal National Rose Society on fire, but it was judged to be the joint Rose of the Year in 1987 by the Rose Growers Association. The flowers are beautifully formed and velvety, but are not particularly large. Obviously there had to be more to explain its success — important features are its strong growth, stiff stems, general good health, attractive foliage and pleasant perfume. It should be a favourite for years to come.

HYBRID TEA ROSES

Height in feet

RUBY WEDDING

Ruby Wedding proves that a variety can have popular appeal without large blooms, novel colouring nor a strong fragrance. The blooms, though nicely shaped, are rather small for a Hybrid Tea. The bush is spreading and below average height. A rose for the small garden or the front of the border — the flowers are borne on stiff stems and the growers recommend it for cutting. There are better red roses to choose from, unless you have a ruby wedding to celebrate.

Blooms:	30 petals Ruby red Medium-sized Slightly fragrant
Foliage:	Dark green Glossy
Health:	Average disease resistance
Growth:	Vigorous Bushy
Awards:	

SHOT SILK

A pre-War favourite which still keeps its place in some rose catalogues. Its main claim to fame is the unique colour of its blooms, still unmatched after more than half a century. The flowers, high-centred at first but soon opening wide, are freely borne on the neat bushes. The foliage is bronze-tinted when young. Unfortunately this old variety has now lost its vigour and is likely to be a disappointing selection. Choose the climbing sport which has retained the original vigour.

Blooms:	30 petals Salmon pink, shaded gold Medium-sized Very fragrant
Foliage:	Medium green Glossy
Health:	Average disease resistance
Growth:	Moderately vigorous Bushy
Awards:	RNRS

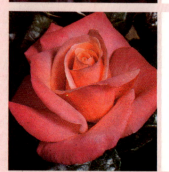

SILVER JUBILEE

The only sad note in the story of this rose was the death of its breeder shortly before its introduction in 1978 — Alec Cocker did not live to see the universal acclaim given to *Silver Jubilee*. Few newcomers gained such instant popularity, and there are several reasons. Shapely blooms on short stems, unusually long petals which do not lose their colour in hot weather, remarkably dense foliage and an outstandingly free-flowering habit combine to make it a splendid bedding variety.

Blooms:	25 petals Coppery salmon pink, shaded peach Large Fragrant
Foliage:	Medium green Glossy
Health:	Good disease resistance
Growth:	Vigorous Bushy
Awards:	RNRS RNRS JM B

SILVER LINING

The elegant blooms of *Silver Lining* can be seen at flower shows and they sometimes win prizes, but there are better varieties nowadays for exhibition. It is a useful variety for flower arrangers, as it is strongly scented and the blooms keep well in water. It is sometimes recommended as a bedding variety for general garden display, but it can be distinctly disappointing. It has lost its original vigour, flowering is no longer prolific and the display can be ruined by wet weather.

Blooms:	30 petals Silvery pink; silver reverse Large Very fragrant
Foliage:	Dark green Glossy
Health:	Prone to disease
Growth:	Moderately vigorous Branching
Awards:	RNRS

SILVER WEDDING

Silver Wedding and *Ruby Wedding* have several features in common — both were introduced by Gregory in the 1970s and both bear medium-sized flowers which are recommended for cutting. The flowers, of course, are completely different. *Silver Wedding* blooms are creamy white with a pinkish blush on the outside — the centre is a pale honey colour. These blooms are borne in clusters rather than singly and the bushes have a neat growth habit and bronze-tinted young leaves.

Blooms:	35 petals Creamy white Medium-sized Slightly fragrant
Foliage:	Dark green Semi-glossy
Health:	Good disease resistance
Growth:	Vigorous Bushy
Awards:	

HYBRID TEA ROSES

Blooms: 30 petals Yellow Large Slightly fragrant	
Foliage: Medium green Glossy	
Health: Good disease resistance	
Growth: Vigorous Bushy	
Awards:	

SIMBA
Other Names: HELMUT SCHMIDT, KORBELMA

This clear yellow rose from Kordes won gold medals in Switzerland and Belgium but not in Britain. Its most outstanding feature is the high centre of the very large bloom. There is nothing particularly delicate about this flower — it is remarkably weather resistant for a yellow rose and it also lasts well when cut. The stems are firm and *Simba* is a good garden rose, but the flowers do tend to appear in distinct flushes rather than continually.

Blooms: 30 petals Yellow, edged pink Medium-sized Slightly fragrant	
Foliage: Bronze-tinted Semi-glossy	
Health: Good disease resistance	
Growth: Vigorous Bushy	
Awards:	

SOLITAIRE
Other Name: MACYEFRE

This McGredy rose certainly started off with a flourish — it received the Royal National Rose Society's top award in 1985. It is a rather tall statuesque bush with classic-shaped blooms. Its growers predict that it will become one of the big names in the 1990s — a smaller version of *Peace*, to which it is not related. Better-shaped blooms and freer-flowering, they say, but it is still rather tall for the average bed. A great start in life but not yet widely grown.

Blooms: 35 petals Deep yellow Medium-sized Slightly fragrant	
Foliage: Dark green Semi-glossy	
Health: Average disease resistance	
Growth: Moderately vigorous Upright	
Awards:	

SUMMER SUNSHINE
Other Name: SOLEIL D'ETE

The demand for *Summer Sunshine* continues because of its colour — the deepest of all the yellow Hybrid Teas. The purity and brilliance remain from the bud stage to open flower and these blooms are freely produced and reasonably rain-resistant. They are borne singly on long stems. Unfortunately the constitution of the plant does not match the quality of the flower. It is an unreliable and indifferent grower, dying out quite quickly in some areas.

Blooms: 30 petals Golden yellow Medium-sized Slightly fragrant	
Foliage: Medium green Semi-glossy	
Health: Good disease resistance	
Growth: Vigorous Upright	
Awards:	

SUNBLEST
Other Name: LANDORA

There are not many pure yellow Hybrid Tea varieties and this one is highly recommended for bedding. It is not a great rose — its blooms are not large and its scent is slight — but it has no serious drawbacks. The shape of the blooms is good, the petals hold their colour and the tall bushes bear abundant flowers. It is an excellent variety for cutting — the slender buds are borne on long straight stems. There is nothing against it and there is nothing to make it a star.

Blooms: 35 petals Orange vermilion Medium-sized Fragrant	
Foliage: Medium green Semi-glossy	
Health: Prone to disease	
Growth: Vigorous Upright	
Awards:	

SUPER STAR
Other Name: TROPICANA

This variety was the super star of the 1960s with world-wide acclaim for the beautifully shaped blooms which seem almost fluorescent. It is found in countless gardens as a rather tall bedding rose, and its long stems make it excellent for cutting. It was never perfect — flowering begins rather late and the petals turn purple with age. Nowadays it has distinct drawbacks — the foliage is susceptible to mildew and old bushes tend to produce few flowers.

HYBRID TEA ROSES

Height in feet

SUSAN HAMPSHIRE
Other Name: MEINATAC

Susan Hampshire appears in some catalogues under its unattractive 'official' name — *Meinatac*. It was bred in France by Meilland and was introduced in 1974. This variety has a number of good points — the petals are an unusual shade of pink and the blooms are full enough and large enough for the show-bench. The fragrance has an old-fashioned quality and the leaves do not succumb easily to mildew. Despite its virtues, it has not become a popular rose.

Blooms:	40 petals Fuchsia pink Large Fragrant
Foliage:	Medium green Matt
Health:	Good disease resistance
Growth:	Vigorous Upright
Awards:	

SUTTER'S GOLD

An old favourite, but still perhaps the most fragrant of all the yellow roses. The tall pointed buds appear very early in the season, and flowering is prolific. The long stems, pleasant perfume and attractive colouring make *Sutter's Gold* an excellent variety for flower arranging, but there is a list of drawbacks. New bushes are slow to establish, and the growth habit is often lanky with sparse foliage. A disadvantage is the speed with which the buds open and the petals fade.

Blooms:	30 petals Pale orange yellow, shaded pink Large Very fragrant
Foliage:	Dark green Glossy
Health:	Average disease resistance
Growth:	Moderately vigorous Upright
Awards:	RNRS G US P

SWEET PROMISE
Other Name: SONIA

This is the pink rose of the cut flower world, sold in florist shops everywhere. The slim blooms, borne on long stems, are amongst the most highly acclaimed roses for flower arrangers. Unfortunately, *Sweet Promise* is distinctly unhappy outdoors in a wet, cool summer and is therefore best grown under glass. But if your garden is in a mild part of the country and if you are keen on roses for cutting then *Sweet Promise* is well worth trying.

Blooms:	30 petals Rosy salmon Small Slightly fragrant
Foliage:	Dark green Glossy
Health:	Average disease resistance
Growth:	Moderately vigorous Upright
Awards:	

TENERIFE

This rose was bred by an amateur from two famous parents — *Fragrant Cloud* provided the sweet perfume and *Piccadilly* provided the bi-colour effect. It is not a rare variety, but it has not reached the popularity one might have expected from its parentage. The colour of the blooms is variable, and there are some doubts about its claim to be free-flowering. Rain resistance is only average, and perhaps its major fault is its susceptibility to disease.

Blooms:	35 petals Deep coral salmon; peach reverse Large Very fragrant
Foliage:	Medium green Glossy
Health:	Prone to disease
Growth:	Vigorous Upright
Awards:	RNRS

THE LADY
Other Name: FRYJINGO

Roses have been named after people, places and products — this one commemorated the centenary of a magazine. The flower is of classic shape and is high centred with reflexed pale-coloured petals. Despite the delicate appearance these blooms stand up to wet and cool conditions remarkably well. The flowers are of exhibition quality when well grown and are borne freely over a long period, appearing singly or in small clusters. Fragrance is sweet but not strong.

Blooms:	35 petals Honey yellow, edged salmon Large Slightly fragrant
Foliage:	Medium green Semi-glossy
Health:	Good disease resistance
Growth:	Moderately vigorous Bushy
Awards:	RNRS BB

HYBRID TEA ROSES

Blooms: 30 petals
Orange bronze, shaded red
Large
Fragrant

Foliage: Medium green
Glossy

Health: Good disease resistance

Growth: Vigorous
Upright

Awards:

Blooms: 35 petals
Pink and copper; yellow base
Large, rather globular
Fragrant

Foliage: Medium green
Semi-glossy

Health: Good disease resistance

Growth: Vigorous
Branching

Awards:

Blooms: 30 petals
White
Medium-sized
Slightly fragrant

Foliage: Dark green
Matt

Health: Prone to disease

Growth: Moderately vigorous
Branching

Awards:

Blooms: 35 petals
Deep reddish pink
Large
Very fragrant

Foliage: Dark green
Glossy

Health: Average disease resistance

Growth: Vigorous
Branching

Awards:

Blooms: 30 petals
Golden apricot
Medium-sized
Very fragrant

Foliage: Bronze-tinted
Glossy

Health: Prone to disease

Growth: Vigorous
Bushy

Awards:

TROIKA

Other Name: ROYAL DANE

If you like copper-coloured roses then this is the one to choose. There is none of the die-back and disease which plague the older varieties in this colour group. The blooms are large enough for exhibition and the buds are long and shapely enough to make them excellent for cutting. But *Troika* is best considered as a bedding rose — the blooms appear early, rain resistance is good and the petals do not fade with age.

TYPHOON

Other Name: TAIFUN

An excellent bedding variety, with large open blooms. Each petal is a blend of orange, salmon and yellow — appealing to some but unfortunately not liked by people who expect their rose blooms to be a single pure colour. The compact bush generally produces plenty of blooms throughout the season and the display is especially good in autumn. The fragrance is variable — usually slight but occasionally strong.

VIRGO

Other Name: VIRGO LIBERATIONEM

One of the best loved white roses. Since the 1940s it has provided free-flowering bushes for garden display and beautiful long buds for cutting. The white flowers, occasionally tinged with pale pink, are best grown under glass. It is a poor choice nowadays for bedding — the bush is usually unattractive and sparse, and the foliage mildews badly. The blooms spoil badly in wet weather and today there are much better white varieties to replace this old favourite.

WENDY CUSSONS

This British-bred variety is almost the perfect bedding rose. Its list of star qualities is most impressive — outstanding perfume, large well-shaped blooms on large handsome bushes, a prolific flowering habit and above average resistance to rain. *Wendy Cussons* has an excellent reputation for longevity and reliability, but it is still not quite the perfect bedding rose — the strong cerise pink clashes badly with the colours of many other varieties.

WHISKY MAC

Much has been written about the *Whisky Mac* phenomenon. Experts have often described the drawbacks of this variety — unreliability when grown in average or poor soil, susceptibility to mildew, blooms which quickly become open-cupped and the loss of the free-flowering habit after a few years. Yet *Whisky Mac* has proven to be one of the most popular of all Hybrid Teas. The reason is simple — a unique colour plus an attractive and unusual scent.

HYBRID TEA ROSES

FLORIBUNDA ROSES
(Cluster Flowered Bushes)

A Danish hybridist, Svend Poulsen, once dreamt of producing a new race of roses, with modern flowers borne in large trusses continually throughout the season. He crossed Polyanthas (pompon roses) with Hybrid Teas and his first hybrid, *Else Poulsen*, appeared in 1924 — a Hybrid Polyantha. This was followed by other Poulsen roses and the Floribundas were born, but it was not until 1952 that this term was generally adopted.

An expert wrote recently that if he had to begin again, he would plant more Floribundas than Hybrid Teas. At first this may seem surprising, because the basic drawbacks of the typical Floribunda remain from the days when he planted his first rose garden. The blooms lack the size, beauty and fragrance of their more elegant rivals — the Hybrid Teas.

If the drawbacks remain, so do the advantages. Above all, there is continuity of bloom — varieties in this class flower almost continually throughout the summer and autumn, whereas Hybrid Teas tend to bloom in distinct flushes. And it is not only frequency of blooming, it is also quantity of

flowers — the Floribunda trusses generally provide a much larger splash of colour on the bush than is found on a Hybrid Tea. The benefits do not stop there. The average Floribunda is hardier, easier to care for and more reliable in wet weather than its Hybrid Tea counterpart.

The increase in popularity amongst expert and ordinary gardener alike has been due to the flood of new varieties in recent years. These have maintained the benefits, introduced new colours and have started to overcome the drawbacks listed earlier. *Margaret Merril* and *Fragrant Delight* rival the sweet-smelling Hybrid Teas for fragrance…*Paddy McGredy* and *Margaret Merril* rival the Hybrid Teas for elegance. These latter roses (Floribunda-H.T. type) have blurred the dividing lines and made classification difficult — you will find *Sunsilk* classed as a Floribunda in one book and as a Hybrid Tea in another. Large Floribundas with shapely H.T. blooms, such as *Queen Elizabeth*, are called Grandifloras in the U.S.

The Floribunda is the rose *par excellence* for providing colour in the garden. It can be grown as a bush or standard, in both formal and informal settings. There are tall varieties for providing hedges, and there are dwarf varieties (known as Patio Roses) for providing neat 1½ ft bushes for the front of the border. Interest in these Patio Roses increased dramatically during the 1980s.

KEY TO THE ROSE GUIDES

Size of Bloom
Large = over 3½ in.
Medium = 2 – 3½ in.

Fragrance
See page 6

Height in ft
Bush height under average growing conditions

Number of Petals
See page 5

Colour
See page 76

Foliage
Leaf colour and surface quality (see page 6)

Blooms: 40 petals
Orange scarlet
Medium-sized
No fragrance

Foliage: Medium green
Semi-glossy

Health: Good disease resistance

Growth: Moderately vigorous
Bushy

Awards:

Awards
Major awards from Britain and overseas (see page 105)

Growth
Vigour (= robustness) and growth habit (spreading, upright, bushy, etc.)

Health
Resistance to mildew and black spot

Blooms: 20 petals
Buttercup yellow
Small
Slightly fragrant

Foliage: Medium green
Glossy

Health: Good disease resistance

Growth: Moderately vigorous
Branching

Awards:

ALLGOLD

Although it won its Gold Medal in the 1950s, *Allgold* is still recommended in many catalogues. Flowering begins early, and goes on almost continually until late autumn. Even in rainy weather the colour of the blooms remains pure and unfading until the petals fall. However, there are better compact yellow Floribundas these days — the blooms are rather short of petals and the foliage may be distinctly sparse. Choose *Amber Queen, Baby Bio* or *Ard's Beauty*.

Blooms: 40 petals
Amber yellow
Large
Fragrant

Foliage: Dark green
Glossy

Health: Good disease resistance

Growth: Moderately vigorous
Bushy

Awards:

AMBER QUEEN
Other Name: HAROONEY

This new star won the 1984 Rose of the Year award and it's not hard to see why. The dark-leaved bush is neat and compact, and the many-petalled blooms are large and cup-shaped when fully open. The trusses bear many flowers and *Amber Queen* has got a good reputation for being free-flowering. The foliage is large and plentiful, making it a good bedding rose. It *is* fragrant, but the Hague Fragrance Medal was perhaps a surprise.

Blooms: 30 petals
Salmon pink
Large
Slightly fragrant

Foliage: Medium green
Glossy

Health: Good disease resistance

Growth: Vigorous
Bushy

Awards:

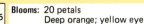

ANISLEY DICKSON
Other Names: DICKIMONO, DICKY

A bold and showy variety which won the Royal National Rose Society's top honours in 1984. The large trusses bear numerous warm-coloured flowers, and these are set off by the abundant foliage. A multi-purpose rose — grow it as a hedge or in a bed or border. In addition it is recommended for both cutting and exhibiting. *Anisley Dickson* has never quite reached the popularity which was expected — some blame the hard-to-remember name.

Blooms: 20 petals
Deep orange; yellow eye
Small
Slightly fragrant

Foliage: Dark green
Glossy

Health: Good disease resistance

Growth: Moderately vigorous
Bushy

Awards:

ANNA FORD
Other Name: HARPICCOLO

One of the new generation of small roses which is difficult to classify — a Miniature in some catalogues, a Patio Rose in others and a Floribunda here and elsewhere. A splendid small bush, covered with small leaves and trusses bearing many small flowers. Each yellow-eyed bloom is orange-red at first, fading slowly to orange. As an edging plant or a specimen in a pot, you can't do much better. Lasts well in water when used as a cut flower.

Blooms: 35 petals
Vermilion
Small
No fragrance

Foliage: Medium green
Semi-glossy

Health: Average disease resistance

Growth: Vigorous
Upright

Awards:

ANNE COCKER

All catalogue and textbook descriptions of *Anne Cocker* highlight its outstanding feature — the length of time its flowers stay fresh on the bush or in a vase. Obviously it is popular with both exhibitors and flower arrangers, but it is also a fine bedding rose. The large trusses are bright and colourful, and the individual blooms are borne on unusually long stalks. The quality of each bloom is excellent, but the flowering season begins rather late and there is no fragrance.

ANNE HARKNESS
Other Name: HARKARAMEL

August is a poor month for many roses, but this is the time when *Anne Harkness* is at its prime. Slow to come to flower, it compensates for the drawback by providing a fine mid- and late-summer display. The flowers are borne in large trusses, capable of braving both wind and rain. The flower stems are remarkably long, and the blooms last well when cut. Not surprisingly, it has become a favourite flower arranger and exhibitor rose, but it is also a good choice for hedging.

Blooms:	25 petals Apricot yellow Medium-sized Slightly fragrant
Foliage:	Medium green Semi-glossy
Health:	Good disease resistance
Growth:	Vigorous Upright
Awards:	

ARD'S BEAUTY
Other Name: DICJOY

They say that Pat Dickson was quite surprised when his yellow Floribunda was awarded the supreme award of the Royal National Rose Society in 1983. It has remained something of a Cinderella ever since — you will find it in only a handful of catalogues. It is an attractive and healthy bush with a free-flowering habit and medium-sized trusses of nicely-shaped flowers. But there is nothing unusual nor spectacular, and so it has missed popular acclaim.

Blooms:	20 petals Canary yellow Large Fragrant
Foliage:	Medium green Glossy
Health:	Good disease resistance
Growth:	Vigorous Bushy
Awards:	

ARTHUR BELL

Arthur Bell well deserves its reputation and popularity. The tall bush is well-clothed with an abundance of leathery leaves and the flowers are large and weather-resistant. The strength of the fragrance is rarely matched by any other Floribunda and it has a good record for mildew and black spot resistance. Flowering starts very early in the season and continues well into the autumn. Its failing is well known — the golden blooms fade to pale cream as they age.

Blooms:	20 petals Golden yellow Large Very fragrant
Foliage:	Medium green Glossy
Health:	Good disease resistance
Growth:	Vigorous Upright
Awards:	

BABY BIO

This dwarf Floribunda is a fairy story rose. Bred by an engine driver (Mr Smith of Sandiacre) in his small greenhouse, it was awarded a Certificate of Merit by the Royal National Rose Society in 1976. Masses of flowers are borne freely and continually throughout the season, and it has been called the best of the dwarf yellows. Its popularity has increased steadily over the years. The probable reason is the remarkable fullness and size of the blooms on such a small bush.

Blooms:	40 petals Golden yellow Large Slightly fragrant
Foliage:	Dark green Semi-glossy
Health:	Good disease resistance
Growth:	Vigorous Bushy
Awards:	

BEAUTIFUL BRITAIN
Other Name: DICFIRE

This 1983 Rose of the Year appears in most of the popular catalogues and has become a firm favourite. The blooms are borne in large trusses — each flower is not large but it has the classic H.T. shape. The colour is most unusual — hence the general appeal. But it has more than an out-of-the-ordinary colour to commend it — it flowers freely and the bush is well-clothed with leaves. A good choice, but there is little fragrance and not many petals.

Blooms:	20 petals Tomato red Medium-sized Slightly fragrant
Foliage:	Medium green Semi-glossy
Health:	Good disease resistance
Growth:	Vigorous Bushy
Awards:	

FLORIBUNDA ROSES

Blooms:	10 petals
	Red; cream eye
	Small
	No fragrance
Foliage:	Medium green
	Semi-glossy
Health:	Average disease resistance
Growth:	Vigorous
	Bushy
Awards:	

BOYS' BRIGADE
Other Name: COCDINKUM

Another Patio or dwarf Floribunda Rose — neat, compact and with trusses of flowers covering the small leaves. The number of flowers in each truss is unusually large and the bloom is unusual for a modern rose. Petals are few and there is a distinct white, cream or pale yellow eye. *Boys' Brigade* has never become a popular rose — it is difficult for single and semi-double types to reach the best-seller lists. Still, it *does* make a change from the others!

Blooms:	15 petals
	Yellow
	Medium-sized
	Slightly fragrant
Foliage:	Medium green
	Glossy
Health:	Good disease resistance
Growth:	Vigorous
	Bushy
Awards:	

BRIGHT SMILE
Other Name: DICDANCE

Bright Smile was introduced by Dickson in 1980, but it took several years before the public took much notice. This is a common problem with all few-petalled roses — the photographs in the catalogues do not do them justice. This low-growing Floribunda became increasingly popular during the late 1980s when its virtues were properly appreciated. The list is impressive – neat shape, early flowering, abundant foliage, absence of disease and a plentiful supply of flowers.

Blooms:	20 petals
	Cream, flushed buff and pink
	Medium-sized, cupped
	Fragrant
Foliage:	Dark green
	Glossy
Health:	Good disease resistance
Growth:	Vigorous
	Branching
Awards:	

CHANELLE

The peaches-and-cream Floribunda, much loved by gardeners who favour pastel colours in their roses. The bushes bear abundant glossy foliage which is exceptionally disease resistant. The blooms are nicely formed in bud, looking like miniature Hybrid Teas, but they open into flat, open blooms. These flowers have good rain resistance, and the flowering season carries on well into autumn. *Chanelle* has a good reputation as a reliable Floribunda, but it is hard to find.

Blooms:	35 petals
	Crimson
	Large
	Slightly fragrant
Foliage:	Dark green
	Glossy
Health:	Good disease resistance
Growth:	Vigorous
	Bushy
Awards:	

CHORUS
Other Name: MEIJULITA

Some of the experts have expressed surprise that this rose of the mid 1970s never became a best-seller. Its list of good qualities is most impressive — the blooms and trusses are large and the colour is dazzling. The bushes are attractive, the foliage is healthy and there is no shortage of flowers throughout the season. It is a good choice if you want a rich red Floribunda for the show-bench or a reliable red-flowering bush of average height for bedding.

Blooms:	35 petals
	Velvety orange scarlet
	Small
	No fragrance
Foliage:	Medium green
	Glossy
Health:	Good disease resistance
Growth:	Moderately vigorous
	Branching
Awards:	

CITY OF BELFAST

City of Belfast is a compact bush with attractive glossy leaves, red when young and medium green when mature. It is often recommended for the small garden where not many roses can be grown, because its free-flowering habit produces a constant splash of colour throughout the season. Rain has little effect on the slightly frilled petals, and both mildew and black spot are rarely a problem. Die-back, however, can be troublesome. It is a good rose for exhibiting and cutting.

FLORIBUNDA ROSES

Height in feet

CITY OF LEEDS

One of the popular Floribundas, widely recommended where the gardener wants a massed planting of a single variety or the beginner requires an easy-to-grow variety. *City of Leeds* proves that a rose does not have to be perfect to be popular. The scent is hardly noticeable, the foliage is small and the flowers spot after heavy rain. These drawbacks, however, are soon forgotten when you see the trusses of rich pink flowers covering the attractive bushes throughout the season.

Blooms: 20 petals
Rich salmon pink
Medium-sized
Slightly fragrant

Foliage: Dark green
Semi-glossy

Health: Average disease resistance

Growth: Vigorous
Upright

Awards:

COPPER POT

The pale coppery shades of this variety were a novelty when it was first introduced in the late 1960s, and the display late in the season can be very attractive. With the advent of new varieties it is no longer in many catalogues and is not a good choice. The tall stems are generally lanky and unattractive, and the flower trusses perched on top are sometimes quite small. Fragrance is virtually absent and you would do much better to choose *Iced Ginger*, which is a richer copper colour.

Blooms: 18 petals
Orange yellow; copper reverse
Medium-sized
Slightly fragrant

Foliage: Dark green
Glossy

Health: Average disease resistance

Growth: Vigorous
Upright

Awards:

DAME OF SARK

The reasons for choosing any particular rose can be many and varied. If your main object is to find a Floribunda which will appear striking and colourful from a distance, then there is no better choice than *Dame of Sark*. But the large flowers may not be things of beauty when examined at close range and *Dame of Sark* continues to lose her place in the catalogues. Choose this rose for low hedging or a large bed — health and rain resistance are good and it is reasonably free-flowering.

Blooms: 35 petals
Golden yellow, flushed scarlet
Large
Slightly fragrant

Foliage: Medium green
Glossy

Health: Good disease resistance

Growth: Very vigorous
Upright

Awards:

DEAREST

For many years *Dearest* was the top-selling pink Floribunda, but its popularity has waned. Its virtues are still there — beautiful pink blooms which are camellia-like and filled with spicy fragrance, trusses which are large and bushes which are clothed with dark and shiny foliage. As always, a good choice for bedding, cutting or exhibiting, but there are faults. This variety does not like wet weather and the foliage is susceptible to both rust and black spot.

Blooms: 30 petals
Salmon pink
Large
Fragrant

Foliage: Dark green
Glossy

Health: Prone to disease

Growth: Vigorous
Branching

Awards:

DISCO DANCER
Other Name: DICINFRA

Many rose blooms have a cool and tranquil appearance — others are warm and rich. *Disco Dancer* is different — the flowers are vivid with a luminescent quality. This may sound an excellent property, but the bright orange-scarlet can make surrounding plants look dull. The trusses bear a large number of blooms — this variety is often recommended for hedging. The *Disco Dancer* story is strange — it has won many awards but not popular appeal.

Blooms: 25 petals
Orange-scarlet
Medium-sized
Slightly fragrant

Foliage: Medium green
Glossy

Health: Good disease resistance

Growth: Vigorous
Bushy

Awards:

Blooms:	35 petals Orange salmon Medium-sized Fragrant
Foliage:	Dark green Semi-glossy
Health:	Prone to disease
Growth:	Moderately vigorous Upright
Awards:	

ELIZABETH OF GLAMIS
Other Name: IRISH BEAUTY

It is hard to be disloyal to one of the great roses of our time and one which has been grown in countless gardens since its introduction in 1964, but it has problems these days. It is now only a sound choice for reasonably good soil — it is definitely unsuitable for cold soils or clays. When well-grown, the high-centred buds open into lovely flat blooms borne in large fragrant clusters. You must remember to spray to keep disease at bay, and die-back can be a problem.

Blooms:	35 petals Silver pink, edged deeper pink Medium-sized Very fragrant
Foliage:	Dark green Glossy
Health:	Good disease resistance
Growth:	Very vigorous Bushy
Awards:	

ENGLISH MISS

An appropriate name for an English-bred rose which has petals of delicate blush pink. The classical pink Floribunda *Dearest* is one of its parents, but *English Miss* is much healthier and is less susceptible to rain. The buds open to form camellia-like flowers which possess a strong, sweet scent. The bush is densely clothed with shiny, leathery leaves which have a purplish tinge. *English Miss* is free-flowering and there is a quick repeat between flushes.

Blooms:	12 petals Rosy lilac; white eye Large Fragrant
Foliage:	Light green Glossy
Health:	Average disease resistance
Growth:	Vigorous Bushy
Awards:	

ESCAPADE

Some Floribundas are difficult to identify, even for an expert, but anyone can tell *Escapade* at a glance. The reason is its unique colouring — a white-centred ring of lilac petals surrounding a group of yellow stamens. The large flat blooms have a distinct musk-like perfume, and the bush is almost always in flower throughout the season. There is an abundance of foliage. *Escapade* is a good choice for cutting and for garden display, but its resistance to disease has declined.

Blooms:	40 petals Deep crimson Medium-sized, rosette-shaped Slightly fragrant
Foliage:	Bronze-tinted Glossy
Health:	Prone to disease
Growth:	Vigorous Branching
Awards:	

EUROPEANA

The red Floribunda which is easy to recognize. The foliage is distinct and outstandingly attractive — deep reddish purple when young and glistening bronzy green when mature. The huge trusses of deep red flowers bow down under their own weight, especially in rainy weather. A real eye-catcher, but you must know how to treat it. Plant *Europeana* in groups, with no more than 1¾ ft between the plants, so that the trusses will be supported. Spray regularly against mildew.

Blooms:	30 petals Vivid scarlet Medium-sized Slightly fragrant
Foliage:	Dark green Glossy
Health:	Average disease resistance
Growth:	Vigorous Branching
Awards:	

EVELYN FISON
Other Name: IRISH WONDER

One of the older bright red Floribundas but regarded by a few experts as still the best. It has an excellent reputation for reliability, and neither bright sun nor heavy rain seem to damage the blooms. The trusses are large and well-spaced, and it is extremely prolific. *Evelyn Fison* is hard to fault as a bedding rose — perhaps the amount of foliage is sometimes inadequate and the reputation for outstanding disease resistance is a little overrated.

FLORIBUNDA ROSES

Height in feet

EYE PAINT

This rose is one of the most unusual of all Floribundas, and you will need to know something about its growth and flowering habit before planting it in the rose garden. The small flowers are borne in great profusion, looking quite unlike the blooms which appear on modern roses. The bush is extremely vigorous, soon reaching 4 ft or more, and it is best grown as a hedge or in the shrub border, where its bright flowers from June to September make a welcome addition.

Blooms: 7 petals
Scarlet; white eye
Small
No fragrance

Foliage: Medium green
Semi-glossy

Health: Average disease resistance

Growth: Very vigorous
Bushy

Awards:

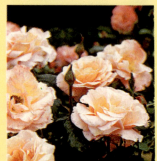

FRAGRANT DELIGHT

If you like Floribundas, strong fragrance and copper-coloured blooms, then *Fragrant Delight* is undoubtedly the rose for you. This offspring of *Chanelle* and *Whisky Mac* was introduced in the late 1970s, and the fine shape of the young blooms, together with the small size of the trusses led at least one grower to include it in the Hybrid Tea section of his catalogue. The young leaves are bronzy green, turning mid-green and remaining very shiny as they mature.

Blooms: 20 petals
Coppery salmon; yellow at base
Large
Very fragrant

Foliage: Medium green
Glossy

Health: Good disease resistance

Growth: Very vigorous
Upright

Awards:

FRENSHAM

For many years after the War, *Frensham* was the most popular red Floribunda. Now it is available from only a few growers, because the new reds offer disease resistance and fuller blooms. *Frensham's* problem is that it has become susceptible to mildew, but if you are prepared to spray then this old favourite will provide large bushes for hedging or borders. Glossy foliage is abundant, the freedom and continuity of flowering are remarkable and the trusses are large.

Blooms: 15 petals
Deep crimson
Medium-sized
No fragrance

Foliage: Medium green
Glossy

Health: Prone to disease

Growth: Very vigorous
Branching

Awards:

GENTLE TOUCH
Other Name: DICLULU

The outstanding feature of this Patio Rose is the beautiful form of the blooms — high-centred with a classic Hybrid Tea shape. With age, however, these flowers open flat. The trusses are strong and sturdy with a score of pink flowers — these clusters appear all season long. The professional growers judged it to be The Rose of the Year for 1986. *Gentle Touch* can be used anywhere in the garden where you need a compact variety, but keep a watch for mildew in late summer.

Blooms: 17 petals
Pale pink
Small
Slightly fragrant

Foliage: Medium green
Semi-glossy

Health: Average disease resistance

Growth: Moderately vigorous
Bushy

Awards:

GERALDINE
Other Name: PEAHAZE

The catalogues describe this one as 'real' orange. This means that it is the colour of orange peel — near, but not quite. Stems are strong and the clusters are colourful with shapely flowers. These blooms last well in water — *Geraldine* is well worth considering if flower arranging or winning prizes at shows is your main interest. This variety also makes an attractive specimen bush for garden display and created a good deal of public interest at the Chelsea Flower Show when introduced.

Blooms: 20 petals
Orange
Medium-sized
Slightly fragrant

Foliage: Light green
Semi-glossy

Health: Good disease resistance

Growth: Vigorous
Bushy

Awards:

FLORIBUNDA ROSES

Blooms:	25 petals Golden amber Medium-sized Slightly fragrant
Foliage:	Dark green Glossy
Health:	Good disease resistance
Growth:	Vigorous Upright
Awards:	

GLENFIDDICH

Glenfiddich is one of the most popular Floribundas and is grown all over Britain, but it is truly a flower of Scotland. Raised by Cocker of Aberdeen, it was named after the Scotch Whisky which is reminiscent of its colour, and it is in Scotland and the northern counties where it is most successful. The well-formed flowers appear singly or in groups and there is good continuity throughout the season. In the south *Glenfiddich* is less reliable and the flowers are somewhat paler.

Blooms:	20 petals Rich orange; golden yellow reverse Medium-sized Fragrant
Foliage:	Medium green Glossy
Health:	Good disease resistance
Growth:	Moderately vigorous Branching
Awards:	

GOLDEN SLIPPERS

An American variety which won top honours in its native country but has not caught the public fancy in Britain. Its supporters speak very highly of its excellence in a small bed — pointed buds appearing freely throughout the season, opening into bi-coloured blooms on dwarf bushes. But it also has its critics, who have been disappointed in its spreading and slight growth plus its unreliability in sunny summers and infertile soil. Good mildew resistance, but watch for black spot.

Blooms:	15 petals Chartreuse green Large No fragrance
Foliage:	Dark green Semi-glossy
Health:	Prone to disease
Growth:	Vigorous Upright
Awards:	

GREENSLEEVES
Other Name: HARLENTEN

Strictly for the flower arranger who likes to use material which is different. Cut the trusses when the buds are tinged with pink — as the blooms open the colour changes to green. Obviously a great talking point, but of little value for general garden display. The growth is unattractive and leggy, the dull blooms are flat when mature and regular spraying against disease is necessary. Still, there is nothing else like it and a bush or two will surprise your friends.

Blooms:	30 petals White, edged dark pink Large Slightly fragrant
Foliage:	Dark green Glossy
Health:	Average disease resistance
Growth:	Vigorous Bushy
Awards:	

HANNAH GORDON
Other Name: KORWEISO

It is surprising that this rose has not become more popular. The Climber *Handel* became a favourite soon after its introduction because of its unusual colouring — cream blooms edged with rosy pink. Now here is a Floribunda with quite similar colouring, but only a small number of growers have it in their catalogues. There are no obvious drawbacks — the flowers are large, the foliage is bronze-tinted when young and growth habit is quite attractive.

Blooms:	40 petals Canary yellow Medium-sized, rosette-shaped Slightly fragrant
Foliage:	Light green Glossy
Health:	Good disease resistance
Growth:	Vigorous Upright
Awards:	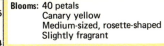

HONEYMOON
Other Name: HONIGMOND

Appropriately named, as it sometimes fails to live up to the promise of the first flush. It does not repeat as quickly as it should, and there can be a disappointing gap between flushes. The trusses are small and the perfume is slight. The colour fades rather quickly in hot weather, and *Honeymoon* should be seen in the northern counties in order to appreciate its virtues to the full. Vigorous growth, abundant shiny foliage and lovely flat blooms filled with petals.

FLORIBUNDA ROSES

Height in feet

ICEBERG
Other Name: SCHNEEWITTCHEN

Still the most popular white Floribunda of our time. The pink-tinged buds open to flat white blooms, the quantity and continuity being quite outstanding. *Iceberg* is seen everywhere, but unfortunately it is often denied the chance to show how beautiful it can be. It needs space where it can be grown, lightly pruned, as a tall specimen bush — then the blooms cover the whole plant and the chance of disease is reduced. It is also a good choice for a hedge or standard.

Blooms:	25 petals White Medium-sized Slightly fragrant
Foliage:	Medium green Glossy
Health:	Prone to disease
Growth:	Vigorous Branching
Awards:	RNRS · RHS · BB

ICED GINGER

There is a bewildering array of Floribundas from which you can choose, but if you are a keen flower arranger then *Iced Ginger* should be near the top of your list. Beautiful blooms, Hybrid Tea in shape with ivory, pink, yellow and copper all blended together, plus an ability to last in water which is unmatched by any other Floribunda. The blooms are large and disease resistance is above average, but there are drawbacks — the tall bush can look leggy and it is not always free-flowering.

Blooms:	45 petals Ivory tinted coppery pink; pink reverse Large Fragrant
Foliage:	Light green Semi-glossy
Health:	Good disease resistance
Growth:	Vigorous Upright
Awards:	

KORONA

An example of a rose which is in its declining years. Once it was the most popular vermilion Floribunda — now it is offered by very few growers. It still retains many of its good points — the trusses are large and are borne freely, although the colour fades in hot weather. The resistance to rain is excellent and established bushes are hardy. However, it now does badly in some areas for no apparent reason, and much of its strong constitution seems to have gone.

Blooms:	20 petals Orange scarlet Medium-sized Slightly fragrant
Foliage:	Dark green Glossy
Health:	Average disease resistance
Growth:	Vigorous Upright
Awards:	RNRS

KORRESIA
Other Names: FRIESIA, SUNSPRITE

No rose could have got off to a less promising start — unknown parentage and no awards in Britain. Yet within a few years it became a star of the rose world — the first serious challenger to *Allgold* for its crown as the top yellow Floribunda. *Korresia* scores over its rival by having flowers which are larger, more fragrant and fully double. Continuity is very good, the trusses of unfading blooms appearing over a long period. A good cutting rose — the buds open slowly indoors.

Blooms:	35 petals Bright yellow Large Fragrant
Foliage:	Medium green Glossy
Health:	Good disease resistance
Growth:	Moderately vigorous Bushy
Awards:	BB

LADY TAYLOR
Other Name: SMITLING

Yet another Patio Rose — this time the flowers are soft vermilion in colour and Hybrid Tea in shape. The usual features of a Patio Rose are there — compact growth, attractive foliage, short sturdy stems and so on. Unlike some other varieties in this popular group, the flowers are both double and fragrant. *Lady Taylor* is offered by few growers, and yet it is a top seller for one of the nurseries which offers it. Growers and public don't always agree on what should be in the catalogue.

Blooms:	25 petals Vermilion Medium-sized Fragrant
Foliage:	Medium green Semi-glossy
Health:	Good disease resistance
Growth:	Moderately vigorous Bushy
Awards:	

FLORIBUNDA ROSES

LAUGHTER LINES
Other Name: DICKERRY

A "hand painted" rose with a kaleidoscope of colour. Pink or cherry red is the usual base, with splashes and veins in a variety of other shades. Blooms appear early, and both the abundance and continuity of flowering are outstanding. Foliage is plentiful and the flowers soon open flat to reveal their colourful petals. *Laughter Lines* is a worthy addition to the "hand painted" group, although some experts doubt whether it will live up to its awards.

Blooms:	15 petals Pink and white, veined red Medium-sized Slightly fragrant
Foliage:	Medium green Semi-glossy
Health:	Good disease resistance
Growth:	Vigorous Bushy
Awards:	

LILLI MARLENE

A good bedding rose, justifiably popular for more than 20 years. The bush is well-clothed with abundant foliage and the flowers are plentiful. The black buds open into velvety dark red blooms which shrug off the effects of rain or hot sun. It has a good reputation for reliability and hardiness, which makes it a suitable Floribunda for beginners. Each individual open bloom is not particularly beautiful, but the overall effect of red blooms and coppery foliage is excellent.

Blooms:	25 petals Deep crimson Medium-sized Slightly fragrant
Foliage:	Bronze-tinted Semi-glossy
Health:	Prone to disease
Growth:	Vigorous Bushy
Awards:	

MARGARET MERRIL
Other Name: HARKULY

At last, a rose to challenge *Iceberg* for the white Floribunda crown. It does not have the height nor the abundance of flowers associated with *Iceberg*, but it beats its famous rival in two important ways — flower form and scent. The pearly flowers are high-centred beauties borne in small trusses, and the fragrance is considered by some to be the sweetest of any modern rose. The blooms do not stand up to rain like *Iceberg* and the disease bogy has not been overcome.

Blooms:	28 petals Pearly white Medium-sized Very fragrant
Foliage:	Dark green Glossy
Health:	Average disease resistance
Growth:	Very vigorous Bushy
Awards:	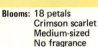

MARLENA

A popular and reliable dwarf Floribunda, sometimes described as the ideal edging rose. Its bushy and compact growth habit and the profusion of its rich red flowers make it an excellent choice for ground cover or the front of the bed or border. The blooms are devoid of perfume — always unfortunate but perhaps less of a drawback for a dwarf than for a tall bush with nose-high blooms. It does have the essential feature of a good ground cover rose — lots of attractive foliage.

Blooms:	18 petals Crimson scarlet Medium-sized No fragrance
Foliage:	Bronze-tinted Glossy
Health:	Good disease resistance
Growth:	Vigorous Branching
Awards:	

MASQUERADE

There is a handful of roses which everybody can name, and *Masquerade* is one of them. This was the first of the multi-coloured varieties, and after 30 years it is still a popular choice for hedging or wherever a larger than average bush is required. The yellow buds quickly turn to salmon pink as they open and eventually to deep red, with each large truss bearing a medley of these colours. Flowering is profuse, but you must dead-head regularly or it will cease.

Blooms:	15 petals Yellow, changing to pink and red Medium-sized Slightly fragrant
Foliage:	Dark green Glossy
Health:	Average disease resistance
Growth:	Vigorous Branching
Awards:	

FLORIBUNDA ROSES

Height in feet

MATANGI

One of the group of roses bred by McGredy which is described as "hand painted" (see page 5). Well-shaped buds open wide to reveal the unusual red and white coloration, the flowers being borne singly or in small trusses. A definite improvement on its parent *Picasso*, as its blooms appear in great profusion throughout the season and its foliage is glossy. An excellent bedding rose, healthy and rain-resistant, but unsuitable for cutting as it will not last in water.

Blooms: 23 petals
Vermilion; white eye; silver reverse
Medium-sized
Slightly fragrant

Foliage: Dark green
Glossy

Health: Good disease resistance

Growth: Vigorous
Upright

Awards:

5—
4—
3—
2—
1—

MEGIDDO

The sole claim to fame for this English-bred rose is the dazzling effect of its flowers in bright sunlight. Luminous red with a deeper reverse, the blooms are large and nicely formed. Borne in well-spaced trusses, the effect of a group of bushes can be quite spectacular when well grown. Continuity of flowering is good, but there are no other special virtues. Disease resistance is not good, there is no noticeable perfume and the blooms are only moderately full.

Blooms: 22 petals
Scarlet red
Large
No fragrance

Foliage: Dark green
Glossy

Health: Prone to disease

Growth: Vigorous
Upright

Awards:

5—
4—
3—
2—
1—

MEMENTO
Other Name: DICBAR

A welcome addition to the light red range, *Memento* provides a compact bush of average height which is densely clothed with glossy leaves. The number of flowers is quite remarkable, and the trusses continue to appear throughout the season. The clusters are large, bearing flat medium-sized flowers which have only a trace of perfume. Resistance to rain is outstanding, and disease resistance is reasonable. A good choice for bedding and cutting.

Blooms: 23 petals
Salmon vermilion
Medium-sized
Slightly fragrant

Foliage: Medium green
Glossy

Health: Average disease resistance

Growth: Vigorous
Upright

Awards:

5—
4—
3—
2—
1—

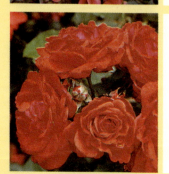

METEOR
Other Name: GERTRUD WESTPHAL

Meteor was introduced more than 20 years ago, and with its full blooms and neat growth habit it became the first dwarf Floribunda to appear in the best-seller lists. Many other dwarf Floribundas have been launched since then, but *Meteor* remains one of the best. Free-flowering, extremely long flowering season, abundant foliage and good resistance to disease are its main virtues. The secret of success is to feed regularly with a good rose fertilizer.

Blooms: 40 petals
Orange scarlet
Medium-sized
No fragrance

Foliage: Medium green
Semi-glossy

Health: Good disease resistance

Growth: Moderately vigorous
Bushy

Awards:

5—
4—
3—
2—
1—

MOUNTBATTEN
Other Name: HARMANTELLE

In the world of the tall Floribunda *Queen Elizabeth* reigned during the 1960s and 1970s. In the 1980s the crown passed to *Mountbatten*. Both praise and awards have been heaped on this variety, but make sure you have space to do it justice. Grow it as a hedge or in a border or large bed — few varieties are healthier or easier to grow. The leaves are semi-evergreen — the flowers are borne in small clusters. In this book, as elsewhere, an unqualified recommendation.

Blooms: 45 petals
Mimosa yellow
Large
Fragrant

Foliage: Medium green
Glossy

Health: Good disease resistance

Growth: Vigorous
Upright

Awards:

5—
4—
3—
2—
1—

FLORIBUNDA ROSES

Height in feet

Blooms: 18 petals
Beetroot purple
Large
Slightly fragrant

Foliage: Medium green
Matt

Health: Average disease resistance

Growth: Vigorous
Bushy

Awards:

NEWS

Perhaps "wine red" could have been a more flattering description of the unique colouring of *News*, rather than its official listing as "beetroot purple". The red buds open into large flat flowers, revealing showy golden stamens, and the petals of the mature blooms turn deep purple with age. The flowering season is an extremely long one and *News* is an attractive bedding Floribunda, especially when planted close to a cream or golden variety. Keep watch for rust and black spot.

Blooms: 24 petals
Light vermilion; gold at base
Medium-sized
Fragrant

Foliage: Light green
Matt

Health: Prone to disease

Growth: Vigorous
Branching

Awards:

ORANGE SENSATION

If carroty vermilion appeals to you, then choose *Orange Sensation* or *Orangeade*. There are many reasons why your choice should be *Orange Sensation* — the colour is vivid, the petals are more numerous and the perfume is strong and sweet. The spreading growth habit means that wide spacing between plants is acceptable, and the trusses are large. The drawbacks are duller foliage and a rather later start to the flowering season. Both black spot and mildew can be problems.

Blooms: 10 petals
Light vermilion
Medium-sized
Slightly fragrant

Foliage: Dark green
Semi-glossy

Health: Prone to disease

Growth: Vigorous
Branching

Awards:

ORANGEADE

Like *Orange Sensation*, this light vermilion rose was introduced 30 years ago and is still popular for bedding where a splash of bright colour is required. The trusses are large and are borne very freely, the open blooms darkening with age. One of the secrets of success is to dead-head regularly, or flowering may cease quite quickly. Rain resistance is excellent, but the susceptibility of *Orangeade* to black spot, mildew and rust is a problem.

Blooms: 35 petals
Deep rose pink
Large
Slightly fragrant

Foliage: Dark green
Semi-glossy

Health: Prone to disease

Growth: Moderately vigorous
Branching

Awards:

PADDY McGREDY

A low-growing Floribunda with a difference — each individual flower is as large and as well-formed as an average Hybrid Tea. Flower shape is not the only virtue — a well-fed and healthy bush will bear enough blooms in the first flush to cover nearly all the foliage. Unfortunately there is usually a delay before the next flush, and this variety does have its share of faults. Rain resistance is not good, the colour fades in hot sun and there is little resistance to the common diseases.

Blooms: 20 petals
Apricot
Small
Slightly fragrant

Foliage: Medium green
Semi-glossy

Health: Average disease resistance

Growth: Moderately vigorous
Bushy

Awards:

PEEK A BOO
Other Names: BRASS RING, DICGROW

A trickle of modern Patio Roses began to appear at the start of the 1980s, and the trickle has now become a flood. *Peek a Boo* was one of the early ones, and it remains one of the best for rockery and tub use. The bush is neat and rounded, and the clusters bear many flowers. The bush is small even for a Patio Rose — you may find this variety in the Miniature section of the catalogues. As the flowers mature the petals change from coppery apricot to pink.

FLORIBUNDA ROSES

Height in feet

PICASSO

The first of the "hand painted" roses — pink on a white background with irregular splashes of cherry red. The shades and intensity vary with the time of the year and the age of the bloom. The stems are slender and light pruning is recommended. The flowers are produced over a long season, but many people feel the newer roses of the *Picasso* type are a better choice. These recent ones have glossier foliage, more flowers and the blooms (e.g. *Laughter Lines*) may be more attractively coloured.

Blooms:	25 petals Deep pink, blotched red; silver reverse Medium-sized No fragrance
Foliage:	Medium green Matt
Health:	Prone to disease
Growth:	Vigorous Bushy
Awards:	

PICCOLO
Other Name: *TANOLOKIP*

The flower shape is good and the shade of orange-red is a welcome addition to the Patio Rose range. This Tantau rose, however, has missed the attention of the judges who grant awards and it has missed the popular acclaim given to other newer dwarf ones such as *Gentle Touch*, *Sweet Magic* etc. It's a good-enough rose — the leaves are reddish-green at first and the blooms appear reasonably freely. On the drawback side there is the absence of scent plus a lack of compactness.

Blooms:	20 petals Coral red Medium-sized No fragrance
Foliage:	Deep green Glossy
Health:	Good disease resistance
Growth:	Moderately vigorous Upright
Awards:	

PINK PARFAIT

Pinks and creams blend in variable amounts in this delightful American-bred Floribunda. A great favourite found in many catalogues, there seems to be little agreement on the height you can expect it to grow. However, all the books agree that it is an excellent choice for the bed or border, or grown lightly pruned as a specimen bush. Flowering is extremely prolific and it is one of the best of all Floribundas for cutting. The blooms resist rain, and the stems are slender and almost thornless.

Blooms:	22 petals Pink; cream at base Medium-sized No fragrance
Foliage:	Medium green Semi-glossy
Health:	Good disease resistance
Growth:	Vigorous Branching
Awards:	

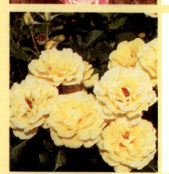

PRINCESS ALICE
Other Name: *HARTANNA*

It is appropriate that one of the keenest gardeners in the Royal Family should have a variety named after her by one of the rose world's great names. A pity, perhaps, that it should be another healthy, yellow Floribunda, because there are so many around these days. *Princess Alice* scores over most of its rivals by producing beautiful clusters in which each bloom is arranged to form a natural bouquet. No yellow is more eye-catching, but *Princess Alice* has not become a top seller.

Blooms:	25 petals Yellow Medium-sized Slightly fragrant
Foliage:	Medium green Glossy
Health:	Good disease resistance
Growth:	Vigorous Upright
Awards:	

QUEEN ELIZABETH

An American-bred rose named in the 1950s after Britain's young monarch, *Queen Elizabeth* has become one of the world's great roses. It will grow almost anywhere, but your garden might not be the right place. It is not suitable for a small bed, as it grows 6 ft or more. Plant it as a specimen shrub or as a hedge; best of all put it at the back of the border with lower-growing roses in front. Fine foliage, lovely blooms, excellent keeping qualities in water — an outstanding rose.

Blooms:	35 petals Light pink Large Slightly fragrant
Foliage:	Dark green Glossy
Health:	Good disease resistance
Growth:	Very vigorous Upright
Awards:	

FLORIBUNDA ROSES

Blooms: 25 petals Golden yellow, edged cherry red Medium-sized Slightly fragrant	
Foliage: Medium green Semi-glossy	
Health: Prone to disease	
Growth: Vigorous Upright	
Awards:	

RED GOLD

The name of this Floribunda aptly describes the young flowers — red on the petal edges and gold on the inside. The colours fade and merge with age and the mature blooms are an overall pale orange. *Red Gold* is a reliable variety which has attractive red-tinted young foliage as well as gay flowers, making it a useful rose for bedding. It is also a good exhibition variety as the flowers are exceptionally long-lasting. Flowering is generally prolific and the blooms have good rain resistance.

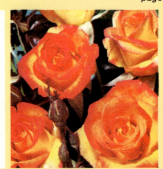

Blooms: 20 petals Pale pink; white eye Large Fragrant	
Foliage: Medium green Glossy	
Health: Good disease resistance	
Growth: Moderately vigorous Bushy	
Awards:	

REGENSBERG
Other Name: MACYOUMIS

A colourful Patio Rose from McGredy. The bush is short and spreading — the leaves occasionally bronze-tinted. The flowers are remarkable — surprisingly large for such a small plant and opening flat to reveal the prominent white centres. *Regensberg* has a good reputation for bearing blooms all season long, but each truss bears few blooms. Like its parent *Old Master* the petals have a silvery reverse. You will find this rose in most but not all of the popular catalogues.

Blooms: 22 petals Scarlet crimson Large Slightly fragrant	
Foliage: Dark green Semi-glossy	
Health: Prone to disease	
Growth: Vigorous Upright	
Awards:	

ROB ROY

It has been claimed that *Rob Roy* has the finest red colour to be found in any rose. The blooms appear freely, and continuity is good. Both cold and wet weather are tolerated, yet this Scottish-bred rose has never become really popular. Perhaps the bush is a little too tall — it is better planted as a hedge or in the border than in an average-sized bed. Perhaps the wide spacing of blooms in the truss is a drawback — whatever the reason for the lack of appeal, it is still a fine rose.

Blooms: 35 petals Rosy red Large, rosette-shaped Fragrant	
Foliage: Bronze-tinted Matt	
Health: Prone to disease	
Growth: Vigorous Branching	
Awards:	

ROSEMARY ROSE

A post-War rose with an old-fashioned look. The trusses are large and the blooms have been described as camellia-like. The medium-sized bush has a rather spreading growth habit, with leaves which are remarkably different. They are bronze red, similar in shade to the foliage of a copper beech. A lovely Floribunda if you like red foliage and 19th century flowers, but *Rosemary Rose* is not widely grown because it is prone to infection by mildew, black spot and rust.

Blooms: 25 petals Orange scarlet Medium-sized, globular Slightly fragrant	
Foliage: Dark green Semi-glossy	
Health: Good disease resistance	
Growth: Vigorous Upright	
Awards:	

SCARLET QUEEN ELIZABETH

A tall red-flowering Floribunda which is used for hedging or as a specimen shrub. It is available from most nurserymen, but its popularity is no doubt due to its famous name rather than its beauty. Unlike the blooms of its pink parent, the flowers are loose and open, and appear later in the season than most other Floribundas. Flowering is not particularly free and the blooms are often hidden by the foliage. Not a great rose, but health and weather resistance are good.

FLORIBUNDA ROSES

SCENTED AIR

As you would expect from its name, fragrance is the outstanding quality of this pink Floribunda. The perfume is rich and fruity, and the flowers are large and usually plentiful. At first the blooms are shapely but they quickly become open and loose. The foliage is a notable feature — large glossy leaves which are much healthier than the average Floribunda. A good and reliable bedding rose for the larger bed, but its colour and flower form are nothing special.

Blooms:	20 petals Deep salmon pink Large Very fragrant
Foliage:	Dark green Glossy
Health:	Good disease resistance
Growth:	Vigorous Upright
Awards:	

SEA PEARL
Other Name: FLOWER GIRL

The young flowers of *Sea Pearl* have the classic shape and beauty of a well-formed H.T. bloom. These flowers lose their pointed shape as they mature and their colour is variable. The blends of pink, peach and yellow can be most attractive, especially in autumn, and flowers are generally plentiful. But there are faults — there is a short pause between flushes and flowers can be spotted by heavy rain. Plant as an eye-catching group of 2 or 3, not as a massed bed.

Blooms:	25 petals Pink; yellow reverse Large Slightly fragrant
Foliage:	Medium green Glossy
Health:	Good disease resistance
Growth:	Vigorous Upright
Awards:	

SHEILA'S PERFUME
Other Name: HARSHERRY

There has long been a need for a strongly scented red-and-yellow rose — and it took an amateur (John Sheridan) to raise it. The flowers have a classic H.T. shape and are borne singly or in small clusters. Healthy, vigorous, attractively clothed with leaves .... but *Sheila's Perfume* has never reached the top rank. Perhaps the problem is that there are not enough petals for an H.T.-type flower — but then *nobody* can tell you what turns a rose into a star.

Blooms:	20 petals Yellow, edged red Large Very fragrant
Foliage:	Dark green Semi-glossy
Health:	Good disease resistance
Growth:	Vigorous Bushy
Awards:	

SHONA
Other Name: DICDRUM

There is really nothing special about *Shona*. The pink colour is attractive but not unusual. Petals are not plentiful and the H.T. form of the opening buds is soon lost. The trusses, however, are large and there is a distinct air of neatness about the bush. The stems are densely clothed with leaves and that means *Shona* makes a reliable and colourful low-growing hedge. Not in every catalogue, but you should have no trouble in finding it.

Blooms:	20 petals Coral pink Medium-sized Slightly fragrant
Foliage:	Medium green Semi-glossy
Health:	Average disease resistance
Growth:	Vigorous Bushy
Awards:	

SOUTHAMPTON

Introduced in 1971, *Southampton* has become one of the leading Floribundas. It combines the marmalade colour beloved by flower arrangers with the robust good health desired by all gardeners. The slightly ruffled blooms are borne singly at the start of the season, but more usually they occur in trusses. Growth is taller than average, so use *Southampton* for the large bed, border or hedge. Although growth is upright the effect is not gaunt as side shoots are plentiful.

Blooms:	25 petals Apricot orange, flushed scarlet Large Slightly fragrant
Foliage:	Dark green Semi-glossy
Health:	Good disease resistance
Growth:	Very vigorous Upright
Awards:	

FLORIBUNDA ROSES

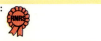

Blooms: 20 petals
Carmine, pink and white
Large
Slightly fragrant

Foliage: Medium green
Matt

Health: Average disease resistance

Growth: Moderately vigorous
Bushy

Awards:

SUE LAWLEY
Other Names: MACSPASH, SPANISH SHAWL

Another Sam McGredy "hand painted" rose — older ones such as *Old Master* and *Priscilla Burton* tend to disappear from the catalogues and newer ones such as *Regensberg* and *Sue Lawley* appear. Always white-eyed, the pinks and reds and the degree of "crayoning" over the petal surface are variable. The large flowers open wide when mature — a useful rose for cutting. Regarded highly in the RNRS trials but it has never become a best-seller.

Blooms: 35 petals
Lemon yellow
Large
Slightly fragrant

Foliage: Medium green
Semi-glossy

Health: Average disease resistance

Growth: Vigorous
Upright

Awards:

SUNSILK

A Hybrid Tea, according to some experts. A Floribunda, according to others, including the man who raised it. *Sunsilk* is indeed a borderline variety, with large blooms which have a distinct H.T. shape when young and are often borne singly. Classification, however, is not the gardener's worry and *Sunsilk* is a fine bedding and cutting rose. The colour can fade in hot sun, but in autumn the number and quality of the flowers are excellent. Not a good choice where rust is a problem.

Blooms: 35 petals
Apricot
Medium-sized
Fragrant

Foliage: Medium green
Glossy

Health: Good disease resistance

Growth: Moderately vigorous
Bushy

Awards:

SWEET DREAM
Other Name: FRYMINICOT

Patio Roses certainly catch the eye of the judges for The Rose of the Year award. *Gentle Touch* in 1986, *Sweet Magic* in 1987 and *Sweet Dream* in 1988. This Fryer-bred rose has a number of special qualities. The unusual peachy colour does not fade with age and the well-formed blooms stand up well to rain. Growth is neat and cushion-like — foliage is dense and attractive. It is recommended for edging, low hedging, patio planting, container growth and for use as a cut flower.

Blooms: 17 petals
Orange, blended gold
Small
Fragrant

Foliage: Medium green
Glossy

Health: Good disease resistance

Growth: Vigorous
Bushy

Awards:

SWEET MAGIC
Other Name: DICMAGIC

A star in its first year, as it came to the market with The Rose of the Year award from the Rose Growers' Association. The blooms are borne in large clusters, deep orange fading to golden yellow which gives each flower a glowing effect. A pink flush appears on old petals. An excellent choice for tub planting or edging — leaves, stems and flower size are all in scale. Fragrance is quite pronounced — an unusual feature for a Patio Rose. Obviously one for the best-seller lists of the 1990s.

Blooms: 30 petals
Blood red
Large
Slightly fragrant

Foliage: Dark green
Glossy

Health: Good disease resistance

Growth: Vigorous
Bushy

Awards:

THE TIMES ROSE
Other Name: KORPEAHN

A rose needs more than a pretty face to win the President's International Trophy of the RNRS. The plant itself has to have charm — *The Times Rose* is a bushy and spreading rose with an abundance of attractive foliage which is bronze-tinted when young. The healthy bushes bear large trusses of crimson flowers which are especially attractive in sunlight. A fine bedding rose, but even winners have faults — there is little fragrance and the petals are short.

FLORIBUNDA ROSES

Height in feet

TIP TOP

Dwarf Floribundas have an important place in the garden — they can fill a small bed or edge a border or pathway. When a pink variety is required, the usual choice is *Tip Top*. It blooms over a long season, and the continuity is excellent. The large trusses seem to appear in profusion whatever the weather and the fragrance, although not strong, is sweet and "old-fashioned". Disease is the only problem — susceptibility to mildew is average but black spot can be a menace.

Blooms:	20 petals Salmon pink Medium-sized Slightly fragrant
Foliage:	Medium green Matt
Health:	Prone to disease
Growth:	Vigorous Bushy
Awards:	

TOPSI

Another dwarf Floribunda for planting in a tub or at the front of the bed, and it is one to choose if you want a really brilliant display. It won the RNRS supreme award in 1972 — its foliage is large and attractive, the period of flowering and the rapid repeat between flushes are outstanding and rain resistance is good. The glowing orange red of the petals does not fade, and only its health stops it being an ideal dwarf Floribunda. It is prone to black spot, and die-back can be a problem.

Blooms:	12 petals Bright vermilion Medium-sized No fragrance
Foliage:	Medium green Semi-glossy
Health:	Prone to disease
Growth:	Vigorous Bushy
Awards:	

TRUMPETER
Other Name: *MACTRU*

One of the bright red Floribundas, low-growing and compact. Introduced in 1978, *Trumpeter* has earned a high reputation as a front-of-the-border bedding rose which has almost unequalled disease resistance amongst roses in this group. There are plenty of flowers, and the trusses appear almost continually. Another advantage is the large number of flowers in each truss, but this is a fault in rainy weather as the heads may bow down when wet.

Blooms:	35 petals Bright vermilion Medium-sized Slightly fragrant
Foliage:	Dark green Glossy
Health:	Good disease resistance
Growth:	Vigorous Bushy
Awards:	

WARRIOR

There are many fine dwarf Floribundas these days, and in such distinguished company this red variety has lost some of its earlier appeal. The rather similar *Trumpeter* remains popular. The colour is bright and unfading, and the flowering season is exceptionally long. The leaves are rather pale and not particularly attractive, but the growth habit is compact, so *Warrior* is still a good subject for the front of the border. No health problems have arisen since its introduction in 1978.

Blooms:	30 petals Scarlet Medium-sized Slightly fragrant
Foliage:	Light green Semi-glossy
Health:	Good disease resistance
Growth:	Vigorous Bushy
Awards:	

WOBURN ABBEY

A popular and long-established orange Floribunda, taller than average and pleasantly perfumed. The colour and not the beauty of the blooms is the reason for the popularity of *Woburn Abbey*, as the flowers are rather untidy and appear crowded in the trusses. Lack of good flower shape is not the major drawback — disease is a more important problem. Mildew, black spot and rust can all be serious, and regular spraying is needed if you grow this variety.

Blooms:	25 petals Coppery orange, shaded gold Medium-sized Fragrant
Foliage:	Dark green Semi-glossy
Health:	Prone to disease
Growth:	Vigorous Branching
Awards:	

MINIATURE ROSES

Miniature Roses are becoming more popular in Britain, but this slowly-awakening interest for these scaled-down versions of "normal" roses does not begin to match the enthusiasm in the U.S. The rose has for many years been Britain's favourite flower, and it is therefore surprising that we should have lagged behind. Some people believe that the price is to blame — a tiny bush does not seem good value when it costs almost as much as a Floribunda. Others feel that we don't need Miniatures in the same way — we set out to fill our gardens whereas the Americans have apartments to decorate.

It can't be that simple. A major factor may be the way we raise our plants — in the U.S. they are propagated from cuttings and so grow on their own roots. Such plants are rather slow-growing and can be somewhat tender, but they do remain truly miniature all their lives. In Britain we generally raise our Miniatures as grafted plants on rootstocks — these plants are hardier, more drought-resistant and quicker-growing. Unfortunately, they also tend to be too vigorous and the fairy-like form may be lost.

Another disappointment has been their failure as reliable house plants. So many people have bought them, put them on the sideboard and expected them to bloom quite merrily from June to November like their outdoor counter-parts. Miniature Roses may not be as easy to grow indoors as some people expect, but they are not as difficult as some experts claim — just follow the rules on page 118.

Miniature Roses most certainly do have a place in our gardening scene. Buy plants in pots — they do not like root disturbance. The best time for planting outdoors is spring or early summer and they will reward you each year by coming into leaf in March, opening their first flowers in midsummer and continuing to bloom until the first frosts arrive.

Even Miniatures have their dwarfs and giants. "Small" varieties grow up to 9 in. high under average conditions — "tall" Miniatures reach 18 in. "Small" blooms are less than 1 in. across — "large" ones are about 2 in.

There is an impressive list of uses. Edging beds and planting in rockeries can both be recommended, but perhaps the most successful use is planting in a raised bed devoted entirely to Miniatures.

The plants you buy will probably be grafted on to a rootstock — you will be able to see the join at the base. If you want to grow Miniatures as pot plants, take cuttings as described on page 115 — the success rate is high and the resulting plants will remain compact and dwarf.

Maintenance is straightforward, but not quite as easy as some books suggest. Pruning (page 92) is no problem, but you must keep a careful watch for pests and diseases. The major nuisances are mildew, black spot, die-back and greenfly. Don't forget to water in dry weather — they don't have the root system of their big sisters. Feeding is necessary — use a liquid fertilizer on a little-and-often basis for Miniatures in pots.

The history of Miniatures is as fascinating as the plants themselves. They were popular pot plants in Victorian times — *Pompon de Paris* was a well-known variety. Then they went out of fashion and disappeared at the end of the 19th century, apparently lost for ever. In 1918 Major Roulet saw a tiny rose growing in a pot in Switzerland. This survivor became *R. roulettii* and the modern Miniature story began — hybridists have given us the wide choice available today.

ANGELA RIPPON
Other Name: OCARU

Bred in Holland and introduced in 1978, this rose is popular for both bedding and showing. Growth is compact and bushy, reaching about 12 in. in height. The double blooms are pale carmine pink, freely borne amongst the healthy foliage. The blooms are quite fragrant.

APRICOT SUNBLAZE
Other Name: SAVAMARK

The blooms of this new variety are small, but they are crowded with petals and the colour break is a new one for Miniatures. The cup-shaped blooms are borne singly or in clusters and there is some fragrance. Growth is neat and bushy — stems are thin and prickly.

BABY GOLD STAR

An unpredictable rose, growing to 1½ ft when grafted on a stock or reaching less than 1 ft when grown on its own roots. The leaves may stay healthy or be covered in black spot — the stems may be numerous or very sparse. Even the slightly fragrant blooms are changeable, fading from golden yellow to cream.

BABY MASQUERADE

One of the top Miniatures in many ways — in popularity, ease of cultivation, number of blooms and length of flowering season. It is rather tall and bushy, reaching 15 in. or more. The double and slightly fragrant blooms change from yellow to pink and finally to rosy red. Dead-head regularly.

CINDERELLA

Tiny flowers crowded with petals, white with touches of pink. A most attractive plant, with abundant shiny foliage and blooms which look like miniature Hybrid Teas. The thornless stems are upright, with the slightly scented flowers being borne in clusters. *Cinderella* blooms last well in water.

COLIBRI 79
Other Name: MEIDANOVER

A free-flowering variety, very bushy and about 10 in. tall. The double blooms are brightly coloured — golden apricot with pinkish tones. There is some confusion over names — *Colibri* (very large, straw-coloured blooms) was introduced shortly before *Colibri 79*.

CORALIN

Coralin is one of the many introductions from Pedro Dot, the Spanish hybridist. The orange-red flowers are large for a Miniature Rose — many-petalled and attractive but devoid of fragrance. The well-branched bush is abundantly clothed with small bronze-tinted leaves. This variety grows 12–15 in.

DARLING FLAME
Other Name: MINUETTO

Introduced in 1971, this variety has become one of the most popular Miniature Roses in Europe. It has all the requirements for success — there are beautiful double flowers, rich orange vermilion with a golden reverse, borne in profusion on a healthy bushy plant which reaches 12 in.

EASTER MORNING

Large ivory white flowers set amongst small shiny leaves. The blooms have 60 petals or more, yet resistance to rain as well as to disease is excellent. This American-bred variety is not a profuse bloomer, but it is highly recommended for edging the front of the border. It reaches a height of about 12 in.

MINIATURE ROSES

FIRE PRINCESS

A splendid choice for edging, exhibiting or growing as a pot plant. The bushes are tall and upright with glossy, dark green foliage, but it is the flower colour which makes this an outstanding Miniature. Brilliant orange-red with a touch of gold, the hues strengthening rather than fading with age. Fragrance is slight.

GREEN DIAMOND

You will either love or hate this American-bred Miniature — flowers which turn lime green as they open are not everybody's choice. The blooms are small and full — the colour is strongest under cool conditions. Popular with exhibitors, but rather anaemic for bedding outdoors. Grows about 12 in. high.

HULA GIRL

A tall bushy plant with blooms made to order for the show-bench. The flowers are unusually large — the salmon-orange pointed petals are very numerous (45–50) and tightly packed to provide an eye-catching bloom. Fragrance is not strong. The attractive buds are unusually long. An easy-to-grow plant for indoors or outdoors.

JOSEPHINE WHEATCROFT
Other Name: ROSINA

A lovely bright yellow Miniature, with blooms which are perfectly shaped when young. The fragrance is slight and there are not many petals, but this variety has been a favourite for many years. The trusses appear freely, bearing up to 10 blooms. Height is about 15 in.

LITTLE BUCKAROO

A rather tall-growing variety (15–18 in.), well-suited to the front of the border. It has a spreading growth habit, with shiny bronze-tinted leaves. The blooms are bright red with a white centre, small in size and pleasantly scented. There are about 25 petals. One of the early Miniatures (1956), but disease resistance is still good.

LITTLE FLIRT

A bi-coloured Miniature Rose, with small *Piccadilly*-like blooms. The petals are orange-red with a yellow reverse, and 40–50 are packed into each small fragrant bloom. The bush bears abundant foliage, light green and glossy, and the height is above average – about 15 in. A popular rose for more than 25 years.

MAGIC CARROUSEL

A striking and unusual Miniature, excellent for indoor decoration and the show-bench. The shapely flowers have white petals, and each petal has a clearly defined red edge. The fragrance is slight and the growth is above average, reaching about 15 in. *Magic Carrousel* is a hardy and reliable variety.

MR BLUEBIRD

You will find *Mr Bluebird* in many catalogues, and it has its friends. Occasionally you can see why — dark green foliage studded with pale lavender flowers. In most cases it is frankly disappointing — spindly growth, poor colouring and shyness in flowering. Choose *Lavender Lace* or *Lavender Jewel* instead.

NEW PENNY

Aptly named, with shining leaves and coppery pink flowers. A most attractive Miniature — ideal for growing as a pot plant. The red buds are freely produced, opening into semi-double blooms which fade with age. There is no fragrance. The plant is well-branched and vigorous, but rarely exceeds 10 in.

MINIATURE ROSES

ORANGE SUNBLAZE
Other Name: SUNBLAZE

A French Miniature which appeared in the 1980s and soon became a popular variety in the catalogues. The flowers are large and full with orange-red petals. The blooms last longer than most Miniatures when stood in water. A salmon pink sport (*Pink Sunblaze*) is available.

POUR TOI
Other Name: PARA TI

A favourite Miniature, highly rated for the beauty of its flowers and the attractive nature of the bush. The foliage is glossy and the growth habit short (7–9 in.) and very bushy. The flowers appear profusely, white with a creamy yellow tinge at the base of the petals. Fragrance is slight.

RED ACE
Other Name: AMRUDA

There are, of course, a number of red Miniatures — both old and new. This De Ruiter variety of the 1980s broke new ground — the semi-double blooms are darker than other Miniatures and the surface is velvety. Good for cutting and showing — bush height 12 in.

RISE 'N' SHINE

This variety is considered by many to be the best yellow Miniature. The long-pointed buds are attractive and appear abundantly under good growing conditions. The large blooms have a classic H.T. form and the deep yellow colour does not fade with age. You will have to spray to keep disease at bay.

SCARLET GEM

Scarlet Gem has the reputation for being one of the brightest red Miniatures. It is a popular pot plant, producing a mass of very full flowers throughout the season. The blooms keep their colour in bright sunlight and the attractive foliage is dark and glossy. Proneness to mildew is its major fault.

SHERI ANNE

The long-lasting flowers are made up of orange-red petals with a yellow base. These petals are not numerous (15–20), but there is more fragrance than you would expect from a Miniature. The catalogues recommend *Sheri Anne* for showing and cutting, but its grow-anywhere vigour makes it a good bedding rose.

STARINA
Other Name: MEIGABI

Starina remains one of the queens of the Miniature world — well-formed bright vermilion flowers cover the plant from early summer until November. It is renowned for its vigour, and can be grown as a pot plant, dwarf bush for bedding or as a miniature standard.

STARS 'N' STRIPES

You cannot fail to recognise this one — each flower is striped with white and strawberry red. The blooms do not have an abundance of petals but they are very large. There is no scent. Rather too garish for some people, but a good bedding variety if you like your plants to be striking. Lax, bushy growth reaching about 15 in.

YELLOW DOLL

A fine creamy yellow variety, popular on the show-bench and as a pot plant. The attractive buds are borne singly or in clusters, opening into fragrant blooms crowded with 50 or more narrow petals. The dwarf bush has a spreading growth habit and reaches about 10 in. Keep watch for black spot.

MINIATURE ROSES

CLIMBERS & RAMBLERS

About a century ago, the standard horticultural text book described climbing roses as the most precious flowers that have ever adorned the garden. No longer true, perhaps, but they are still regarded as indispensable for some purposes. Their main use is, of course, to cover part of the house — occasionally helping to bring the garden indoors by framing a window. Other uses include covering arches, poles, fences, pergolas and old trees.

There is much more to succeeding with this group than simply picking a pretty picture from a catalogue and then planting the specimen. It is an area where there are pitfalls for the unwary and where you can't afford to make a mistake. A wall, fence or pergola which suddenly loses its floral cover can look extremely bare. To ensure an abundance of leaves *and* flowers you must learn to choose wisely and then care for the plants in the proper way.

There are two basic types of climbing rose — Ramblers and Climbers. Ramblers have been around since Victorian times, their long pliable stems bearing huge trusses of small flowers. Growth is very vigorous and they can be a mass of colour in summer, but there is only one flush of flowers. Ramblers

are no longer a popular choice — their mildew-prone leaves need regular spraying and pruning can be a tiresome chore. Blooms are borne on new wood, so that each year the old wood should be cut out. If you want to cover a wall or screen, it is usually better to choose a Climber, but Ramblers do have a few special uses. They make splendid weeping standards, and can also be left to trail along the soil as ground cover or to clamber up dead trees as born-again foliage and flowers.

Climbers have much stiffer stems, larger flowers and smaller trusses than Ramblers. Flowers are borne on the framework of mature wood which is more or less permanent, so pruning and maintenance is much easier. As you will see from the A–Z guide (pages 52–60) there are several types — the extremely tough and disease-resistant Kordesii Climbers, which like the Climbing Bourbon and Climbing China Roses are repeat flowering, and the Large-flowered Climbers —the most important group of all.

Of course it is a temptation to buy a Climbing Hybrid Tea — the idea of covering a wall with well-known beautiful blooms is appealing. Unfortunately, the climbing form has usually lost much of the repeat flowering nature of the bush form, and there may be little blossom after the first or second flush.

Don't guess with climbing roses — choose carefully, plant properly and don't expect too much in the first year. Train the stems to stimulate flowering (see page 89) and prune as directed.

KEY TO THE ROSE GUIDES

Number of Petals See page 5	**Colour**
Fragrance See page 6	**Foliage** Leaf colour (see page 6)

Blooms:	Double Deep velvety crimson Very fragrant
Foliage:	Medium green
Introduction:	1946
Type:	Climbing Hybrid Tea
Pruning:	Climber — Method 2
Flowering Period:	Repeat flowering

Introduction Year of introduction in Britain

Type Type of climbing rose

Height in ft

Flowering Period Repeat flowering, or time of blooming if once flowering (see page 6)

Pruning Correct pruning method – see page 92

Height in feet

ALBERIC BARBIER

A great old favourite, seen in gardens everywhere. It has a well-deserved reputation for flourishing under poor conditions and in difficult situations when there is little direct sunlight. It blooms profusely in late June or July, the small yellow buds opening into flat creamy white flowers. The foliage is dark and glossy, lasting through most of the winter. Grow it on a pillar rather than on a wall.

Blooms:	Double Cream Fragrant
Foliage:	Dark green
Introduction:	1900
Type:	Rambler
Pruning:	Rambler — Method 2
Flowering Period:	Midsummer

25 — 20 — 15 — 10 — 5

ALBERTINE

One of the great names in Rambler Roses — vigorous branching growth which stretches over walls or up old trees and then bursts into bloom in June. The coppery buds open into medium-sized flowers which scent the air, and when not in flower the reddish young foliage keeps the plant attractive. There are difficulties — mildew can be a serious problem and the blooms are often ruined by heavy rain.

Blooms:	Double Pale pink Very fragrant
Foliage:	Dark green
Introduction:	1921
Type:	Rambler
Pruning:	Rambler — Method 2
Flowering Period:	Early summer

25 — 20 — 15 — 10 — 5

ALOHA

If you want a pink climber like *Albertine* with more beauty in the flowers but with much less vigour in the stems, then choose *Aloha*. It is recommended for pillars or walls where slow and restricted growth is required — its only fault is that occasionally it remains bushy and fails to climb at all. The foliage is attractive and healthy, the flowers are very full and sweetly scented. The Hybrid Tea-type blooms are resistant to rain.

Blooms:	Double Rose pink Fragrant
Foliage:	Medium green
Introduction:	1949
Type:	Large-flowered Climber
Pruning:	Climber — Method 2
Flowering Period:	Repeat flowering

25 — 20 — 15 — 10 — 5

ALTISSIMO

A short climber, sturdy and healthy, with eye-catching blooms. They first appear in June, and the plant stays in flower until autumn. There is no sudden flush of a myriad small flowers — instead there are large blooms here and there on the stems and each one is a thing of beauty. The petals are a rich red and at the centre of each flower is a boss of golden stamens. It is suitable for walls, posts and fences.

Blooms:	Single Blood red Slightly fragrant
Foliage:	Dark green
Introduction:	1967
Type:	Large-flowered Climber
Pruning:	Climber — Method 2
Flowering Period:	Repeat flowering

25 — 20 — 15 — 10 — 5

AMERICAN PILLAR

Before the War everyone agreed that *American Pillar* was an excellent choice as a climbing rose, but now the experts are divided. A few feel that its remarkable profusion of flower trusses in late June or July still earn it a place in the garden, but most feel that more modern varieties, such as *Dortmund*, should be used in its place. The faults are serious — there is no resistance to mildew and a good deal of pruning is required.

Blooms:	Single Deep pink; white eye No fragrance
Foliage:	Dark green
Introduction:	1902
Type:	Rambler
Pruning:	Rambler — Method 1
Flowering Period:	Midsummer

25 — 20 — 15 — 10 — 5

BANTRY BAY

Bantry Bay can be grown against a wall, as it has good resistance against mildew, but it is usually recommended for clothing a pillar or fence. Don't expect a rampant grower which will quickly cover large areas — its growth habit has been described as "restrained". The shapely buds open into flat pink blooms, which are well-spaced in the truss. These fairly large flowers are borne in profusion throughout the season.

Blooms:	Semi-double Pale rose pink Slightly fragrant
Foliage:	Medium green
Introduction:	1967
Type:	Large-flowered Climber
Pruning:	Climber — Method 2
Flowering Period:	Repeat flowering

25 — 20 — 15 — 10 — 5

Height in feet

Blooms:	Double Apricot Fragrant
Foliage:	Medium green
Introduction:	1982
Type:	Large-flowered Climber
Pruning:	Climber — Method 2
Flowering Period: Repeat flowering	

BREATH OF LIFE

A climber of the 1980s from Harkness — a prize winner from Munich to Tokyo and a popular choice in Britain. Both the flower colour and perfume are unusual in the world of the climbers and the large Hybrid Tea-type blooms are most attractive. All the catalogues recommend it as a cut flower — the blooms are carried singly or in small clusters. Where there is no wall or pillar to spare you can prune the plant and grow it as a bush.

Blooms:	Double Primrose yellow Slightly fragrant
Foliage:	Dark green
Introduction:	1963
Type:	Large-flowered Climber
Pruning:	Climber — Method 1
Flowering Period: Repeat flowering	

CASINO

The catalogue description will make you want to rush out and buy one — deep yellow buds, Hybrid Tea in shape, opening to produce lovely full flowers which are soft yellow in colour and pleasantly scented. Foliage is healthy and the flowering season is prolonged. But there is a strong word of caution — *Casino* can be delicate so don't choose it if you live in the colder part of the country or if the planting site is exposed to cold winds.

Blooms:	Double Shell pink Slightly fragrant
Foliage:	Dark green
Introduction:	1894
Type:	Climbing China Rose
Pruning:	Climber — Method 2
Flowering Period: Repeat flowering	

CECILE BRUNNER, CLIMBING

Cécile Brunner is a dainty bush, just 2½ ft x 2½ ft. The climbing sport is a giant, capable of reaching 20 ft x 20 ft. Although technically described as repeat flowering, there is an impressive flush of small pink flowers in June but only sporadic flowering later in the season. The young blooms are beautifully shaped, but there is usually much more leaf than flower in summer. It is a good choice for growing up trees.

Blooms:	Double Pink, shaded apricot Very fragrant
Foliage:	Dark green
Introduction:	1973
Type:	Large-flowered Climber
Pruning:	Climber — Method 2
Flowering Period: Repeat flowering	

COMPASSION

During the past 10 years this fine variety bred by Harkness has become Britain's favourite climbing rose. The flowers are beautifully shaped with forty petals, and the apricot pink colouring is unusual in this group. The scent is outstanding and the profusion of flowers is excellent. It produces new shoots freely from the base but it will not cover the side of the house — see it at its best on a pillar or against a white wall.

Blooms:	Double Deep velvety crimson Very fragrant
Foliage:	Medium green
Introduction:	1946
Type:	Climbing Hybrid Tea
Pruning:	Climber — Method 2
Flowering Period: Repeat flowering	

CRIMSON GLORY, CLIMBING

Once the bush form of *Crimson Glory* was Britain's favourite red rose, but now it has been replaced by many newer reds without its faults. The faults are to be found in the climbing form — flowers which purple with age and leaves which are susceptible to mildew. But *Climbing Crimson Glory* has virtues which are still unmatched — velvety, dark red flowers borne in such profusion that the whole garden is scented.

Blooms:	Double Crimson Slightly fragrant
Foliage:	Light green
Introduction:	1951
Type:	Rambler
Pruning:	Rambler — Method 1
Flowering Period: Late summer	

CRIMSON SHOWER

An excellent choice for people who like Rambler Roses but don't like mildew. It is free-flowering, the small rosette-shaped blooms appearing in large clusters when other Ramblers have passed their flowering season. From late July to early September the red flowers will clothe trellises, arches or pillars. *Crimson Shower* makes an excellent weeping standard. The fragrance is very faint.

CLIMBERS & RAMBLERS

Height in feet

DANSE DU FEU
Other Name: SPECTACULAR

One of the first of the modern repeat-flowering climbers and still one of the most popular. The blooms are not large, but the colour is vivid and the freedom of flowering is outstanding. Trusses appear until well into the autumn and this variety is well-known for the ability to bloom in its first season. Its major fault is also well-known — the flowers turn purple with age.

Blooms:	Double / Orange scarlet / No fragrance
Foliage:	Bronze-tinted
Introduction:	1954
Type:	Large-flowered Climber
Pruning:	Climber — Method 2
Flowering Period:	Repeat flowering

DOROTHY PERKINS

Ninety years after its introduction you will still find the most famous name amongst Rambler Roses in some catalogues. Grow it for sentimental reasons, but it is no longer a good choice for garden display. It is extremely prone to mildew, making it unsuitable for growing against a wall. The small flowers appear in large clusters in late July, and the best use for *Dorothy Perkins* is to screen an open fence or arch.

Blooms:	Double / Rose pink / No fragrance
Foliage:	Medium green
Introduction:	1901
Type:	Rambler
Pruning:	Rambler — Method 1
Flowering Period:	Late summer

DORTMUND

A healthy and hardy rose, which is excellent for covering a pillar or it can be kept pruned as a large specimen bush. The big flowers have five petals, white-centred with a boss of yellow stamens. The trusses appear throughout the summer and autumn, but dead flowers should be removed or the flowering season will be shortened. The foliage is glossy and abundant, but the flowers have no noticeable scent.

Blooms:	Single / Red; white eye / No fragrance
Foliage:	Dark green
Introduction:	1955
Type:	Kordesii Climber
Pruning:	Climber — Method 2
Flowering Period:	Repeat flowering

DUBLIN BAY

You will find this McGredy-bred rose in most catalogues, where you can read about its virtues — rich red and beautifully formed flowers borne profusely on healthy stems which are clothed with abundant glossy foliage. Unfortunately it has a drawback — at first its growth habit is inclined to be bush-like, and on some occasions it remains as an upright bush instead of a vigorous Large-flowered Climber.

Blooms:	Double / Deep red / Slightly fragrant
Foliage:	Dark green
Introduction:	1976
Type:	Large-flowered Climber
Pruning:	Climber — Method 2
Flowering Period:	Repeat flowering

EMILY GRAY

An old favourite, with two outstanding reasons for keeping its place in the catalogues. The flowers, with their unique chamois-leather colouring and the foliage, red at first and then dark and glossy when mature. These leaves are almost evergreen — a great advantage when it is used to clothe a wall or screen. *Emily Gray* is a reasonably healthy rose, but it is not free-flowering. The secret is to prune very lightly.

Blooms:	Double / Buff yellow / Fragrant
Foliage:	Dark green
Introduction:	1918
Type:	Rambler
Pruning:	Rambler — Method 3
Flowering Period:	Midsummer

ENA HARKNESS, CLIMBING

The drooping nature of the blooms, a disadvantage in the bush form of *Ena Harkness*, becomes a positive virtue in the climbing form. All the advantages of this old but much-loved Hybrid Tea are there — beauty of colour, form and fragrance. It flowers freely in summer but the autumn display may be disappointing. Plant it against a south-facing wall and enjoy the sweetly-scented blooms in May.

Blooms:	Double / Crimson scarlet / Fragrant
Foliage:	Medium green
Introduction:	1954
Type:	Climbing Hybrid Tea
Pruning:	Climber — Method 1
Flowering Period:	Repeat flowering

Blooms:	Double Deep red Very fragrant
Foliage:	Dark green
Introduction:	1931
Type:	Climbing Hybrid Tea
Pruning:	Climber — Method 1
Flowering Period:	Repeat flowering

ETOILE DE HOLLANDE, CLIMBING

The bush form of *Etoile de Hollande* was the Queen of the Reds between the Wars, and its climbing sport still remains popular. In fact, it is often recommended as the best of all climbing red roses for clothing the wall of a house. There the hanging flowers, velvety red and richly fragrant, can be enjoyed to the full. The summer flush of flowers is impressive, but the quantity of autumn flowering is unpredictable.

Blooms:	Double Rosy crimson; white centre No fragrance
Foliage:	Medium green
Introduction:	1909
Type:	Rambler
Pruning:	Rambler — Method 1
Flowering Period:	Midsummer

EXCELSA

Other Name: RED DOROTHY PERKINS

The red Rambler of yesteryear — its place has now been taken by the much healthier *Crimson Shower*. But *Excelsa* still keeps its place in many catalogues as it makes an excellent weeping standard. When grown in this way or on an arch or pillar it is festooned with small globular flowers, white-centred with crimson petals, during July. It is a rampant grower.

Blooms:	Double Pale pink Fragrant
Foliage:	Bronze-tinted
Introduction:	1906
Type:	Rambler
Pruning:	Rambler — Method 1
Flowering Period:	Early summer

FRANCOIS JURANVILLE

This old Rambler remains an excellent choice to cover a large structure such as a pergola or large screen. It is a very vigorous grower, reaching 20 ft or more. The flowers are large for a Rambler Rose, and have a heavy old-world fragrance. They appear in late June, at first deep salmon pink but soon fading to pale pink. The long flexible stems have few thorns and the leaves are small and shiny.

Blooms:	Double Pink Slightly fragrant
Foliage:	Medium green
Introduction:	1966
Type:	Large-flowered Climber
Pruning:	Climber — Method 2
Flowering Period:	Repeat flowering

GALWAY BAY

This offspring of *Queen Elizabeth* has the properties you would expect in a modern pillar rose — restrained growth reaching about 8 ft high and leaves with good disease resistance. Although there is nothing special about the growth habit of *Galway Bay*, the flowers are noteworthy. They are large, well-formed and borne in remarkable profusion. The small clusters appear regularly during the summer and autumn.

Blooms:	Double Buff yellow Fragrant
Foliage:	Medium green
Introduction:	1853
Type:	Noisette Climber
Pruning:	Climber — Method 2
Flowering Period:	Repeat flowering

GLOIRE DE DIJON

Victorian rose experts wrote about the great beauty of this old climbing rose, and you can see why if you look at a mature and vigorous plant in June. The flowers are large, strikingly coloured and sweetly scented. Having started early in the season, flowering continues until the autumn. Recommended for walls, but watch out for mildew. Many modern stocks have deteriorated, so buy from a reputable supplier.

Blooms:	Double Golden yellow Fragrant
Foliage:	Dark green
Introduction:	1956
Type:	Large-flowered Climber
Pruning:	Climber — Method 2
Flowering Period:	Repeat flowering

GOLDEN SHOWERS

By far the most popular yellow climbing rose — you can buy it anywhere. There are several reasons for its universal appeal — resistance to rain, bright flowers and foliage, and above all the prolonged flowering season from June until the frosts arrive. It is excellent for a small garden as it is easily kept in check. It has faults — the blooms soon become loose and growth at first is bushy rather than climbing.

CLIMBERS & RAMBLERS

Height in feet

GUINEE

You will love or hate this blackest of all garden roses. Velvety deep red, the blooms may look dull on a cloudy day but can glow in full sunshine. These flowers are large, opening flat and emitting a strong perfume. Very free-flowering in June, but the later flushes are disappointing. Foliage is leathery and plentiful, but you must watch for mildew. A good variety for walls and screens — stems are stiff and quite rigid.

Blooms:	Double Very dark red, shaded black Very fragrant
Foliage:	Medium green
Introduction:	1938
Type:	Large-flowered Climber
Pruning:	Climber — Method 2
Flowering Period:	Repeat flowering

HANDEL

Handel is a star of the climbing rose world. The secret of its appeal lies in the unique colouring of its blooms, for it has no other unusual feature. The flowers are nicely shaped, but are rather short of petals. The stems are relatively thornless and the leaves are glossy, but mildew and black spot can be problems. The flowers are borne singly or in clusters over a long period, and are not spoilt by rain.

Blooms:	Double Cream, edged rosy pink Slightly fragrant
Foliage:	Bronze-tinted
Introduction:	1965
Type:	Large-flowered Climber
Pruning:	Climber — Method 2
Flowering Period:	Repeat flowering

HIGHFIELD

Highfield is a sport of the most popular of all modern climbing roses — *Compassion*. It has many of the properties of its illustrious parent, including its free-flowering habit. The flowers are medium-sized, sometimes tinged with pink or peach. It is not a rampant grower, so it is best on a pillar, fence or arch rather than against a large wall. You will find it in a number of catalogues, but it has never matched the popularity of *Compassion*.

Blooms:	Double Pale yellow Fragrant
Foliage:	Dark green
Introduction:	1981
Type:	Large-flowered Climber
Pruning:	Climber — Method 2
Flowering Period:	Repeat flowering

ICEBERG, CLIMBING

This sport of the most successful white Floribunda of our time has not become really popular. Surprising, perhaps, because it has many admirers and is regarded as one of the most reliable climbing sports of recent years. It will clothe a wall with abundant glossy foliage studded with large trusses of flat white blooms, and this display continues until the autumn. Spraying against mildew may be necessary.

Blooms:	Double White Slightly fragrant
Foliage:	Medium green
Introduction:	1968
Type:	Climbing Floribunda
Pruning:	Climber — Method 2
Flowering Period:	Repeat flowering

LADY SYLVIA, CLIMBING

A climbing sport appeared a few years after the introduction of *Lady Sylvia*. The Climber has the same long buds and attractive foliage as its bushy parent, but the fragrance is even stronger. Make sure you have enough space for this one — it is a vigorous grower and will reach 20 ft or more. Don't try to keep it in check by pruning heavily — flowers will be few and far between if you do so. Tolerates poor conditions better than most.

Blooms:	Double Pale pink; yellow at base Very fragrant
Foliage:	Medium green
Introduction:	1933
Type:	Climbing Hybrid Tea
Pruning:	Climber — Method 2
Flowering Period:	Late summer

LEVERKUSEN

As you would expect from a Kordesii Climber, the leaves are healthy and the flowers appear freely. Even on an exposed site or in one of the colder areas of the country *Leverkusen* can be relied upon to provide an attractive display on a pillar or wall. Large clusters of blooms appear in June and further flushes follow — the autumn show is outstanding for a rose in this German-bred group.

Blooms:	Semi-double Pale yellow Slightly fragrant
Foliage:	Medium green
Introduction:	1954
Type:	Kordesii Climber
Pruning:	Climber — Method 2
Flowering Period:	Repeat flowering

Blooms:	Double White, flushed pink Very fragrant
Foliage:	Light green
Introduction:	1879
Type:	Noisette Climber
Pruning:	Climber — Method 2
Flowering Period:	Repeat flowering

MADAME ALFRED CARRIERE

In Victorian times a wide range of Noisette Climbers were used to clothe cottages and castles; today very few remain in the catalogues. *Madame Alfred Carrière* is one, because its ability to clothe a north-facing wall of a house has not been matched by many modern varieties. It grows quickly, and the large, fragrant blooms open regularly during summer and autumn. A century old, but as vigorous as ever.

Blooms:	Double Pink; shaded crimson Very fragrant
Foliage:	Medium green
Introduction:	1927
Type:	Large-flowered Climber
Pruning:	Climber — Method 1
Flowering Period:	Early summer

MADAME GREGOIRE STAECHELIN
Other Name: SPANISH BEAUTY

A sight to behold — a full-grown specimen of *Madame Grégoire Staechelin* in full flower. The H.T.-type blooms are large, with frilled pink petals and a scent which is heavy and sweet. These blooms smother the abundant foliage of this very vigorous variety in June, but the flowering season lasts for only a few weeks after which the large hips begin to develop.

Blooms:	Semi-double Bronze yellow Fragrant
Foliage:	Medium green
Introduction:	1953
Type:	Large-flowered Climber
Pruning:	Climber — Method 2
Flowering Period:	Early summer

MAIGOLD

Maigold has many virtues, and it is not surprising to find it in the best-seller lists of climbing roses. It comes to flower in May, when roses are so welcome. It also blooms early in the life of the plant — a problem with many climbers. The foliage is healthy and attractive, and the fragrance is strong. There are drawbacks — the stems are thorny, the blooms are unshapely and flowering after the first flush is unlikely.

Blooms:	Semi-double Yellow, then pink and red Slightly fragrant
Foliage:	Dark green
Introduction:	1958
Type:	Climbing Floribunda
Pruning:	Climber — Method 2
Flowering Period:	Repeat flowering

MASQUERADE, CLIMBING

The visual effect of large trusses bearing yellow, pink and deep red flowers is even more spectacular on the climbing sport of *Masquerade* than on the more familiar bush form. This variety is suitable for a fence or pillar, and has a good reputation for reliability. There is a profuse flush in June, but if you fail to remove the dead flowers before the hips form then there will be few flowers later in the season.

Blooms:	Semi-double Pink; apricot at base Fragrant
Foliage:	Dark green
Introduction:	1954
Type:	Large-flowered Climber
Pruning:	Climber — Method 2
Flowering Period:	Repeat flowering

MEG

A Large-flowered Climber to grow for its beautiful blooms — 5 in. across, apricot and pink with a large boss of red stamens. The many-flowered clusters appear in June, but even with regular dead-heading the later flushes are disappointing. *Meg* is a good choice for a pergola, pillar or fence, but you must remember to tie it in regularly as the stems are wide-spreading and rigid. The leaves are large and glossy.

Blooms:	Single Primrose yellow Fragrant
Foliage:	Medium green
Introduction:	1918
Type:	Large-flowered Climber
Pruning:	Climber — Method 1
Flowering Period:	Repeat flowering

MERMAID

The giant of the climbing rose world — a plant to cover the wall of a large house. It should, however, be a west- or south-facing wall as *Mermaid* can be killed by frost. This lack of hardiness is not the only fault of *Mermaid* — the stems are brittle and thorny, and a new plant will take a couple of years to establish. But in full flower it is supreme — the very large blooms are eye-catching and fragrant.

CLIMBERS & RAMBLERS

Height in feet

MORNING JEWEL

The pink of the large blooms has been described in many ways — "rich", "glowing" and so on. With a backcloth of shiny leaves this Scottish-bred variety gives an eye-catching display during the summer months. The autumn show can be disappointing. New shoots appear readily from the base — a useful Large-flowered Climber for fences or pillars. Not very popular — perhaps the continuity of flowering is not good enough.

Blooms:	Semi-double Pink Slightly fragrant
Foliage:	Medium green
Introduction:	1969
Type:	Large-flowered Climber
Pruning:	Climber — Method 2
Flowering Period:	Repeat flowering

MRS SAM McGREDY, CLIMBING

Mrs Sam McGredy has almost disappeared from the catalogues — the climbing form is the way to enjoy once again her former glory. Here is the old vigour, and here are the bronze buds, the copper red blooms and the purple young foliage. The blooms are borne in large numbers and the flowering period lasts well into the autumn. Really colourful and reliable on a wall — the only drawback is susceptibility to black spot.

Blooms:	Double Coppery orange, flushed red Fragrant
Foliage:	Bronze-tinted
Introduction:	1937
Type:	Climbing Hybrid Tea
Pruning:	Climber — Method 2
Flowering Period:	Repeat flowering

NEW DAWN

Dr W. van Fleet was once a popular Rambler, but it has now been replaced by its sport *New Dawn*. There are two distinct advantages with the newer variety — the growth is much less rampant and the flower clusters continue to appear throughout the summer. The blooms are small, but they are present in great numbers above the shiny leaves. A multipurpose rose — use as a hedge, specimen shrub or climber.

Blooms:	Semi-double Shell pink Fragrant
Foliage:	Medium green
Introduction:	1930
Type:	Rambler
Pruning:	Rambler — Method 2
Flowering Period:	Repeat flowering

PARKDIREKTOR RIGGERS

This variety has the profusion of flowers and the hardiness associated with Kordesii Climbers, but it does not have the family resistance to disease — both mildew and black spot can be problems. The large clusters of glowing crimson blooms are borne with remarkable freedom, and this has led to the popularity of this climbing rose. Once the flowers are dead remove them to ensure continuous flowering.

Blooms:	Semi-double Blood red Slightly fragrant
Foliage:	Dark green
Introduction:	1957
Type:	Kordesii Climber
Pruning:	Climber — Method 1
Flowering Period:	Repeat flowering

PAUL'S SCARLET CLIMBER

The top climbing red rose for many years, *Paul's Scarlet* is sadly past its prime. There are newer red varieties which don't dull with age, and there are varieties which have much better resistance to disease. Still, it remains an eye-catching rose in June, with masses of cupped red flowers which last for a month or more and then they are gone — there is no repeat flowering. It is less vigorous than the average old-fashioned Rambler.

Blooms:	Semi-double Scarlet, shaded crimson Slightly fragrant
Foliage:	Medium green
Introduction:	1916
Type:	Rambler
Pruning:	Rambler — Method 2
Flowering Period:	Early summer

PINK PERPETUE

A best-selling variety, due to its free-flowering nature and the ability to produce an autumn display of flower trusses which rivals the summer show. *Pink Perpétue* does not grow very tall, but it is vigorous and wide-spreading which makes it a good choice for covering a fence or wall. The blooms are not large, but they have plenty of petals and an attractive globular shape. Rust can be a serious problem.

Blooms:	Double Rose pink; carmine reverse Slightly fragrant
Foliage:	Dark green
Introduction:	1965
Type:	Large-flowered Climber
Pruning:	Climber — Method 2
Flowering Period:	Repeat flowering

Blooms:	Single Creamy white Fragrant
Foliage:	Medium green
Introduction:	1954
Type:	Rambler
Pruning:	Rambler — Method 3
Flowering Period:	Midsummer

ROSA FILIPES KIFTSGATE

A rambling giant of a rose, tall and wide-spreading, used for covering sheds or for growing up old trees. In July there is a cascade of bloom – enormous clusters of small fragrant flowers. These blooms are followed by bright red hips in the autumn. Treat it as an enormous bush — don't try to keep it in bounds in a small garden by pruning and don't try to flatten it against the side of the house.

Blooms:	Double Deep rose pink Fragrant
Foliage:	Dark green
Introduction:	1968
Type:	Large-flowered Climber
Pruning:	Climber — Method 2
Flowering Period:	Repeat flowering

ROSY MANTLE

A well-bred rose — it has the reliable climbing habit of *New Dawn* and some of the floral beauty of its other parent, *Prima Ballerina*. The large and shapely blooms are borne in small clusters throughout the season, and the display is especially good in autumn. The glossy leaves are rarely troubled by disease, but the wiry stems need regular attention to ensure that they are trained properly.

Blooms:	Double Deep yellow Slightly fragrant
Foliage:	Medium green
Introduction:	1957
Type:	Large-flowered Climber
Pruning:	Climber — Method 2
Flowering Period:	Repeat flowering

ROYAL GOLD

A variety which sounds irresistible in the catalogue — fragrant golden blooms, high-centred like a Hybrid Tea and 4 in. in diameter. But *Royal Gold* in the garden is not as desirable as its catalogue description — it does not flower freely and vigour is distinctly lacking if the soil is not fertile. The major problem is lack of hardiness — this is a rose for a south or west wall on a sheltered site.

Blooms:	Double White Fragrant
Foliage:	Light green
Introduction:	1912
Type:	Rambler
Pruning:	Rambler — Method 1
Flowering Period:	Midsummer

SANDERS' WHITE RAMBLER

Despite its great age this fine old Rambler has kept both its health and its place in the catalogues. The rosette-shaped flowers are small but they are both sweet smelling and filled with petals. The large clusters of flowers appear in August and this variety is usually recommended for clothing arches, pillars and fences rather than walls. It is particularly good as a weeping standard where its glossy attractive leaves can be appreciated.

Blooms:	Double Apricot orange Fragrant
Foliage:	Dark green
Introduction:	1964
Type:	Large-flowered Climber
Pruning:	Climber — Method 2
Flowering Period:	Repeat flowering

SCHOOLGIRL

It is not surprising that *Schoolgirl* should have become so popular. Good orange climbing roses are extremely rare, and the blooms of this McGredy-bred rose are large and fragrant. The leaves are glossy and abundant, and the flowers appear throughout the summer and autumn. Its main fault is the loss of the lower leaves, so that the stems appear leggy. Another drawback is the failure to produce a mass of flowers.

Blooms:	Single White Fragrant
Foliage:	Medium green
Introduction:	1907
Type:	Rambler
Pruning:	Rambler — Method 1
Flowering Period:	Midsummer

SEAGULL

Another oldie, but you should have no difficulty in locating a supplier. Its parentage is unknown — technically it is classed as a Climbing Wild Rose. The small flowers bear prominent golden stamens and they appear in large numbers in summer. Growth is vigorous and the trusses are large. The continuing popularity of *Seagull* is probably due to the frequent references in the catalogues to its ability to scramble up and clothe old trees.

CLIMBERS & RAMBLERS

Height in feet

SUPER STAR, CLIMBING

It is fashionable these days to dwell on the faults rather than to extol the virtues of this fading star. Foliage is sparse and dull — the leaves and buds are prone to mildew. Still, you will find it listed in many catalogues as the large, high-centred and luminescent flowers have kept their charm. Fragrance is still there and grow it if you must, but there are really much better climbing roses to grow as mildew control can be difficult.

Blooms:	Double Orange vermilion Fragrant
Foliage:	Medium green
Introduction:	1965
Type:	Climbing Hybrid Tea
Pruning:	Climber — Method 2
Flowering Period:	Repeat flowering

SWAN LAKE

One of the best white climbers you can buy — the flowers are large and shapely, and the foliage is abundant. The blooms are not spoilt by wet weather — an unusual advantage for a white rose. The flowers, bearing fifty petals or more, are borne freely throughout the season, but the foliage is prone to attack by mildew and black spot so spraying is necessary. A good choice for an arch or pillar.

Blooms:	Double White, tinged pink Slightly fragrant
Foliage:	Medium green
Introduction:	1968
Type:	Large-flowered Climber
Pruning:	Climber — Method 2
Flowering Period:	Repeat flowering

VEILCHENBLAU
Other Name: VIOLET BLUE

A black and white photograph of *Veilchenblau* in bloom reveals a very ordinary rose — small, semi-double and cupped flowers. In the garden, grown against a wall shaded from the noon-day sun, it is a most unusual variety — one of the closest yet to the elusive "blue" rose. The mature bloom is perhaps more grey than blue, but it is worth growing if you like out-of-the-ordinary roses.

Blooms:	Semi-double Violet, fading to slate grey Fragrant
Foliage:	Light green
Introduction:	1909
Type:	Rambler
Pruning:	Rambler — Method 2
Flowering Period:	Midsummer

WEDDING DAY

The only small thing about this rose is the flower — 5-petalled, cream-coloured fading to pinky white and studded with golden stamens. Everything else is on the grand scale — growth is extremely vigorous, the flower trusses in July and August are large and the rampant stems will cover 2-storey buildings or massive old trees. A rival to *Rosa Filipes Kiftsgate* for hiding unsightly objects, but a bad choice for small gardens.

Blooms:	Single Creamy white Fragrant
Foliage:	Medium green
Introduction:	1950
Type:	Rambler
Pruning:	Rambler — Method 3
Flowering Period:	Midsummer

WHITE COCKADE

Like *Swan Lake*, this Scottish-bred variety is one of the best modern white climbers available. The blooms are beautifully formed with a pleasant fragrance, and there is a prolonged flowering period. It is a short-growing climber — obviously not a rose to cover the side of the house. Use it to clothe a low pillar or fence, or grow it as a tall bush. Disease resistance is good, and the glossy foliage is attractive.

Blooms:	Double White Slightly fragrant
Foliage:	Medium green
Introduction:	1969
Type:	Large-flowered Climber
Pruning:	Climber — Method 2
Flowering Period:	Repeat flowering

ZEPHIRINE DROUHIN
Other Name: THORNLESS ROSE

Zephirine Drouhin deserves its place in the Rose Hall of Fame — after more than 100 years it still appears in nearly all the catalogues, and the praise from the experts is as loud as ever. Grow it as a climber, or keep it pruned as a tall bush or hedge. Dead-head regularly, and there will be a succession of blooms from June onwards. Spray regularly with a fungicide.

Blooms:	Semi-double Carmine pink Very fragrant
Foliage:	Light green
Introduction:	1868
Type:	Climbing Bourbon Rose
Pruning:	Climber — Method 2
Flowering Period:	Repeat flowering

CLIMBERS & RAMBLERS

SHRUB ROSES

It has been estimated that for every 25 Hybrid Teas and Floribundas purchased in Britain, only one Shrub Rose is bought. The reason is, of course, the faults which everybody knows — Shrub Roses only bloom once, they are far too large for an average garden and they are far too old-fashioned for a modern garden.

Not one of these allegations is true. Consider the first misconception — lack of repeat flowering. Some Shrubs, such as the Species Roses, the Gallicas and the Centifolias do produce only one spectacular showing, but other Shrub Roses are repeat flowering, and many examples are listed on pages 62–72. Even the once flowering varieties should not be decried. The flowering period often lasts for many weeks and the timing, as with *Canary Bird* in May, may not be achievable with a Floribunda or Hybrid Tea. Furthermore, the sight of some of the once flowering varieties in full bloom in June or July exceeds the display value of most of the shrubs we grow.

The second incorrect idea about Shrub Roses concerns their size. Some indeed are giants, like *William Lobb, Nevada* and *Frühlingsmorgen*, but there are others which could look up to an average Floribunda — dainty Shrubs such as *Cécile Brunner* and *The Fairy*.

Finally, the question of the old-fashioned look. Of course there are cottage-type roses — pink, overblown and full of fragrance, and that's their charm. But every flower form is available, from *Fred Loads* with its 5-petalled blooms to *Fountain* with its high-centred, H.T.-type flowers.

A feature of the 1980s was the marked increase in the number of ground cover varieties available. Ten are listed here and most have been recently introduced. For more details of this group, see page 82.

Shrub Roses are underestimated, under-utilized and misunderstood. One of the problems is that they are not a clear-cut group — quite frankly they are a rag-bag of varieties which do not belong in any of the other classes. Included are the Species Roses (wild varieties and their near relatives) and the Old-Fashioned Roses (varieties dating back to the pre-Hybrid Tea era). Finally there are the Modern Shrub Roses, which usually have a flower form rather similar to a Floribunda or Hybrid Tea. Somewhere in this class is a variety for nearly every garden. Many Shrubs will thrive in conditions which would not support a Hybrid Tea, and both pruning and upkeep are simple.

KEY TO THE ROSE GUIDES

Foliage Leaf colour (see page 6)

Number of Petals See page 5

Colour

Fragrance See page 6

Introduction Year of introduction in Britain

Type Type of Shrub — for descriptions see page 78

Blooms: Semi-double / Pale crimson / No fragrance

Foliage: Medium green

Introduction: Before 1300

Type: Gallica Rose

Growth Type: Upright

Flowering Period: Midsummer

Height in ft **Width in ft**

Flowering Period Repeat flowering, or time of blooming if once flowering (see page 6)

Growth Type Growth habit (upright, trailing, spreading etc.)

Height in feet   Width in feet

ANGELINA

A rounded bush which is quite small for a Shrub Rose. *Angelina* is suitable for planting at the front of the shrub border or as a hedge, but despite its good points and compact size it has not become popular. The blooms are borne in trusses, appearing regularly until early autumn. There are not many petals, but the slightly cupped blooms with their prominent stamens are most attractive. Growth is vigorous and healthy.

Blooms:	Semi-double Deep pink; white eye Slightly fragrant
Foliage:	Light green
Introduction:	1975
Type:	Modern Shrub Rose
Growth Type:	Bushy
Flowering Period:	Repeat flowering

AUSTRIAN COPPER
Other Name: *R. FOETIDA BICOLOR*

The brightest of the Species Roses — a superb sight in full bloom. Unfortunately the flowering season lasts for only a couple of weeks and for the rest of the summer the bush is rather dull and highly susceptible to black spot. The smell is neither strong nor pleasant. Some (but not all) experts believe it to be the original parent of all orange H.T.s.

Blooms:	Single Coppery orange; yellow reverse No fragrance
Foliage:	Medium green
Introduction:	Before 1590
Type:	Species Rose
Growth Type:	Arching
Flowering Period:	Midsummer

BALLERINA

Masses of tiny flowers are borne in hydrangea-like heads which appear all summer long. The bush bears an abundance of small glossy leaves, and this healthy variety is suitable for either the herbaceous border or rose bed. It can also be planted as a hedge or grown as a standard. There is a pleasant musk-like perfume and for lovers of *Ballerina* there is now a similar red variety *(Marjorie Fair)* available.

Blooms:	Single Pale pink; white eye Slightly fragrant
Foliage:	Light green
Introduction:	1937
Type:	Modern Shrub Rose
Growth Type:	Bushy
Flowering Period:	Repeat flowering

BLANC DOUBLE DE COUBERT

This old French-bred Shrub remains popular. Its flowers are large and sweet-smelling, first appearing in June and continuing into the autumn. The great virtue is outstanding disease resistance, making spraying unnecessary. There are drawbacks — the papery petals are easily damaged by rain, the foliage is too sparse and the stem bases are too bare to make it either a reliable hedge or an attractive bush.

Blooms:	Semi-double Pure white Very fragrant
Foliage:	Medium green
Introduction:	1892
Type:	Rugosa Shrub
Growth Type:	Bushy
Flowering Period:	Repeat flowering

BLANCHE MOREAU

Over a hundred years old and still one of the best of all Moss Roses. The white blooms are large and full with a green button centre, standing out against the dark and prickly stems. The buds are covered in brownish moss. The flowers appear in clusters in June — it is not repeat flowering but a few blooms may be produced in autumn. This Shrub Rose is suitable for use as a specimen bush or as a hedge.

Blooms:	Double White Fragrant
Foliage:	Dark green
Introduction:	1880
Type:	Moss Rose
Growth Type:	Open
Flowering Period:	Midsummer

BONICA
Other Name: *MEIDOMONAC*

[Ground Cover]

There is some confusion here. The original *Bonica* was a scarlet-flowered bush the 'Bonica' of the catalogues is really *Bonica 82*. This variety bred by Meilland is a ground cover rose of the 1980s. It has been awarded top honours in the U.S. — an excellent choice where a ground-covering bush is required. Flowers appear from June until September and the leaves are healthy.

Blooms:	Semi-double Pink Slightly fragrant
Foliage:	Dark green
Introduction:	1984
Type:	Modern Shrub Rose
Growth Type:	Procumbent
Flowering Period:	Repeat flowering

SHRUB ROSES

Blooms:	Double Ivory Very fragrant
Foliage:	Dark green
Introduction:	1867
Type:	Bourbon Rose
Growth Type:	Upright
Flowering Period:	Repeat flowering

BOULE DE NEIGE

The English translation of the name of this French-bred Bourbon Rose is Snowball — and how appropriate it is. The red-tinged buds, borne in small clusters, open into white, ball-like blooms about 2½ in. across. The petals are silky, the fragance is strong — undoubtedly one of the best Bourbons you can buy. The main problem is balling (see page 96) in wet weather — black spot can also be a problem.

Blooms:	Double Pale apricot Fragrant
Foliage:	Purple-tinted
Introduction:	1939
Type:	Hybrid Musk
Growth Type:	Arching
Flowering Period:	Repeat flowering

BUFF BEAUTY

The flowers are borne in large clusters, buff yellow at first then fading to a warm ivory. They are shapely in bud, but soon become confused and formless as they mature. *Buff Beauty* is a good choice for a hedge or for cutting — the perfume is pleasant and the foliage is attractive. The spreading branches will need spraying against mildew — if kept healthy, the autumn display is outstanding.

Blooms:	Single Canary yellow Fragrant
Foliage:	Grey green
Introduction:	After 1907
Type:	Species Rose
Growth Type:	Arching
Flowering Period:	Late spring

CANARY BIRD

Other Name: R. XANTHINA SPONTANEA

The popular choice for the rose to herald in the flowering season. In May the dainty yellow blooms appear in profusion along the arching stems. The period of flowering lasts for about a month. The ferny foliage makes an attractive bush when flowering is over. *Canary Bird* makes a good hedge — grow it as a standard where space is limited. Die-back occasionally occurs.

Blooms:	Semi-double Pink No fragrance
Foliage:	Medium green
Introduction:	1982
Type:	Modern Shrub Rose
Growth Type:	Procumbent
Flowering Period:	Repeat flowering

CANDY ROSE

Ground Cover

A wide-spreading ground cover from Meilland. It has the great advantage of being repeat flowering — a property lacking in the older ground covers. The flower clusters are small, the petals are few and there is no perfume, but it grows well in quite shady conditions and makes a good dwarf hedge. Health is good and the leaves are glossy. *Candy Rose* is a good choice to cover the ground beneath a tree.

Blooms:	Double Shell pink Slightly fragrant
Foliage:	Dark green
Introduction:	1881
Type:	China Rose
Growth Type:	Open
Flowering Period:	Repeat flowering

CECILE BRUNNER

Other Name: SWEETHEART ROSE

A hundred years old, and it remains a favourite in many gardens. You will still find it in some catalogues, for nothing has replaced the charm of the small bush bearing tiny pink flowers which are perfectly formed at the bud stage. Excellent for cutting or as a buttonhole rose — the clusters are large but the foliage is sparse. Flowering is from June until October.

Blooms:	Double Blush pink Fragrant
Foliage:	Grey green
Introduction:	About 1780
Type:	Alba Rose
Growth Type:	Upright
Flowering Period:	Midsummer

CELESTIAL

Other Names: CELESTE, MINDEN ROSE

Like all the Albas, *Celestial* is robust, hardy and trouble-free. It is free-flowering, the richly scented pink blooms appearing at the end of June to provide a midsummer display. The blooms have about 25 petals, opening to reveal the stamens within — a favourite old-fashioned variety which is excellent for hedging or as a tall specimen bush.

SHRUB ROSES

Height in feet   Width in feet

CHAPEAU DE NAPOLEON
Other Name: R. CENTIFOLIA CRISTATA

A true Centifolia Rose — full, globular blooms with a pleasant old-fashioned perfume. The buds are unique — a winged extension on the buds giving the appearance of "Napoleon's hat". The bush is hardy and spreading, the flowers appearing in June or July in drooping clusters. The stems may need support and protection from mildew.

Blooms:	Double Rose pink Fragrant
Foliage:	Medium green
Introduction:	1827
Type:	Centifolia Rose
Growth Type:	Open
Flowering Period:	Midsummer

CHINATOWN
Other Name: VILLE DE CHINE

A popular large bush rose — you will find it in the Floribunda or Shrub section of the catalogue. The fragrant flowers will withstand rainy weather and the bush is healthy and tolerant of exposed situations. The flowers are borne in large trusses and appear freely throughout the season — a good choice for hedging, the back of the border or as a specimen bush.

Blooms:	Double Yellow, edged pink Fragrant
Foliage:	Medium green
Introduction:	1963
Type:	Modern Shrub Rose
Growth Type:	Bushy
Flowering Period:	Repeat flowering

COMMON MOSS ROSE
Other Name: R. CENTIFOLIA MUSCOSA

The original and perhaps the best of the Moss Roses, sometimes called *Old Pink Moss.* The large, globular blooms open flat when mature, appearing in June or July. Both the buds and stems bear green "moss" and this variety has a distinct old-fashioned look. It is suitable for the smaller garden, where it can be used as a hedge or as a specimen bush. Keep watch for mildew.

Blooms:	Double Rose pink Fragrant
Foliage:	Medium green
Introduction:	About 1700
Type:	Moss Rose
Growth Type:	Open
Flowering Period:	Midsummer

COMPLICATA
Other Name: R. GALLICA COMPLICATA

The outstanding feature of this age-old variety is the size of the blooms which appear in June — 4 or 5 in. across, single and with a pleasing if not strong perfume. The stems bearing these blooms are long and lax, and this variety is best grown next to an old tree so that it can clamber upwards without artificial support. Easily rooted from cuttings.

Blooms:	Single Pink; white eye Slightly fragrant
Foliage:	Light green
Introduction:	Unknown
Type:	Gallica Rose
Growth Type:	Arching
Flowering Period:	Midsummer

CORNELIA

Grow *Cornelia* as a hedge — if you have lots of space you can grow it as a specimen bush. It is recognised by the unusually dark appearance of its stems and leaves plus its small and fragrant pink flowers, which first appear in June. These blooms are resistant to rain, and the best floral display occurs in autumn. The large trusses and free-flowering habit make *Cornelia* a popular Shrub Rose.

Blooms:	Double Apricot pink Very fragrant
Foliage:	Dark green
Introduction:	1925
Type:	Hybrid Musk
Growth Type:	Spreading
Flowering Period:	Repeat flowering

DOROTHY WHEATCROFT

A rather gaunt Shrub (a Floribunda in some catalogues) which should be planted at the back of the border. Its glory is the profusion of large heads of bright flowers on long stems, so large that they often bow down under their own weight, so some support may be necessary. Rain resistance is good despite the size of the flowers, but spraying is essential if you live in a black spot area. Fragrance is unfortunately very slight.

Blooms:	Semi-double Orange red, flushed scarlet Slightly fragrant
Foliage:	Medium green
Introduction:	1960
Type:	Modern Shrub Rose
Growth Type:	Upright
Flowering Period:	Repeat flowering

Height in feet   Width in feet

FELICIA

Blooms: Double, Apricot pink, Very fragrant
Foliage: Medium green
Introduction: 1928
Type: Hybrid Musk
Growth Type: Spreading
Flowering Period: Repeat flowering

A Hybrid Musk which is noted for its long flowering season — the first sweet-smelling blooms appear in June and flowering continues throughout the summer. The best display is in the autumn and flowers are still found on the wide-spreading bushes in November. The blooms are shapely, like a Hybrid Tea, and are borne in large trusses. Excellent for cutting, *Felicia* makes a good hedge or specimen bush.

FIONA

Other Name: MEIBELUXEN

Ground Cover

Blooms: Double, Blood red, Slightly fragrant
Foliage: Dark green
Introduction: 1983
Type: Modern Shrub Rose
Growth Type: Procumbent
Flowering Period: Repeat flowering

One of the largest of the ground cover roses — it is described as a bush in some of the catalogues. The flowers are small and only moderately full, but the rich red colour makes up for the lack of substance. These blooms appear freely throughout the summer months, small clusters appearing amongst the small and semi-glossy leaves. Grow it in the border or plant it as a hedge.

F.J. GROOTENDORST

Other Name: NELKENROSE

Blooms: Double, Crimson, No fragrance
Foliage: Light green
Introduction: 1918
Type: Rugosa Shrub
Growth Type: Open
Flowering Period: Repeat flowering

In most ways this Shrub has very little to offer. There is neither fragrance nor hips, and the flowers are small and rather dull. The foliage is pale and small, although it is attractive in the autumn months. The unique feature of *F.J. Grootendorst* is the distinct frill at the edge of the petals, giving a carnation-like effect. Like all Rugosas, it is reliable under poor conditions.

FOUNTAIN

Blooms: Double, Blood red, Fragrant
Foliage: Dark green
Introduction: 1972
Type: Modern Shrub Rose
Growth Type: Upright
Flowering Period: Repeat flowering

The blooms of this upright Shrub helped it to gain the supreme British awards in 1971. Large, velvety, blood red — the H.T.-type flowers are borne singly or in small trusses throughout the season. The bush is abundantly clothed with dark foliage which is reddish when young. It has a good reputation for reliability and resistance to disease, but the tall shoots occasionally snap in autumn storms.

FRAU DAGMAR HARTOPP

Other Name: FRU DAGMAR HASTRUP

Blooms: Single, Shell pink, Very fragrant
Foliage: Dark green
Introduction: 1914
Type: Rugosa Shrub
Growth Type: Bushy
Flowering Period: Repeat flowering

Frau Dagmar Hartopp lacks the height of many of the Rugosas, but it is considered by many experts to be one of the best. It has all the good properties of the group — freedom from disease, continuous flowering, blooms which are attractive and strongly scented and finally hips which are red and large. The bush will grow almost anywhere and is ideal as a low-growing hedge.

FRAU KARL DRUSCHKI

Other Name: SNOW QUEEN

Blooms: Double, White, No fragrance
Foliage: Medium green
Introduction: 1901
Type: Hybrid Perpetual
Growth Type: Upright
Flowering Period: Repeat flowering

Frau Karl Druschki appeared nearly 90 years ago, but it is still going strong and is widely offered for sale. Its everlasting appeal is at first surprising — there is no scent and no resistance to mildew. But its virtues can be seen in a large garden — a stately bush covered with masses of pure white blooms opening from red-splashed buds. Prune lightly; peg down long shoots.

SHRUB ROSES

	Height in feet	Width in feet

FRED LOADS

This variety has become really popular, even though it has only five petals. The reason is that it makes up for its shortage of petals with bright colouring and huge trusses which can exceed 18 in. across. The flowers are large and unfading, and the bush is well-clothed with leaves. Healthy and vigorous, *Fred Loads* is an excellent choice, although it can look rather top heavy in full flower.

Blooms: Single
Orange vermilion
Fragrant

Foliage: Light green

Introduction: 1967

Type: Modern Shrub Rose

Growth Type: Upright

Flowering Period: Repeat flowering

FRÜHLINGSGOLD
Other Name: SPRING GOLD

Kordes bred a number of splendid hybrids from *R. spinosissima*, the Scotch Briar. *Frühlingsgold* is perhaps the finest — a mature bush in full flower in May is one of the great sights of the rose world. The arching branches are festooned with saucer-sized flowers, and the air is filled with fragrance. The flowering period lasts for only a fortnight, and ample space is essential.

Blooms: Semi-double
Creamy yellow
Fragrant

Foliage: Light green

Introduction: 1937

Type: Species Rose

Growth Type: Arching

Flowering Period: Early summer

FRÜHLINGSMORGEN
Other Name: SPRING MORNING

Another Kordes hybrid, smaller and bushier than its yellow sister described above. The small-leaved Shrub is not particularly attractive, but the flowers are — large, scented and colourful. The pale centre of each pink-edged petal highlights the maroon stamens. The second flush of flowers in September are smaller and not as prolific as the early summer flush.

Blooms: Single
Deep pink; yellow centre
Fragrant

Foliage: Grey green

Introduction: 1942

Type: Species Rose

Growth Type: Open

Flowering Period: June & September

GOLDEN WINGS

A popular and highly praised variety, perhaps the best of all the large-flowered yellow Shrubs. From June onwards the blooms appear in regular flushes provided the old flowers are dead-headed. The flowers are large and sweet-smelling — light primrose with prominent buff yellow stamens. These blooms are not damaged by rain, but they do fade slightly with age. Disease resistance is good — an excellent choice.

Blooms: Single
Pale yellow
Fragrant

Foliage: Light green

Introduction: 1956

Type: Modern Shrub Rose

Growth Type: Bushy

Flowering Period: Repeat flowering

GRAHAM THOMAS
Other Name: AUSMAS

This English-bred rose was named after a leading authority on old-fashioned roses, and nearly everything about it is unusual. There is the colour — almost unique amongst blooms with an old-fashioned look. Then there is the fragrance — tea-like rather than sweet. Each flower has the form of a Paeony and the flowering season extends from early summer to late autumn.

Blooms: Double
Deep yellow
Fragrant

Foliage: Pale green

Introduction: 1983

Type: Modern Shrub Rose

Growth Type: Arching

Flowering Period: Repeat flowering

GROUSE
Other Name: KORIMRO

Ground Cover

One of the "game bird" group of ground cover roses bred by Kordes — others are *Partridge* (white flowers) and *Pheasant* (rose pink). All are truly prostrate, producing ground-hugging branches which can be used to cover banks, trail over walls etc. Weeds are suppressed by the abundant glossy foliage — a real breakthrough. Flowers are small, appearing in summer.

Blooms: Single
Pale pink
Fragrant

Foliage: Medium green

Introduction: 1984

Type: Modern Shrub Rose

Growth Type: Procumbent

Flowering Period: Repeat flowering

JOSEPH'S COAT

Seen at its best in June or July, this offspring of *Circus* bears medium-sized blooms in large trusses. The petals change from yellow to orange and finally to cherry red as they age. This bright but gaudy variety can be trained as a climber, reaching 10 ft high, or it can be grown as a hedge or 6 ft specimen shrub. It can also be kept pruned as a 4 ft bush for the small garden, but it is happiest when grown as a shrub.

Blooms:	Semi-double Yellow, edged red Slightly fragrant
Foliage:	Dark green
Introduction:	1964
Type:	Modern Shrub Rose
Growth Type:	Open
Flowering Period:	Repeat flowering

LADY PENZANCE

R. rubiginosa (the Sweet Briar of Eglantine) is a wild English rose with a most unusual property — the foliage emits an apple-like odour after rain. The best hybrid for the ordinary garden is *Lady Penzance* which blooms in early June. The flowers are small and the flowering period lasts for only a week or two — this variety is grown for its fragrant foliage and not for its blooms. Choose it if novelties appeal to you.

Blooms:	Single Copper; yellow centre Very fragrant
Foliage:	Dark green
Introduction:	1894
Type:	Species Rose
Growth Type:	Open
Flowering Period:	Early summer

LITTLE WHITE PET
Other Name: WHITE PET

An old Polyantha Rose — like *The Fairy* it keeps its place in numerous catalogues despite the superior blooms of the modern Floribundas. The flowers are indeed small and pompon-like, but they are borne in huge trusses throughout the summer months. Plant it as a standard or grow the bushes in groups of 3 or 4 in the border. An excellent choice for a small old-world garden.

Blooms:	Double White Fragrant
Foliage:	Dark green
Introduction:	1879
Type:	Polyantha Rose
Growth Type:	Spreading
Flowering Period:	Repeat flowering

MADAME HARDY

A lovely old-fashioned rose — full of petals and fragrance. *Madame Hardy* is a Damask Rose, with the dull foliage and lax stems which characterize the group. The blooms are borne in large clusters during June and July. Considered by some to be the most beautiful of all white Shrub blooms, they are certainly not the hardiest. Both rain and strong winds damage them and stems may need support against bad weather.

Blooms:	Double White Fragrant
Foliage:	Medium green
Introduction:	1832
Type:	Damask Rose
Growth Type:	Open
Flowering Period:	Midsummer

MADAME ISAAC PEREIRE

Pity the poor novice who seeks advice from the experts about this Bourbon Rose. For most of them this old-fashioned variety is a joy — huge flowers with a fragrance which is probably unmatched by any other Shrub. To others it is an ugly plant with unattractive foliage and with flowers which are sometimes misshapen... and both sides are telling the truth. The stems need support — it can be grown as a pillar rose.

Blooms:	Double Deep carmine pink Very fragrant
Foliage:	Medium green
Introduction:	1881
Type:	Bourbon Rose
Growth Type:	Open
Flowering Period:	Repeat flowering

MARGUERITE HILLING
Other Name: PINK NEVADA

A sport of the popular Shrub *Nevada*. It is identical to its parent in many ways — the same growth habit, foliage and size. It is, however, more free-flowering and the blooms are pale pink overlaid with a deeper shade of pink. The whole base can be covered by the first flush of blooms in June. The leaves are small and dull, and black spot can be a problem.

Blooms:	Semi-double Pink, shaded deep pink Slightly fragrant
Foliage:	Medium green
Introduction:	1959
Type:	Modern Shrub Rose
Growth Type:	Arching
Flowering Period:	June & September

SHRUB ROSES

	Height in feet	Width in feet

MARJORIE FAIR
Other Name: RED YESTERDAY

Harkness produced this variety by crossing *Ballerina* and *Baby Faurax*. It inherited its carmine flower colour from neither of its parents, but all its growth characteristics come from *Ballerina* (page 62). Here you will find the same large heads of tiny flowers, the mass of glossy leaves and the freedom from disease. It has won awards in several countries, but it is not a best-seller.

Blooms:	Single Red; white centre Slightly fragrant
Foliage:	Light green
Introduction:	1978
Type:	Modern Shrub Rose
Growth Type:	Bushy
Flowering Period:	Repeat flowering

MARY ROSE
Other Name: AUSMARY

A rose of the 1980s, but you would never tell from the flowers. They are large, full and distinctly cupped — an old-fashioned look for a modern rose. The scent is strong, the growth is robust but the foliage is dull. *Mary Rose* has no distinguished parents and it has won no premier awards, but buy it if you want a Victorian-style rose with none of the problems.

Blooms:	Double Rose pink Very fragrant
Foliage:	Medium green
Introduction:	1983
Type:	Modern Shrub Rose
Growth Type:	Bushy
Flowering Period:	Repeat flowering

MAX GRAF

Ground Cover

The first and still a very useful ground cover rose. The prostrate stems spread over the soil surface, rooting as they go, and quickly produce a dense green mat. The single pink flowers appear freely over a long period in June and July, but there is no repeat flowering. The flowers, borne in clusters, have an apple-like fragrance. The stems are thorny, which makes weeding a problem. *Max Graf* is recommended for growing over a wall.

Blooms:	Single Pink; white centre Fragrant
Foliage:	Medium green
Introduction:	1919
Type:	Rugosa Shrub
Growth Type:	Trailing
Flowering Period:	Midsummer

NEVADA

Nevada is one of the great sights of the rose world. In June the whole bush is covered with large creamy white blooms. When mature and well-grown both the small leaves and thornless red stems may be almost completely hidden. Space is essential — trying to keep the bush small by hard pruning leads to disappointing results. If black spot is a problem in your area, regular spraying will be necessary.

Blooms:	Semi-double Creamy white Slightly fragrant
Foliage:	Medium green
Introduction:	1927
Type:	Modern Shrub Rose
Growth Type:	Arching
Flowering Period:	June & September

NOZOMI

Ground Cover

Technically it is a Climbing Miniature, but you will find *Nozomi* amongst the Shrub Roses in the catalogues. This Japanese variety has become popular as a ground cover plant. Its trailing stems bear small glossy leaves, and in summer there are clusters of tiny pearly flowers. Not as wide-spreading as *Max Graf* or *Grouse*, but still very useful for edging. Stems may be pegged down to improve the cover.

Blooms:	Single Pearly pink No fragrance
Foliage:	Dark green
Introduction:	1968
Type:	Modern Shrub Rose
Growth Type:	Trailing
Flowering Period:	Midsummer

PENELOPE

Several Hybrid Musks are described in this section, and *Penelope* is easily the most popular. It can be grown in almost every garden — left unpruned it will produce a large spreading Shrub; regularly pruned it can be grown as a 3 ft bush. It also makes an excellent hedge. Large clusters of pale flowers cover the bush in June — dead-head regularly to ensure that later blooms will appear in early autumn.

Blooms:	Semi-double Shell pink Fragrant
Foliage:	Bronze-tinted
Introduction:	1924
Type:	Hybrid Musk
Growth Type:	Spreading
Flowering Period:	Repeat flowering

PERLE D'OR
Other Name: YELLOW CECILE BRUNNER

Blooms:	Double Apricot Fragrant
Foliage:	Dark green
Introduction:	1884
Type:	China Rose
Growth Type:	Open
Flowering Period:	Repeat flowering

A close relative of *Cécile Brunner*, hence its age-old alternative name. The tiny buds are pointed and classically shaped, opening into miniature flowers which are apricot at first but turn almost white with age. Excellent for cutting for indoor use — outdoors use it for bedding rather than as a specimen Shrub. Growth more robust than *Cécile Brunner*.

PINK BELLS
Other Name: POULBELLS

Ground Cover

Blooms:	Double Pink Slightly fragrant
Foliage:	Dark green
Introduction:	1983
Type:	Modern Shrub Rose
Growth Type:	Procumbent
Flowering Period:	Repeat flowering

Still one more ground cover rose which appeared in the early 1980s. This one (and its close relatives *White Bells* and *Red Bells*) has arching stems which cover the soil below. The blooms are somewhat bell-shaped (hence the name) and are borne in clusters. There is repeat blooming, but the flowering season is quite short, extending from the end of June to early September.

PINK GROOTENDORST

Blooms:	Double Rose pink No fragrance
Foliage:	Light green
Introduction:	1923
Type:	Rugosa Shrub
Growth Type:	Open
Flowering Period:	Repeat flowering

A sport of *F.J. Grootendorst*, with a little more to offer. The novelty of the frilled petals remains, but the colour is much more attractive. The blooms are highly recommended for display as a cut flower. As with its parent, the bush is not attractive but it is tough and hardy. A good choice for hedging in cold and windswept areas — the small clusters of small flowers appear throughout summer and autumn.

RED BLANKET
Other Name: INTERCELL

Ground Cover

Blooms:	Semi-double Rosy red Slightly fragrant
Foliage:	Dark green
Introduction:	1979
Type:	Modern Shrub Rose
Growth Type:	Procumbent
Flowering Period:	Repeat flowering

A good name for a ground cover rose, and it does live up to its name. The medium-sized flowers are produced in clusters — dull pale red against glossy dark leaves. Growth is both vigorous and healthy, and *Red Blanket* now appears in many catalogues. Like *Rosy Cushion* (page 71) it is descended from *Yesterday*, but the blooms are larger than those of its parent.

ROSA GALLICA OFFICINALIS
Other Name: APOTHECARY'S ROSE

Blooms:	Semi-double Pale crimson No fragrance
Foliage:	Medium green
Introduction:	Before 1300
Type:	Gallica Rose
Growth Type:	Upright
Flowering Period:	Midsummer

One of the most ancient roses still grown in our gardens, this original Red Rose of Lancaster is the ancestor of many of today's red H.T.s and Floribundas. In June or July clusters of pale red flowers appear, followed by small round hips. It is available from many rose suppliers, and it can be grown in an average-sized garden. You will have to spray to keep mildew under control.

ROSA HUGONIS
Other Name: GOLDEN ROSE OF CHINA

Blooms:	Single Buttercup yellow Slightly fragrant
Foliage:	Grey green
Introduction:	1908
Type:	Species Rose
Growth Type:	Arching
Flowering Period:	Late spring

A popular wild rose, rather like *Canary Bird* when not in flower. The stems are arching, the leaves are ferny and the bush has a graceful appearance. The flowers appear in May, and have the annoying habit of often remaining half closed. *R. hugonis* is subject to die-back, especially after a hard winter, and it is better to choose *Canary Bird* or *R. cantabrigiensis*.

SHRUB ROSES

| | Height in feet | Width in feet |

ROSA MOYESII GERANIUM
Other Name: GERANIUM

The wild rose *R. moyesii*, grown for its beautiful red flowers and spectacular hips is a gaunt giant of a shrub. It is better to grow the variety *Geranium* — smaller, more compact and with orange red, flagon-shaped hips which are even better than those on the wild variety. The bright red flowers appear among the small leaves in May or June — the 2 in. long hips appear later.

Blooms:	Single Scarlet No fragrance
Foliage:	Medium green
Introduction:	1938
Type:	Species Rose
Growth Type:	Arching
Flowering Period:	Early summer

ROSA MUNDI
Other Name: R. GALLICA VERSICOLOR

By far the most popular of the Gallica Roses, *Rosa Mundi* is a novelty which is more than 300 years old. The small flowers are distinctly striped and they appear on the twiggy, upright bushes for about a month in June or July. Like all Gallicas, this variety will succeed in poor soil but regular spraying against mildew will be necessary. The bushes sucker freely from the base.

Blooms:	Semi-double Pale pink, striped crimson No fragrance
Foliage:	Medium green
Introduction:	1650
Type:	Gallica Rose
Growth Type:	Upright
Flowering Period:	Midsummer

ROSA RUBRIFOLIA
Other Name: R. FERRUGINEA

A wild rose of central Europe, grown in our gardens for the beauty of its foliage. These leaves have a purplish bloom and the stems are practically free from thorns — a favourite material for flower arrangers. The small flowers are insignificant and short-lived, but the clusters of dark red hips are highly decorative. If space is limited, keep in check by pruning.

Blooms:	Single Pink No fragrance
Foliage:	Grey green, tinged purple
Introduction:	Before 1830
Type:	Species Rose
Growth Type:	Arching
Flowering Period:	Midsummer

ROSA RUGOSA ALBA

A typical Rugosa Rose — wrinkled disease-free leaves, fragrant blooms, attractive hips and an iron constitution. *R. rugosa alba* produces large flowers which appear throughout the summer and autumn months, and the orange red tomato-like hips are very large. It forms an attractive hedge, the dense foliage turning gold in the autumn. It can also be grown as a specimen bush, but it must never be hard pruned.

Blooms:	Single White Fragrant
Foliage:	Light green
Introduction:	1870
Type:	Rugosa Shrub
Growth Type:	Bushy
Flowering Period:	Repeat flowering

ROSA RUGOSA SCABROSA
Other Name: SCABROSA

A rival to *Roseraie de L'Haÿ* as the best Rugosa Rose. Both are remarkably healthy, hardy and bear large fragrant flowers. *Scabrosa* scores by producing tomato red hips in the autumn. Flowering begins at the end of spring and continues well into the autumn. Excellent as a hedge or specimen bush — choose it if you do not have the room for its rival.

Blooms:	Single Magenta pink Fragrant
Foliage:	Light green
Introduction:	Before 1939
Type:	Rugosa Shrub
Growth Type:	Spreading
Flowering Period:	Repeat flowering

ROSA SERICEA PTERACANTHA
Other Name: R. OMEIENSIS PTERACANTHA

A tall impenetrable Shrub with a number of unusual features. The small white flowers which appear fleetingly in early June are four-petalled, and the leaves are ferny. The most unusual and decorative features are the thorns on young wood — large and triangular with 1 in. red bases. Another unusual feature is the need for regular pruning to ensure a supply of new wood.

Blooms:	Single White No fragrance
Foliage:	Light green
Introduction:	1890
Type:	Species Rose
Growth Type:	Bushy
Flowering Period:	Early summer

ROSERAIE DE L'HAŸ

One of the best of the Rugosas, and one of the best Shrub Roses for hedging. The plant is densely clothed with tough foliage which remains free from disease. It will grow in poor soil, salt-laden air and in exposed sites. Its toughness, however, is not reflected in its blooms — large, velvety and sweetly scented. Flowering is prolific; its only fault compared with other Rugosas is the lack of hips.

Blooms:	Double Wine red Fragrant
Foliage:	Light green
Introduction:	1902
Type:	Rugosa Shrub
Growth Type:	Bushy
Flowering Period:	Repeat flowering

ROSY CUSHION

Other Name: INTERALL

Ground Cover

This Dickson-bred rose resembles its relative *Red Blanket* in growth habit and flower form, but its flowers have a distinct white or ivory eye. Its blooms are also smaller and there are only 7–10 petals. Leaf colour and form are similar — the catalogues often recommend these two varieties as partners along a path or in a border. They are also recommended for hiding unsightly objects.

Blooms:	Semi-double Pink; white centre Slightly fragrant
Foliage:	Dark green
Introduction:	1979
Type:	Modern Shrub Rose
Growth Type:	Procumbent
Flowering Period:	Repeat flowering

SALLY HOLMES

Two outstanding Shrub Roses (*Sally Holmes* and *Fred Loads*) were raised by the amateur rose breeder R.A. Holmes. This one is quite distinctive — the large open flowers are borne on tall clusters which stand above the foliage. An unusual delphinium-like effect for a rose, and the catalogue description has made this variety increasingly popular. Take care — it is temperamental and needs wind protection.

Blooms:	Single Creamy white, tinged pink Fragrant
Foliage:	Dark green
Introduction:	1976
Type:	Modern Shrub Rose
Growth Type:	Upright
Flowering Period:	Repeat flowering

SARAH VAN FLEET

The large cupped flowers are borne in clusters on healthy stems. Like all Rugosa Roses it is strongly recommended for hedging — the flowers are sweetly scented and the foliage is dense. An added advantage is that *Sarah Van Fleet* is one of the earliest roses to flower — a distinct benefit if you like to beat your neighbours. Unlike some other early bloomers, the show goes on — the soft pink flowers are borne continuously during summer.

Blooms:	Double Pink Very fragrant
Foliage:	Light green
Introduction:	1926
Type:	Rugosa Shrub
Growth Type:	Upright
Flowering Period:	Repeat flowering

SCHNEEZWERG

The smallest of the Rugosa Roses, and not the most attractive. The scent is weak, and the foliage is dull and uninteresting. The flowering season, however, is excellent — from late May until the end of autumn the white anemone-like blooms appear. In autumn new flowers open among the small scarlet hips, but the foliage does not take on the attractive autumn colouring of other Rugosas.

Blooms:	Semi-double White Slightly fragrant
Foliage:	Light green
Introduction:	1912
Type:	Rugosa Shrub
Growth Type:	Spreading
Flowering Period:	Repeat flowering

STANWELL PERPETUAL

Very prickly, as you would expect from a rose with *Rosa spinosissima* as one of its parents. A large straggly bush, useful as a pillar rose. The leaves are unusually small and numerous — the flowers are medium-sized and fade from pink to white. Nobody is quite sure about its parentage — it appeared by chance in an Essex garden about 150 years ago... and the full fragrance is still there. A notable feature is the continuity of flowering.

Blooms:	Double Pale pink Very fragrant
Foliage:	Light green
Introduction:	1838
Type:	Species Rose
Growth Type:	Arching
Flowering Period:	Repeat flowering

SHRUB ROSES

	Height in feet	Width in feet

SWANY

Other Name: MEIBURENAC

`Ground Cover`

A wide-spreading, low growing rose which covers large areas of ground with small glossy leaves and large trusses of flowers. Each small flower is cupped and bears scores and scores of petals. *Swany* is very vigorous and has become a popular ground cover. Fragrance is only slight, but absence of scent is not a problem with a low-growing rose.

Blooms:	Double White Slightly fragrant
Foliage:	Bronze-tinted
Introduction: 1978	
Type:	Modern Shrub Rose
Growth Type: Procumbent	
Flowering Period: Repeat flowering	

THE FAIRY

The Fairy is one of the few remaining Polyanthas and it has its enthusiasts. They praise the profusion of blooms which appear in the heat of late summer plus the attraction of the glossy box-like foliage. The flowers are very small and rosette-shaped, but they are borne in large clusters throughout the late summer and autumn. There is a major drawback — flowering does not start until mid or late July.

Blooms:	Double Pale pink No fragrance
Foliage:	Medium green
Introduction: 1932	
Type:	Polyantha Rose
Growth Type: Spreading	
Flowering Period: Repeat flowering	

UNCLE WALTER

Some catalogues call it a Hybrid Tea, but it is more generally classed as a Shrub Rose. It is a tall and untidy bush, but the flowers are neat and attractive — velvety, high-centred and full of petals. The colour does not fade nor turn blue with age, and the foliage has good resistance to disease. Too tall for bedding — use it as a specimen bush or hedge. *Uncle Walter* is highly recommended for cutting.

Blooms:	Double Crimson scarlet Slightly fragrant
Foliage:	Bronze-tinted
Introduction: 1963	
Type:	Modern Shrub Rose
Growth Type: Upright	
Flowering Period: Repeat flowering	

WILLIAM LOBB

Other Name: OLD VELVET MOSS

A gaunt giant of a Moss Rose, used as a large specimen bush or as a pillar rose. There is a single flush of flowers, in late June or early July, with wide trusses of large blooms — at first fuchsia purple and finally slate grey in colour. The buds and flower stalks are mossy, but there is little moss on the stems and leaves. Choose *Common Moss Rose* if you want mossy stems.

Blooms:	Semi-double Purple magenta Fragrant
Foliage:	Dark green
Introduction: 1855	
Type:	Moss Rose
Growth Type: Open	
Flowering Period: Midsummer	

YESTERDAY

Other Name: TAPIS D'ORIENT

It looks old-fashioned, despite its youth. The small flowers are borne in clusters and the bush is almost continually in bloom throughout the season. Each bloom opens flat, and the colour may range from pale pink to deep mauve. This unusual Shrub is good for cutting and has been given premier awards abroad. A good compact bush but it can be trimmed for ground cover.

Blooms:	Semi-double Pink Fragrant
Foliage:	Medium green
Introduction: 1974	
Type:	Modern Shrub Rose
Growth Type: Open	
Flowering Period: Repeat flowering	

YORK AND LANCASTER ROSE

Other Name: R. DAMASCENA VARIEGATA

The old *York and Lancaster Rose*, with its pink and white blooms on the same bush, may be of great interest to the historian but is of little interest to the ordinary gardener. Few flowers are produced and the Shrub is not vigorous. Sometimes there are pink and white petals on a single bloom, but if you want a pink-and-white bloom it is much better to choose *Rosa Mundi*.

Blooms:	Double Pink and white Fragrant
Foliage:	Light green
Introduction: Before 1550	
Type:	Damask Rose
Growth Type: Bushy	
Flowering Period: Midsummer	

SHRUB ROSES

CHAPTER 3
CHOOSING & BUYING ROSES

The secret of success for choosing the right roses is to start early. In summer, look through the selector guides (pages 74—78) and the A—Z sections (pages 7—72). Look through rose catalogues to find larger photographs of your chosen varieties, but never let a pretty picture be your sole guide. Try to see the roses growing in a display garden or nursery — only then will you know if the shape, colour and general form are right for you.

Shop early. If you are buying from a shop or garden centre, the widest selections should be available in autumn. This rule is even more important when shopping by mail order — the grower will substitute a similar variety if the one you have ordered is sold out. If you don't want this to happen, write 'No Substitutes' on your order.

Bargain Offers should be treated with great caution — you really do get what you pay for. Collections are different — they can be a good idea for a beginner but do check on the properties of each variety before buying. Most suppliers offer some form of guarantee system, but do make sure that failure isn't your own fault before claiming.

The type to buy

There are three types of planting material. The **bare-root** bush is lifted at the nursery during the dormant season (October-March) and sold over the counter or by post to the customer. In recent years an increasing number of these bare-root plants have been **prepackaged** for sale through shops, supermarkets and department stores as well as garden centres.

The correct type for some Climbers and Shrubs, most Miniatures and *all* roses during the growing season is the **container-grown** plant.

Bare-root

The traditional type for planting — dug up at the nursery or garden centre and taken home, or put on display with damp peat packed around the roots. Alternatively, the dormant roses are dug up and placed in wax-lined paper containers which are sent by post to the customer. The danger is drying out, see page 86 for instructions on how to deal with this problem.

Prepackaged

Prepackaged roses are bare-root plants with moist peat around the roots and the whole plant housed in a polythene bag and/or a box. There are advantages — reasonable price, ready availability from shops everywhere and coloured pictures plus instructions. But there can be problems — premature growth and shrivelled stems if kept too warm.

Container-grown

Container-grown roses can be bought to provide instant colour, but they are more expensive than bare-root plants and need extra care at planting time. Choose a specimen for its sturdiness and good health — not for the beauty of its few flowers. Make sure it has been grown in the container — not transferred into it from open ground.

What to look for

Bush

Stems should be green and unwrinkled. The wood should be well-ripened (not soft when squeezed between the fingers)

2 stems or more, each no thinner than a pencil

Well-developed and fibrous root system

Climber

Buds should be dormant, and long white shoots should not be present

2 stems or more, each at least 30 in. long

HYBRID TEA SELECTOR

Hybrid Teas are chosen for the reasons given on page 8. Now you have chosen this group, it is necessary to pick the varieties which will suit your situation and personal preferences.

Using the keys on these pages you will obtain a short list of roses, selected on the basis of three fundamental features — colour, height and fragrance. Next, look up each variety in the A—Z guide (pages 9–29) to discover its good and bad points. Note carefully that some roses are recommended for producing exhibition blooms and not for garden display — such varieties often produce only a few blooms and may be easily damaged by bad weather.

WHITES & CREAMS

White   Creamy white

PASCALI
POLAR STAR

START HERE "Do I want a rose which will grow more than 2½ ft high?" **YES** "Do I insist on a rose which is distinctly fragrant?" **YES**

NO

MESSAGE
SILVER WEDDING
VIRGO

ELIZABETH HARKNESS
PEAUDOUCE

REDS

Scarlet

Vermilion

Crimson

ALEXANDER

START HERE "Do I want a rose which will row more than 2½ ft high?" **YES** "Do I insist on a rose which is distinctly fragrant?" **NO**

YES

NO "Do I insist on a rose which is distinctly fragrant?"

ACE OF HEARTS
ALEC'S RED
DEEP SECRET
ERNEST H. MORSE
FORGOTTEN DREAMS
FRAGRANT CLOUD
INGRID BERGMAN
MISTER LINCOLN
PAPA MEILLAND
PRECIOUS PLATINUM
RED DEVIL
ROYAL WILLIAM
SUPER STAR

NO

ABBEYFIELD ROSE
NATIONAL TRUST
RUBY WEDDING

PINKS

Pink

Shell pink

Carmine rose

Rose pink

LOVERS' MEETING

DUKE OF WINDSOR
ENA HARKNESS
JOSEPHINE BRUCE
MME LOUIS LAPERRIERE

YES

NO

START HERE "Do I want a rose which will grow more than 2½ ft high?" **YES** "Do I insist on a rose which is distinctly fragrant?" **YES**

NO

DR MACALPINE
LOVELY LADY
MME BUTTERFLY
OPHELIA

YES "Do I insist on a rose which is distinctly fragrant?"

NO

PINK FAVOURITE

ADMIRAL RODNEY
BLESSINGS
CONGRATULATIONS
LADY SYLVIA
MARY DONALDSON
MULLARD JUBILEE
PINK PEACE
PRIMA BALLERINA
PRISTINE
ROYAL HIGHNESS
SILVER LINING
SUSAN HAMPSHIRE
WENDY CUSSONS

BI-COLOURS

KRONENBOURG
ROSE GAUJARD

START HERE "Do I want a rose which will grow more than 2½ ft high?" **YES** "Do I insist on a rose which is distinctly fragrant?" **NO**

YES

NO

GAY GORDONS
PICCADILLY
ROSY CHEEKS

BOBBY CHARLTON
MY CHOICE
TENERIFE

YELLOWS

Buttercup yellow
Lemon yellow
Canary yellow
Golden yellow

GOLD CROWN
GOLDSTAR
GRANDPA DICKSON
SUMMER SUNSHINE
SUNBLEST

NO

"Do I want a rose which will grow more than 2½ ft high?" — **YES** → "Do I insist on a rose which is distinctly fragrant?"

NO

YES

DIORAMA
DUTCH GOLD
FRAGRANT GOLD
FREEDOM
MISS HARP
POT O' GOLD
SUTTER'S GOLD

START HERE

BELLE BLONDE
KING'S RANSOM ← **YES** — "Do I insist on a rose which is distinctly fragrant?"

NO

SIMBA

ORANGES & BLENDS

Apricot
Blends
Salmon
Peach
Tangerine

CHICAGO PEACE
DORIS TYSTERMAN
L'OREAL TROPHY
MISCHIEF
MOJAVE
PEACE
PEER GYNT
PERFECTA
SOLITAIRE
SWEET PROMISE

NO

START HERE — "Do I want a rose which will grow more than 2½ ft high?" — **YES** → "Do I insist on a rose which is distinctly fragrant?"

NO

YES

APRICOT SILK
DOUBLE DELIGHT
JOHNNIE WALKER
LINCOLN CATHEDRAL
PAUL SHIRVILLE
REBECCA CLAIRE
REMEMBER ME
ROSEMARY HARKNESS
TROIKA

ALPINE SUNSET
BETTINA
CAN CAN
CHAMPION
ROYAL ROMANCE ← **YES** — "Do I insist on a rose which is distinctly fragrant?"
SHOT SILK
SILVER JUBILEE
TYPHOON
WHISKY MAC

NO

BEAUTE
CHESHIRE LIFE
JULIA'S ROSE
JUST JOEY
THE LADY

EASY-TO-GROW VARIETIES
Twenty Hybrid Teas for beginners, poor soils and industrial areas

ALEC'S RED
ALPINE SUNSET
CHESHIRE LIFE
CHICAGO PEACE
ERNEST H. MORSE
GOLD CROWN
JOHNNIE WALKER
JUST JOEY
MISCHIEF
MULLARD JUBILEE
NATIONAL TRUST
PEACE
PEER GYNT
PICCADILLY
PINK FAVOURITE
ROSE GAUJARD
SILVER JUBILEE
TROIKA
TYPHOON
WENDY CUSSONS

LILACS

STRIPES

BLUE MOON

HARRY WHEATCROFT

EXHIBITION VARIETIES
Twenty Hybrid Teas which can win prizes at shows

ADMIRAL RODNEY
ALEC'S RED
ALPINE SUNSET
BOBBY CHARLTON
CHAMPION
ERNEST H. MORSE
FRAGRANT CLOUD
GRANDPA DICKSON
LOVELY LADY
PEACE
PEAUDOUCE
PERFECTA
PINK FAVOURITE
PRISTINE
RED DEVIL
ROSE GAUJARD
ROYAL HIGHNESS
SILVER JUBILEE
SILVER LINING
WENDY CUSSONS

FRAGRANT VARIETIES
Twenty Hybrid Teas renowned for their outstanding perfume

ALEC'S RED
BLUE MOON
CHAMPION
DEEP SECRET
DOUBLE DELIGHT
DUKE OF WINDSOR
ENA HARKNESS
ERNEST H. MORSE
FRAGRANT CLOUD
JOSEPHINE BRUCE
JUST JOEY
LADY SYLVIA
MISTER LINCOLN
MY CHOICE
OPHELIA
PAPA MEILLAND
PRIMA BALLERINA
SUTTER'S GOLD
WENDY CUSSONS
WHISKY MAC

FLORIBUNDA SELECTOR

Floribundas are chosen in preference to Hybrid Teas where a large splash of garden colour is required, especially where the setting is informal.

    The varieties you choose must be right for your garden and right for your personal taste. Use the keys on these pages to obtain a short list, and then look up each variety in the A—Z guide (pages 31–46) for its good and bad points. Check the average height — Floribundas range from 1½ ft dwarfs to 5 ft giants, and catalogues are sometimes a little vague about the meaning of 'short' and 'tall'.

WHITES & CREAMS

White

Creamy white

ICEBERG

START HERE
"Do I want a rose which will grow more than 2½ ft high?" — **YES** → "Do I insist on a rose which is distinctly fragrant?"

NO → CHANELLE

NO (from first question leads) — under Iceberg: **NO**

"Do I insist on a rose which is distinctly fragrant?" **YES** → MARGARET MERRIL

REDS

Vermilion

Scarlet

Crimson

START HERE
"Do I want a rose which will grow more than 2½ ft high?" — **YES** →

ANNE COCKER
CHORUS
DISCO DANCER
EUROPEANA
EYE PAINT
FRENSHAM
KORONA
MEGIDDO
ROB ROY
SCARLET QUEEN ELIZABETH
THE TIMES ROSE

NO → "Do I insist on a rose which is distinctly fragrant?"

YES → LADY TAYLOR
ROSEMARY ROSE

NO →

BEAUTIFUL BRITAIN
BOYS' BRIGADE
CITY OF BELFAST
EVELYN FISON
LILLI MARLENE
MARLENA
MEMENTO
METEOR
PICCOLO
TOPSI
TRUMPETER
WARRIOR

PINKS

Shell pink

Pink

Rose pink

Carmine rose

ANISLEY DICKSON
PINK PARFAIT
QUEEN ELIZABETH

START HERE
"Do I want a rose which will grow more than 2½ ft high?" — **YES** → "Do I insist on a rose which is distinctly fragrant?"

NO → LADY TAYLOR ROSEMARY ROSE *(Carmine rose)*

NO → "Do I insist on a rose which is distinctly fragrant?"

YES → DEAREST
ENGLISH MISS

NO →
CITY OF LEEDS
GENTLE TOUCH
PADDY McGREDY
SHONA
TIP TOP

YES → SCENTED AIR

BI-COLOURS

START HERE
"Do I want a rose which will grow more than 2½ ft high?" — **YES** → COPPER POT
SEA PEARL

NO → GOLDEN SLIPPERS

PATIO ROSES
Floribundas which grow 18 in. tall

ANNA FORD
BOYS' BRIGADE
GENTLE TOUCH
LADY TAYLOR
MARLENA
PEEK A BOO

PICCOLO
REGENSBERG
SWEET DREAM
SWEET MAGIC
TIP TOP
TOPSI

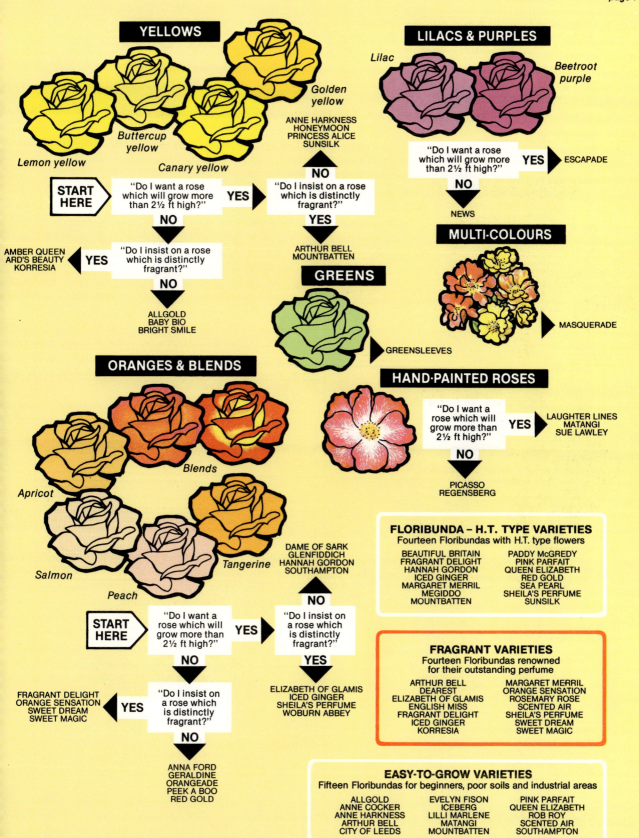

YELLOWS

Lemon yellow
Buttercup yellow
Canary yellow
Golden yellow

ANNE HARKNESS
HONEYMOON
PRINCESS ALICE
SUNSILK

START HERE → "Do I want a rose which will grow more than 2½ ft high?"

YES → "Do I insist on a rose which is distinctly fragrant?"

NO (from first question)

NO (from fragrant question) → ANNE HARKNESS / HONEYMOON / PRINCESS ALICE / SUNSILK

YES → ARTHUR BELL / MOUNTBATTEN

"Do I insist on a rose which is distinctly fragrant?"
YES → AMBER QUEEN / ARD'S BEAUTY / KORRESIA
NO → ALLGOLD / BABY BIO / BRIGHT SMILE

LILACS & PURPLES

Lilac
Beetroot purple

"Do I want a rose which will grow more than 2½ ft high?"
YES → ESCAPADE
NO → NEWS

MULTI-COLOURS

→ MASQUERADE

GREENS

→ GREENSLEEVES

HAND-PAINTED ROSES

"Do I want a rose which will grow more than 2½ ft high?"
YES → LAUGHTER LINES / MATANGI / SUE LAWLEY
NO → PICASSO / REGENSBERG

ORANGES & BLENDS

Apricot
Blends
Salmon
Peach
Tangerine

DAME OF SARK
GLENFIDDICH
HANNAH GORDON
SOUTHAMPTON

START HERE → "Do I want a rose which will grow more than 2½ ft high?"

YES → "Do I insist on a rose which is distinctly fragrant?"
NO → DAME OF SARK / GLENFIDDICH / HANNAH GORDON / SOUTHAMPTON
YES → ELIZABETH OF GLAMIS / ICED GINGER / SHEILA'S PERFUME / WOBURN ABBEY

NO → "Do I insist on a rose which is distinctly fragrant?"
YES → FRAGRANT DELIGHT / ORANGE SENSATION / SWEET DREAM / SWEET MAGIC
NO → ANNA FORD / GERALDINE / ORANGEADE / PEEK A BOO / RED GOLD

FLORIBUNDA – H.T. TYPE VARIETIES
Fourteen Floribundas with H.T. type flowers

BEAUTIFUL BRITAIN	PADDY McGREDY
FRAGRANT DELIGHT	PINK PARFAIT
HANNAH GORDON	QUEEN ELIZABETH
ICED GINGER	RED GOLD
MARGARET MERRIL	SEA PEARL
MEGIDDO	SHEILA'S PERFUME
MOUNTBATTEN	SUNSILK

FRAGRANT VARIETIES
Fourteen Floribundas renowned for their outstanding perfume

ARTHUR BELL	MARGARET MERRIL
DEAREST	ORANGE SENSATION
ELIZABETH OF GLAMIS	ROSEMARY ROSE
ENGLISH MISS	SCENTED AIR
FRAGRANT DELIGHT	SHEILA'S PERFUME
ICED GINGER	SWEET DREAM
KORRESIA	SWEET MAGIC

EASY-TO-GROW VARIETIES
Fifteen Floribundas for beginners, poor soils and industrial areas

ALLGOLD	EVELYN FISON	PINK PARFAIT
ANNE COCKER	ICEBERG	QUEEN ELIZABETH
ANNE HARKNESS	LILLI MARLENE	ROB ROY
ARTHUR BELL	MATANGI	SCENTED AIR
CITY OF LEEDS	MOUNTBATTEN	SOUTHAMPTON

SHRUB ROSE SELECTOR

Shrub Roses suffer by being in the shadow of their universally popular relatives — the Floribunda and Hybrid Tea. Regard them as extremely useful shrubs — alternatives to Lilac and Rhododendron rather than rivals to *Piccadilly* and *Super Star*. There are many groups of Shrub Roses as shown below. Representatives of each one appear in the A—Z guide (pages 62—72).

SPECIES ROSES

All wild roses are included in this group, together with their close relatives. Many are known by their Latin names (e.g. *Rosa rubrifolia*) but some have Common names (e.g. *Canary Bird*). Most Species Roses bloom only once a year, but this flowering period may be earlier than for any bush rose.

The origin of most Species Roses is lost in history, but some are modern. The Kordes hybrids (*Frühlingsgold* and *Frühlingsmorgen*) are 20th century improvements of the Scotch Briar. The Penzance Briars (*Lady Penzance*) are 19th century improvements of the Sweet Briar.

OLD-FASHIONED ROSES

Most Shrub Roses belong here. In general these are the garden roses of yesteryear — dating back to the era when there were no Hybrid Teas or Floribundas. There are two exceptions — both the Hybrid Musks and Rugosa Shrubs are 20th century creations.

RUGOSA SHRUB
Rosa rugosa alba and the modern hybrids are hardy shrubs which will thrive in soils and conditions where hardly any other rose would survive. The leaves are uniquely wrinkled and remarkably disease-free. The repeat flowering stems are dense and thorny, making this group an excellent choice for hedging. The flowers are fragrant, and the hips are usually large.

ALBA ROSE
You can easily recognize an Alba Rose by its soft and drooping grey-green leaves. The vigorous bush resists both pests and diseases, and some rigorous pruning may be necessary to keep it in check. The flowers appear in a single flush in midsummer — pink or white with a rich scent. Alba Roses withstand partial shade better than most other roses.

DAMASK ROSE
The perfume of the white or pink flowers is the glory of the Damask Rose. It has never been really popular — the arching, weak stems bear dull foliage, and the weak flower stalks allow the blooms to droop. The flowers are borne mainly in clusters, and appear as a single flush in midsummer. Damask Roses are very hardy, but need good soil and proper cultivation.

POLYANTHA ROSE
A group of low-growing Shrub Roses, rarely reaching more than 3 ft. The bushes are extremely hardy, and produce large clusters of small blooms more or less continually throughout the summer and autumn. A few Polyanthas remain in the catalogues, but this group has been almost completely replaced by their much showier offspring — the Floribundas.

CENTIFOLIA ROSE
This is the Cabbage Rose, so-called from its double, globular flowers. With its cottage garden colours and heavy fragrance, the Centifolia Rose is the epitome of old-fashioned roses. Unfortunately, this group has none of the robustness of the Rugosas or the Albas — the stems are lax and need support, and the bushes require regular spraying and feeding.

MOSS ROSE
About 300 years ago an unknown Centifolia Rose produced a sport — the Moss Rose. All Moss Roses are rather similar to the parent type but bear distinctive green or brown "moss" (sticky hairs) all over the sepals and flower stalks. The sweet-smelling blooms have an old-fashioned look, appearing once a year in midsummer.

GALLICA ROSE
The first garden rose of all, which has collected many common names on the way — French Rose, Apothecary's Rose and Rose of Provins. The hybrids grown today are usually compact, with rough leaves and semi-double or double blooms. *Rosa Mundi* is the one you are most likely to see, and like other Gallicas it is practically thornless, midsummer flowering, successful in poor soils and prone to mildew.

CHINA ROSE
The importance of China Roses in the development of modern varieties has been described elsewhere (see page 110). *Old Blush*, one of the original imports from China in the 18th century, is still available from a few suppliers and so is the Victorian favourite, *Cécile Brunner*. The hybrids you can buy are slender open shrubs, bearing large clusters of small flowers throughout the summer. Plant in a sunny, protected site.

BOURBON ROSE
In about 1818 a cross occurred between *Autumn Damask* and a China Rose, and the Bourbon group of roses was born. The fragrant globular flowers, large and many-petalled, became the most popular roses in Victorian gardens, for they had the advantage of blooming in autumn as well as June. Eventually they lost their crown to the Hybrid Perpetuals, and today you will find very few varieties in the catalogues.

HYBRID PERPETUAL
At the end of the 19th century the Hybrid Perpetual became the most popular garden rose in Britain. A few of the thousands of varieties are still available, but of course the Floribundas and Hybrid Teas have taken over. The H.P. lost its crown because it is *not* perpetual — there is a summer flush followed by an autumn one. The bush tends to be too vigorous for average gardens and the blooms are cupped, not high-centred.

HYBRID MUSK
Reverend Pemberton introduced and named this group at the beginning of the 20th century. The scent is similar to that of the old Musk Rose, but there is no close relationship. They are suitable for the average-sized garden, provided that their sprawling habit is kept in check. An abundance of trusses appears in June and July, and the autumn show is particularly impressive.

MODERN SHRUB ROSES

A widely diverse group of roses with little in common apart from their 20th century origin. Most, but not all, are repeat flowering and the shape of the blooms is usually modern rather than old-fashioned.

CHAPTER 4

USING ROSES

As everybody knows, roses are for growing in beds and borders, growing up walls and growing over arches and screens. But on this page you will find many more uses for the Queen of Flowers. On the appropriate page you will find a list of rules for each of these uses, but do remember that it is *your* garden to use in any way you like . . . with one proviso. Make sure that the variety or varieties you choose are suitable for the use you have in mind.

PLANTING IN BEDS page 80

PLANTING IN BORDERS page 81

PLANTING AS SPECIMENS page 82

COVERING SCREENS page 84

GROWING UNDER GLASS page 83

COVERING TREES page 84

PLANTING IN ROCKERIES page 81

COVERING WALLS page 84

USING AS CUT FLOWERS page 117

USING AS HOUSE PLANTS page 118

GROWING IN TUBS page 83

PLANTING AS GROUND COVER page 82

PLANTING AS HEDGES page 82

USING IN BUTTONHOLES page 119

USING IN THE KITCHEN page 119

EXHIBITING page 112

MAKING PERFUME page 118

Planting in Beds

A bed is a planted area which is designed to be viewed from all sides.

FLANKING BED

Many gardens have one or more beds which divide the lawn from a path or driveway. These can be turned into attractive flanking beds by using a single line of roses.

Standards and weeping standards are the most important types for this purpose, and the bed must be wide enough to support them.

Underplanting is essential here. Where roses are used, choose compact varieties which will not compete with the standards. Dwarf Floribundas are ideal for this purpose.

Colour

According to some purists, you should only plant one variety per bed. In most gardens this is not practical and would lead to a distinctly dull appearance. It is important to avoid the other extreme — a large bed filled with single plants of many varieties, giving a patchwork quilt effect.

The best plan is to use 3–5 bushes of each variety. You can obtain all sorts of advice from the experts about which colours harmonize and which do not, but the grouping of colour is a matter of taste and you should not worry too much about colour clashes. Reds, however, can be a problem as some shades clash horribly. It is advisable to separate groups of red roses by planting white, cream or pale yellow varieties as dividers between them.

Underplanting

Some rose experts believe that no other plants should be grown in a rose bed. Their reason is usually based on the old tradition that the glory of roses is spoilt by "inferior" flowers, but there are also sound practical reasons for not underplanting. Mulching is made difficult or impossible, reserves of water and nutrients are depleted and walking between the bushes for maintenance work may become a tricky operation.

If you select the right plants, the drawbacks of underplanting become insignificant and the advantages are important — a colourful display when the roses are leafless or flowerless. The plants chosen must be low-growing and shallow-rooting, and when grown as an edging there is no inconvenience.

Spring bulbs are useful — Crocus, Snowdrop, etc., but avoid bulbs which have to be lifted regularly and avoid the larger bulbs with foliage which looks unsightly after flowering. Other favourites for underplanting are Primula Wanda, Auricula, Primrose, Candytuft, Ageratum, Viola, Aubretia, Alpine Phlox and Arabis.

ISLAND BED

Rose beds first began to appear about 100 years ago, and now they are a basic feature of the British garden. Gravel or crazy-paving is sometimes used to surround them, but grass is the traditional and still the best pathway between beds. Avoid lots of tiny beds — large and few is the general rule.

Beds are usually formal, with the roses planted in a strictly geometric pattern. Hybrid Teas or Floribundas can be used, but it is advisable not to mix the two types. Use Hybrid Teas if the bed is close to the house and where each bloom is to be admired. Choose Floribundas where a large splash of continuous colour is the prime need.

Keep things in proportion — small bushes in small beds. An appearance of flatness is a danger, especially in medium-sized or large beds. This can be avoided by planting a standard or a tall-growing variety in the centre.

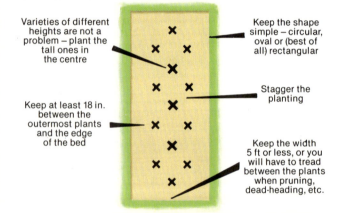

Varieties of different heights are not a problem – plant the tall ones in the centre

Keep the shape simple – circular, oval or (best of all) rectangular

Stagger the planting

Keep at least 18 in. between the outermost plants and the edge of the bed

Keep the width 5 ft or less, or you will have to tread between the plants when pruning, dead-heading, etc.

The Ideal Bedding Rose

Flushes appear in quick succession

Prolific flowering; blooms not damaged by rain

Bushy growth habit

Hardy in cold winters

Blooms borne at various levels, not just at the top of the bush

Abundant foliage; leaves glossy with good disease resistance

Planting in Borders

A border is a planted area which is designed to be viewed from one, two or three sides but not the back.

In the formal border, the rules on page 80 for the formal rose bed apply apart from the fact that the tallest-growing varieties are planted at the back of the border and the shortest at the front. A mass of colour is all-important and so Floribundas are more widely used than Hybrid Teas.

It is much more usual for a rose border to be informal, with the plants grouped and spaced according to their height and width. Here you can choose from the whole of the rose kingdom. In a large border you can use Climbers and Ramblers as well as tall Shrubs to make up the back row — in a smaller garden pillar roses and more modest Shrubs will be used.

Exploit the wide range of roses to the full — as a rough guide fill about half the space with Floribundas and a few Hybrid Teas, planting the rest of the border with roses of other types. Plant *Canary Bird* for flowers in the spring, and *Rosa rugosa* hybrids for red hips in the winter.

Grow Climbers and large Shrubs as single plants

STANDARD BORDER (3 rows)   **NARROW BORDER (2 rows)**

6ft

10ft

Plant Floribundas or Hybrid Teas in groups of 3 or 5

Keep at least 18 in. between the front row and edge of the border

Underplant with other plants. Choose carefully – these plants should never detract from the roses. Good choices are Heather, Alchemilla mollis, spring bulbs, Stachys, Lavender and Rosemary

Planting in Rockeries

Some years ago it would have been unthinkable to grow roses in the rockery, but the wide range of Miniatures now available has changed all that. The taller-growing varieties, such as *Baby Masquerade*, can add height when set amongst low clumps of alpines, in the same way that dwarf Conifers are used. The smaller varieties, such as *Pour Toi*, can be used to form 9 in. mounds of green leaves and semi-double blooms.

Whatever variety is used, Miniature Roses bring the blessing of midsummer flowers to an area of the garden where spring colour is abundant but summer colour is scarce. Careful maintenance is essential. The root run may be restricted, so watering will be necessary in dry weather. Spray against mildew and black spot, and keep the plants properly shaped by pruning with scissors. Do not plant Miniatures amongst rampant growers.

The Mixed Shrub Border

A visit to some of the great gardens of Britain will reveal the full extent of the beauty of a rose border. More modest examples can be seen in large private gardens throughout the country, but the simple truth is that for most people there is only room for one shrub border, and that is made up of Forsythia, Hydrangea, Ribes, Lilac and the rest.

It is surprising that so many of these shrub borders do not contain one Shrub Rose — even though it could provide colour and fragrance in midsummer when so many shrubberies are short of flowers.

For the rose lover a border of roses interspersed with approximately the same number of shrubs is an excellent idea. The roses are helped in three ways:

● Grey-leaved shrubs such as Lavender provide an excellent background for the pinks and purples of old-fashioned roses when in bloom.

● Evergreens such as Conifers provide a leafy skeleton for the border when roses are not in leaf.

● Winter- and early spring-flowering shrubs such as Forsythia and Viburnum tinus provide a floral display when roses are not in bloom.

The Mixed Herbaceous Border

For many people there are rose beds and herbaceous borders, and never the twain shall meet. In recent years the clear-cut barriers have started to break down, and many writers now sing the praises of Floribundas amongst the perennials.

The benefit to the border is obvious — an abundance of flowers throughout the summer to liven up the large blank spaces which sometimes occur.

The roses also benefit — bare stem bases can be successfully hidden and there is surrounding colour before the rose season begins. Careful selection is obviously important. First of all, get the height right — tall varieties such as *Queen Elizabeth* or *Alexander* are for the back of the border, the 1½–3ft Floribundas for the middle region, and the Miniatures for the front of the border where they make a welcome change from low-growing perennials.

Colour should also be carefully watched. Brilliant reds can be too eye-catching — the pinks and creams are especially suitable. Finally, make sure the bushes are given ample space — overcrowding can lead to mildew.

Planting as Hedges

A hedge is a continuous line of bushes in which the individuality of each plant is lost. Unlike a plant-covered fence (see page 84) a hedge requires little or no support.

The text books are right — roses can make a splendid hedge for both large and small gardens. Rose lovers sometimes scorn the all-too-familiar privet and yew, but before digging up your present hedge it would be wise to study the drawbacks of roses used in this way. Firstly, a rose hedge loses its leaves in winter. Next, it is informal and uneven in shape, and must not be chopped into a neat, squared-off outline with shears. Finally, it will not succeed in dense shade.

In the right situation, however, no other living screen will provide such an abundant and continuous display of flowers. Maintenance is simple — just dead-heading in summer and pruning in winter. Pick your variety with care — remember that many shrubs grow more than 5 ft wide. A hedging variety should be hardy, repeat flowering, abundantly supplied with foliage and it should be healthy — nobody wants to spray a hedge every fortnight!

Rugosa Shrubs (see page 78) are the best of all boundary hedges. The prickly stems are animal- and child-proof, the handsome foliage is mildew-free and many varieties bear attractive hips in winter. *Scabrosa* takes pride of place, closely followed by *Roseraie de l'Haÿ*. The Hybrid Musks are another popular group with *Penelope* as the favourite. With this group some support may be necessary, and long summer shoots may have to be cut back. The tall-growing Floribunda *Queen Elizabeth* has become a familiar hedge, but it can be disappointing. The secret is to prune the stems to different lengths. In this way leaves and flowers will be borne at varying heights instead of just at the top.

TALL HEDGE (5ft and over)
Shrub Roses or tall Floribundas
Plant 3ft apart (Exception: Queen Elizabeth — 2ft apart)

Recommended Varieties:

		PINK GROOTENDORST
CANARY BIRD	CORNELIA	QUEEN ELIZABETH
CELESTIAL	FELICIA	ROSA RUGOSA ALBA
CHINATOWN	MOUNTBATTEN	ROSERAIE DE L'HAY

MEDIUM HEDGE (2½ – 5ft)
Floribundas, Hybrid Teas or compact Shrub Roses
Plant 1½ft apart   Single row planting is possible, but 2 staggered rows are better

Rows 1½ft apart

Recommended Varieties:

ALEXANDER	FRAU DAGMAR HARTOPP	PINK PARFAIT
BALLERINA	ICEBERG	SILVER JUBILEE
EYE PAINT	MASQUERADE	SOUTHAMPTON

SMALL HEDGE (under 2½ft)
Dwarf Floribundas or Miniature Roses

Planting as Specimens

A specimen rose is one which is grown to be admired on its own as distinct from being grouped with other plants.

The faults of a rose in a bed or border are partly hidden by its neighbours. Bare stems can be hidden by low-growing plants in the foreground, and lop-sided growth is often compensated for by the stems of nearby plants.

A specimen rose stands on its own. When well-grown it is a thing of unmatched beauty — when badly grown it can be an eyesore. So for all specimen roses careful selection and proper maintenance are especially important.

The basic rule is to keep the plant in balance with its surroundings. An average-sized Hybrid Tea could look insignificant set as a solitary specimen in a large lawn, in the same way that a giant cascading Shrub has no place in the centre of a tiny front garden. A favourite specimen is the standard rose, grown in a circular bed in the lawn. Weeping, full, half and miniature versions are available (see page 4). In addition, many Shrubs make excellent specimen roses where space is adequate. The catalogues sing the praises of *Nevada*, but there are also *Fred Loads*, *Frühlingsgold*, *Joseph's Coat* and *Cornelia*.

For the smaller garden, the choice is made from Floribundas and Hybrid Teas. Of course, there are *Iceberg*, *Masquerade*, *Peace*, and *Queen Elizabeth* as a walk along any suburban road will reveal, but there are many others to choose from, such as *Arthur Bell*, *Mountbatten* and *National Trust*.

Planting as Ground Cover

A ground cover rose is a low-growing and spreading plant which forms a dense leafy mat.

Roses as ground cover plants may seem a modern idea, but some wild roses grow this way in their natural habitat. The uses of these prostrate roses in the garden are quite numerous — such as hiding unsightly mounds and manhole covers, edging rose beds and covering steep banks.

Ground cover roses are weed suppressors, but never regard them as weed eliminators. Planting in couch grass-infested soil will leave you with the hopeless task of trying to pull out grass from a tangled mass of stems.

Ten varieties are listed in the Shrub Roses section (pages 62–72). Some are spreading bushes with arching stems which cover the soil — examples are *Bonica*, *Fiona* and *Rosy Cushion*. Others are prostrate plants with stems which creep across the ground — *Nozomi* and *Max Graf* have been around for years, but are now being challenged by newer ones such as *Grouse*.

If there is a large stretch of land to cover, use one of the "game bird" series such as *Grouse*. Alternatively you can peg down a Rambler such as *Crimson Shower* or *Dorothy Perkins*. Such rampant growers have no place in a bed or border where space is limited — choose *Nozomi*, *Max Graf*, *Pink Bells*, *Bonica* or *Rosy Cushion*.

Growing under Glass

The appearance of the first blooms of the year are eagerly awaited by every rose lover. By growing roses in pots in an unheated greenhouse these first flowers can be obtained in mid April. If the greenhouse is heated, the plants will bloom in March. There are extra benefits — the flowers are perfect, free from wind and rain damage, and delicate varieties such as *Baccara* can be grown.

Planting takes place in October or November. Use a bare-root plant and a 10 in. clay or plastic pot. A clay pot should be soaked in water before use. If a plastic pot is chosen, put a few large pebbles in the bottom to increase stability.

Use John Innes or a peat-based compost. Keep the crown level with the top of the pot and use the end of a blunt stick to firm the compost around the roots. Leave a 2 in. space between the top of the compost and the rim. Finally, water the compost thoroughly.

Stand the pot outdoors on a firm surface (concrete, gravel, ash etc.), not in contact with the soil. The site should be unshaded but protected from strong winds and look after it during the spring and summer as if it was an ordinary tub rose (see below). Water in dry weather, spray when necessary and cut off dead flowers. There are one or two differences — remove nearly all flower buds so that only a few blooms appear and feed by spraying the leaves with a foliar feed such as Fillip.

In November or December cut the stems back to 6 in. and move the pots into the greenhouse. Add 1 oz of Toprose Fertilizer to the surface of the compost in each pot.

Avoid the various pitfalls which are likely during this forcing stage. Water properly — soak the pot thoroughly and then allow the compost to become partly dry before rewatering. On mild sunny days during spring ventilate the greenhouse adequately to avoid mildew. Paint the glass with Coolglass if the weather remains sunny.

From April onwards, use a liquid feed such as Bio Plant Food on a little-but-often basis. Once flowering is over, move the pots outdoors again until November, and then begin the sequence all over again. Repot every three years.

Recommended Varieties:

ALEC'S RED	LADY SYLVIA
ALLGOLD	MADAME BUTTERFLY
AMBER QUEEN	METEOR
BABY BIO	MULLARD JUBILEE
BACCARA	NATIONAL TRUST
BEAUTIFUL BRITAIN	PASCALI
BLESSINGS	PEER GYNT
ENA HARKNESS	PERFECTA
ERNEST H. MORSE	PICCADILLY
FRAGRANT CLOUD	PINK FAVOURITE
FRAGRANT GOLD	RED DEVIL
GRANDPA DICKSON	ROYAL HIGHNESS
JOSEPHINE BRUCE	SUTTER'S GOLD
KORRESIA	WENDY CUSSONS

The Quick Method

The traditional method outlined on the left results in a gap of 18 months between planting and the appearance of the first greenhouse blooms. A quicker but less satisfactory method is to use a container-grown rose instead of a bare-root plant. Pot up the specimen in an 8 in. pot in October, carefully avoiding root disturbance. Bring the pot indoors in December, and treat according to the general rules. After flowering, stand the pot outdoors and at the end of the summer transplant into a 10 in. pot.

Growing in Tubs

Growing roses in tubs on the terrace is a welcome addition to the plants in the beds and borders of the garden, but for balconies and in some town gardens it is the *only* way to grow roses.

The first step is to choose the right container. Some experts believe that wooden casks make the only truly satisfactory type, but you can choose from a large range of materials — plastic, fibreglass, stone, metal and so on. Much more important than material is size — a good root run is essential which means a depth of 9 in. for Miniatures, 12 in. for Patio Roses (dwarf Floribundas) and 15 in. for average-sized Floribundas and Hybrid Teas.

The tub should be stood on blocks to allow free drainage, and a 1–2 in. layer of rubble or crocks placed over the drainage holes. Use a soil-based compost or, if weight is a problem, a peat-based compost.

There is a wide selection of roses to choose from, but reject all varieties which do not have good disease resistance and avoid all varieties which are described as tall and upright. As a general rule the most satisfactory tub roses are the Patio Roses listed on page 76. Standards can be grown, provided firm staking is used.

Edging with spring flowering plants such as Primroses and miniature bulbs or with trailing plants such as Lobelia is a matter of personal taste. The cultural rules, however, must be followed. Place the tub in a sunny spot away from overhanging trees. Water during dry weather but never keep the compost permanently wet. Feed twice a year with Toprose Fertilizer — 2 oz per container when the leaves are beginning to unfold, and 1 oz in June or July. Water the compost before feeding — rake in lightly afterwards.

Covering Screens

There are Climber and Rambler varieties, but no rose has a natural climbing habit of growth. They neither twist around supports nor send out tendrils like a vine, so you will need both a sturdy support and some way of attaching the stems to the support.

Fence

Hardwood stake

— 6 ft —

Galvanized wire. Pull wire taut *before* driving home the staples

Trellis

Treat wooden laths with paint or wood preservative (not creosote)

— 1 ft —

Attach firmly to support

Tripod

Rustic poles

Pillar

8-10 ft

● The basal shoots of climbing roses must be trained as described on page 89. Use plastic-covered wire ties to attach the stems to the support — do not wind the young stems around the straining wires of a fence. Do not twist the wire ties too tightly around the main stems — leave room for the canes to increase in diameter.

● Ensure that all fence posts and pillars are well-anchored. Strong winds can cause havoc when the roses are in full leaf if the underground part of the support is too shallow or rotten.

● Ramblers can be grown on open screens, arches, pergolas, etc. where a large area is to be covered. Try to avoid tangling the stems when training. Before choosing a Rambler, read about the drawbacks on page 51.

Recommended Varieties:

Pillars & Fences

ALOHA	GALWAY BAY	MORNING JEWEL
ALTISSIMO	GOLDEN SHOWERS	NEW DAWN
BANTRY BAY	HANDEL	PARKDIREKTOR RIGGERS
BREATH OF LIFE	HIGHFIELD	PINK PERPETUE
COMPASSION	ICEBERG, CLIMBING	ROSY MANTLE
DANSE DU FEU	LEVERKUSEN	SCHOOLGIRL
DORTMUND	MAIGOLD	SWAN LAKE
DUBLIN BAY	MASQUERADE, CLIMBING	WHITE COCKADE
EMILY GRAY	MEG	ZEPHIRINE DROUHIN

Arches & Pergolas

Ramblers are once flowering, prone to mildew and difficult to prune. For some gardeners, however, the thin pliable stems still make them the first choice for arches and pergolas.

ALBERIC BARBIER	EXCELSA
ALBERTINE	FRANÇOIS JURANVILLE
CRIMSON SHOWER	PAUL'S SCARLET CLIMBER
EMILY GRAY	VEILCHENBLAU

Covering Walls

There were roses growing on the walls of British houses before the birth of Hybrid Teas and Floribundas, and they remain an important feature. But they can be more trouble than they are worth if you don't choose wisely and provide a proper support.

— 4 ft —

At least 3 in. between wire and wall

Vine eye or rustproof nail firmly secured in the wall

1½ ft

Plastic-covered straining wire pulled taut between the vine eyes. Make sure the wire is strong enough for this purpose

Recommended Varieties:

Never choose a variety which is particularly prone to mildew, which rules out most Ramblers.

North & East Walls

BANTRY BAY
DANSE DU FEU
GUINEE
LADY SYLVIA, CLIMBING
LEVERKUSEN
MAIGOLD
MME ALFRED CARRIERE

South & West Walls

The N&E varieties plus —
CASINO
ENA HARKNESS, CLIMBING
ETOILE DE HOLLANDE, CLIMBING
MERMAID
MRS SAM McGREDY, CLIMBING
ROYAL GOLD

Covering Trees

A dead tree is an eyesore in the garden, and if it is weak or rotten it should be felled. If it is sturdy, however, it can be used as a support for a climbing rose in the same way that some living trees can be employed. In this role the vigorous Rambler is supreme — this is no job for the compact modern Climber. Plant the rose on the side of the tree from which the prevailing wind blows, and provide some means of attachment to the trunk. The climbing rose will be self-supporting once its canes become entwined among the branches.

Recommended Varieties:

CECILE BRUNNER, CLIMBING
FRANÇOIS JURANVILLE
ROSA FILIPES KIFTSGATE
SEAGULL

CHAPTER 5
ROSE PLANTING

The number of new roses planted in Britain each year is staggering — if set out as a single row these plants would girdle the equator! So the chances are that you will be planting new roses this year, and with care you can expect them to last for 20 years or more.

Not all rose planting is successful, because there is more to it than digging a hole, spreading out the roots and then replacing the soil. Before you even lift a spade you should have considered several things. Has the soil already grown roses for many years? Does it need improving? Is the site really suitable for roses? This chapter offers you a step-by-step guide to avoiding all the pitfalls.

Picking the right spot

PLENTY OF SUN is required to produce top quality roses, but slight shade during early afternoon is beneficial.
ROSES CANNOT STAND DEEP AND CONTINUOUS SHADE

SHELTER FROM COLD WINDS is helpful. A nearby hedge or fence is useful, but it should not be close enough to shade the bush. Avoid planting in the lowest part of the garden if it is a 'frost pocket'.
ROSES DO NOT THRIVE IN EXPOSED, LOW-LYING SITES

REASONABLY FREE DRAINAGE is essential, so break up the subsoil if necessary.
ROSES CANNOT STAND BEING WATERLOGGED

PLENTY OF AIR is required to produce healthy plants. Bush and standard roses do not like being shut in by walls and overhanging plants.
ROSES CANNOT STAND BEING PLANTED UNDER TREES

SUITABLE SOIL is necessary, and fortunately this can be achieved in nearly all gardens. Ideally it should be a medium loam, slightly acid and reasonably rich in plant foods and humus. A high clay content is not necessary, and is actually harmful if not improved by adding humus. A high lime content is harmful. Soil in which roses have grown for more than 10 years is not suitable — see page 86.
ROSES CANNOT THRIVE IF THE SOIL IS POOR

Timing

Bare-root Plants

← —— PLANTING SEASON —— →

APR	MAY	JUNE	JULY	AUG	SEPT	OCT	NOV	DEC	JAN	FEB	MAR

Soil condition is as important as the calendar. The ground must be neither frozen nor waterlogged. Squeeze a handful of soil — it should be wet enough to form a ball and yet dry enough to shatter when dropped on a hard surface.

BEST TIME in nearly all gardens, as the soil is warm enough to produce some new root growth before winter. Late October is better than November in northern counties.

BEST TIME in very heavy soils and in cold exposed areas with high rainfall.

Container-grown Plants

Can be planted at any time of the year, provided the soil condition is suitable. Spring and autumn are preferred.

Getting the soil ready

The most expensive roses you can buy will grow only as well as the soil allows. Very few soils are naturally ideal, but almost all can be transformed into a satisfactory home for roses with some spadework (especially in clayey gardens) and humus (especially in sandy soils). There is no truth in the old saying that heavy clay is essential for top quality results.

STEP 1

STEP 2

DOUBLE DIGGING is recommended to aerate the top soil and break up the subsoil. The first step is to dig out a trench 18 in. wide and 12 in. deep at one side of the bed or border and transport the soil to the other. Fork over the bottom of the trench to the full length of the prongs, working in garden compost, well-rotted manure, leaf mould or peat. Turn strip A into the trench. Fork over the trench left by the removal of A, again incorporating compost or peat. Turn over strip B and so on, until a final trench is formed which is then filled with the soil from the first one. Do not remove small stones, as they are beneficial in a dry season. Roots of perennial weeds should be removed during digging. To add major and trace nutrients, fork 4 oz of Toprose Fertilizer per square yard into the top soil, and then let the ground settle for at least six weeks before planting.

WARNING: SOILS WHICH HAVE GROWN ROSES FOR MORE THAN 10 YEARS
You may wish to replant an old rose bed or just dig up one or two old bushes and replace them with new ones. In either case the soil is likely to be rose-sick (see page 102) if the plants have been growing in the soil for more than 10 years.
The causes of rose sickness are complex and still not yet fully understood, but a well-known effect is for newly-planted bushes and standards to suffer even though the established roses were thriving before their removal.
It is therefore wise to remove the old soil, digging out a hole 2 ft in diameter and 1½ ft deep for each new plant. Dig in plenty of organic matter and use a planting mixture made up with soil from a part of the garden which has not grown roses in recent years. The old soil from the rose bed can be safely spread in the vegetable or flower garden.

DRAINAGE is all-important, and double digging will help to prevent waterlogging in wet weather. If top soil is shallow and subsoil composed of heavy clay, the simplest plan is to make raised beds with added top soil, surrounded by paths on hardcore bases which will act as soakaways.

LIMING is not usually necessary because roses prefer slightly acid soil (pH 6.0 to 6.5). Only very acid soils need liming and even then only a light dressing will be required. Avoid overliming, or weak growth will result.

WARNING: CHALK SOILS
If there is less than 1½ ft of top soil above the chalk you will have either to add more top soil or excavate a 2 ft hole at each planting site and fill with planting mixture (see page 87). Alternatively, grow chalk-tolerant Shrub Roses — Albas, Damasks and Hybrid Musks.

Getting the plant ready

IF PLANTING IS TO BE DELAYED FOR LESS THAN 10 DAYS –
Leave the package containing the bush or standard unopened in an unheated but frost-proof cellar, garage or shed.

IF PLANTING IS TO BE DELAYED FOR MORE THAN 10 DAYS –
'Heel-in' the roses by digging a shallow V-shaped trench and then spreading the plants as a single row against one side of it. Cover the roots and lower part of the stems with soil and tread down. Label with some form of permanent tag — paper labels attached by the supplier may rot away.

WHEN YOU ARE READY TO BEGIN PLANTING –
Carefully unpack and place the packing material, sacking, etc. over the roots. Then prepare bush as shown in the adjoining diagram.

Cut off any leaves, hips or buds which may still be present

If stems are shrivelled, place all of the bush in water for several hours

Cut off decayed or thin shoots. Pruning takes place in spring — see page 92

Plunge roots in a bucket of water if they appear dry. Roots must never be allowed to dry out before planting. Keep them covered until you are ready to set the bush in its planting hole

Cut back any damaged or very long roots to about 12 in.

Planting

BUSHES

Bare-root Plants

The first step is to mark out the planting stations with canes to make sure that the bushes will be spaced out as planned. Next the planting hole for each rose must be dug, and the commonest mistake at planting time is to dig a hole which is too deep and too narrow.

Round hole when roots spread out in all directions

Fan-shaped hole when roots run in only one direction

Soil at the bottom of the hole is drawn into a small mound

Bud union should be 1 in. below soil level when planting is completed

Two handfuls of planting mixture or Bio Humus placed on top of the soil mound

Make up the **planting mixture** in a wheelbarrow — 1 part soil, 1 part moist peat and 3 handfuls of Bone Meal per barrow load.

Spread out the roots evenly in the planting hole and work a couple of trowelfuls of the mixture around them. Shake the plant gently up and down and then firm the planting mixture with your fists. Place a cane across the top of the hole to ensure that the bud union is level with the surface.

Half-fill the hole with more of the mixture and firm it down by gentle treading. On no account should you stamp heavily — this would destroy the natural soil structure. Start treading at the outer edge of the planting hole, working gradually towards the centre.

Add more planting mixture until the hole is full, tread down once again and then loosen the surface. Spread a little more soil so that the bud union is about an inch below the surface and finally attach a weatherproof label bearing the name of the rose. The job is now finished but if frosty weather occurs after planting, refirming may be necessary.

Transplanting Established Bushes

It is occasionally necessary to move a rose bush from one part of the garden to another. Do this job in late autumn or early spring — shorten stems, cut off old leaves and flowers, and then carefully remove the bush from the soil. There are two methods — two people with forks at opposite sides steadily lever up the plant or one person with a spade cuts straight down on all four sides about 9 in. from the centre of the bush and then carefully lifts it on to a wheelbarrow. Plant immediately — keep the soil ball moist and covered if there is to be any delay.

Container-grown Plants

Never regard container-grown plants as an easy way to plant roses. If the environment surrounding the soil ball is not to the plant's liking then the roots will not grow out into the garden soil. This means that it is not enough to dig a hole, take off the container covering, drop in the plant and replace the soil.

Water thoroughly before planting or removing the container

Layer of planting mixture, moist peat or Bio Humus

Cut down the side of the container when it is stood on the base of the hole. Remove this cover very carefully

Make sure that the soil is moist before digging a planting hole which is large enough and deep enough for the soil ball and a surrounding 3–4 in. layer of planting mixture. The cover of the container should be slit and then gently slid off the soil ball. Never lift up the plant to do this and never break up the compost around the roots.

Fill the space between the soil ball and the sides of the hole with planting mixture (see above) and never with ordinary soil — roots may not move from a peat-based compost into ordinary mineral garden soil. Firm down the planting mixture with your fingers or the handle of the trowel. Water regularly during dry weather in spring and summer until the plant is established.

Planting continued

STANDARDS

If bushes and standards are to be planted in the same bed, deal with the standards first.

Top of stake should be just below head of tree

Stage 1
Drive in stake firmly

Stage 2
Plant firmly as for bushes

Stage 3
Fix ties, using sacking and tarred twine. Proprietary expanding ties are also available. Leave loose – tighten after a few weeks when the plant has settled

The stake should be 1–1½ in. across, and should be placed on the side from which the prevailing wind blows

Plant to old soil mark on stem

Cut off upper ring of roots if present

Bottom 2 ft of stake must be treated with a wood preservative (not creosote) and driven below the soil surface

Two or three handfuls of Bio Humus or planting mixture

CLIMBERS

The planting hole must be kept away from the wall to avoid excessive dryness at the roots.

Prepare the ground thoroughly before planting, and keep well watered in dry weather during the first season after planting.

Do not grow other plants closer than 18 in. from a climbing rose.

Stems tied to support after planting. Read the section on Training (page 89) before attaching the stems to the wall

Roots sloping away from wall

15 in.

Damp Course. Planting must be below this level

Two or three handfuls of Bio Humus or planting mixture

Spacing

ROSE TYPE	DISTANCE BETWEEN SIMILAR PLANTS
MINIATURE ROSES	1 ft
HYBRID TEA & FLORIBUNDA BUSHES Compact varieties	1½ ft
HYBRID TEA & FLORIBUNDA BUSHES Average varieties	2 ft
HYBRID TEA & FLORIBUNDA BUSHES Tall varieties	2½ – 3 ft
LOW-GROWING SHRUBS	3 ft
STANDARDS	4 ft
SHRUBS	average 5 ft or half of expected height
WEEPING STANDARDS	6 ft
CLIMBERS	7 ft
RAMBLERS	10 ft

Bush roses should not be planted closer than 18 in. from the edge of bed or border.

CHAPTER 6

ROSE CARE

The ever-increasing popularity of the Hybrid Tea and Floribunda is no doubt due to the beauty and colours of modern varieties together with their repeat flowering habit. But the simplicity of rose care, compared to the time-consuming job of looking after some other garden favourites is also an important factor.

A number of simple and straightforward tasks have to be carried out during the rose-growing year. Some, such as hoeing and feeding, are generally understood and practised. Others, like mulching and training, are still not widely followed and countless roses suffer as a result. One feature of rose cultivation causes more arguments and concern than all the rest, and that is pruning. Finally, there is one aspect of rose care which does not appear in the textbooks — take time to enjoy your roses by sitting close to them occasionally and doing nothing!

MULCHING

A mulch is a layer of bulky organic material placed on the soil surface around plants. In the rose garden it provides five distinct benefits:

- The soil is kept moist during the dry days of summer.
- Weeds are greatly reduced.
- Soil structure is improved as humus is added to the soil.
- Plant foods are provided by some mulching materials.
- Black spot attacks are reduced.

Suitable materials are moist peat, Bio Humus, hop manure, well-rotted manure, good garden compost and leaf mould. Grass clippings are often recommended and used, but a word of caution is necessary. Do not use them if the lawn contains many weeds or has recently been treated with a weedkiller. If they are used, add only a thin layer at a time and stir occasionally.

The standard time for mulching is late April and early May. Success depends on preparing the soil surface before adding the organic blanket — remove debris, dead leaves and weeds, and then water the surface if it is dry. Apply the spring feed (see page 94) if this has not yet been done, hoe in lightly, and you are ready to apply the mulch. Spread a 2 – 3 in. layer around the roses, keeping it away from the crown of the plants. Lightly prick this dressing into the top inch of soil during October.

Mulching will greatly reduce the need for watering and hoeing, but it cannot replace the need for feeding, as the balance of nutrients in a good rose fertilizer is not generally provided by mulching materials.

Some experts believe that autumn mulching is equal to or even better than late spring mulching, as described above. If you follow this advice, apply the mulch in October before the soil has become cold.

TRAINING

Some shrubs with lax spreading stems may require some form of support after a few years. Use three or more unobtrusive stakes with a secure band or board joining the top of each stake — never rely on a single ugly pole and string.

Climbing roses must be trained from the outset to ensure that they remain attached to their supports and grow in the desired direction. This does not mean that the main stems should be allowed to grow vertically — when this happens the usual result is a mature plant which bears its leaves and flowers at the top.

To prevent this happening, train the main shoots as horizontally as possible. This interruption of the free upward movement of the sap causes lateral branches to appear. It is these laterals which grow upwards to provide both height and cover, and they bear the flowers.

Basal shoots spread out fan-wise to encourage growth of vertical laterals

Fan training is fine for a climbing rose growing against a wall, fence, or screen, but is quite impractical when a pillar or tripod is to be covered. In this case, wind the canes in an ascending spiral around the pole.

The wire ties used to attach the main stems to the supports should not be tied too tightly — these stems thicken with age and a tight tie can strangle growth.

PRUNING

A rose bush, unlike a tree, does not produce shoots which steadily increase in size every year for as long as the plant remains alive. A rose stem grows actively and bears flowers for only a few years, after which the upper portion becomes exhausted. A new shoot then appears from a bud lower down on the stem, and the part above the new shoot dies.

The result is that a rose bush left unpruned becomes a tangled and shapeless mass of live and dead wood, with poor quality blooms borne on weak and twiggy stems. The purpose of pruning is to get rid of old exhausted wood every year and to encourage the regular development of strong and healthy stems. It will not give you more flowers next year — that is the job of feeding, but it will give you a well-shaped bush which will continue to bloom freely for many years to come.

The pruning cut

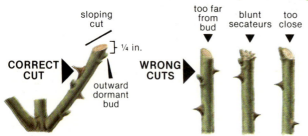

All pruning cuts must be clean — pare off any ragged parts. Sharp secateurs are essential — never force them to cut through thick stems, and relegate them to ordinary garden work once the blades are dull. Cuts more than ½ in. across should be painted with Arbrex to protect them from frost and damp.

It is impossible to avoid making some wrong cuts when pruning several bushes on a cold unpleasant day. As a result snags will form above some of the new shoots which develop — merely cut these dead bits off as they appear.

The tools to use

TWO-BLADED SECATEURS will cut cleanly for many years with proper care. The cut must be made at the centre of the blades.

or

ONE-BLADED SECATEURS are easier to use and will cut at the tip of the blade, but tend to wear out more quickly than the two-bladed variety, as the anvil becomes worn.

GLOVES are necessary to protect your hands from thorns. Buy a stout and flexible pair.

LONG-HANDLED PRUNERS are essential for tall climbers and shrubs. Many gardeners prefer them to a pruning saw for dealing with thick stems.

KNEELING PAD will allow you to get close to the bush when the soil is cold and wet at pruning time. Essential for the over-fifties.

PRUNING SAW if stems over ½ in. diameter have to be cut.

PRUNING KNIFE if you are experienced in its use.

Pruning step-by-step

All bushes and standards should be tackled in the following way:

STEP 1 Cut out completely all dead wood and all parts of stems which are obviously diseased or damaged. Test: Cut surface should be white. If brown — cut back further.

STEP 2 Cut out completely all very thin stems, and remove any branch which rubs against another. Aim to produce an open-centred bush. Remove suckers.

STEP 3 Cut out all unripe stems. Test: Try to snap off several thorns. If they bend or tear off instead of breaking off cleanly, the wood is too soft to be of any use.

STEP 4 Only healthy and ripe stems now remain. Prune these to the length advised on page 92 for the type of rose in question.

Types of pruning

BEFORE	AFTER	TYPE

HARD PRUNING

(other name: Low Pruning)

Stems are cut back to three or four buds from the base. This leaves short, sturdy stems about 5 in. high.

Hard pruning is recommended for newly-planted bush roses and it is often used for established H.T.s grown solely for the production of exhibition blooms.

It is no longer recommended for established roses grown for garden display although it is still used for some very weak-growing H.T.s and for rejuvenating neglected roses. Hard pruning should never be used for established Floribundas.

MODERATE PRUNING

(other name: Medium Pruning)

Stems are cut back to about half of their length. Weaker than average stems should be reduced by more than this amount.

Moderate pruning is recommended for nearly all established H.T.s growing in ordinary soils. Established Floribundas are pruned using a variation of this system (see page 92).

If the roses are well cared for, you can expect exhibition-quality blooms as well as a fine garden display following the use of moderate pruning. Hard pruning is no longer considered to be essential for winning prizes.

LIGHT PRUNING

(other name: High or Long Pruning)

Stems are cut back to about two-thirds of their length. This means that after the removal of all unwanted wood, the remaining stems are merely tipped.

Light pruning is not generally recommended as it produces tall spindly bushes bearing early but poor quality blooms if used year after year.

In special cases, however, light pruning is the only method to use. Very vigorous H.T. varieties such as *Peace* should be tackled in this way, and all roses growing in very sandy or smoky areas should be lightly pruned.

When to prune

BUSHES, STANDARDS & CLIMBERS

Early spring pruning is recommended for autumn- and winter-planted roses and for established plants. If the bushes or standards are to be planted in the spring, prune just before planting.

The best time to prune is when growth is just beginning. The uppermost buds will have begun to swell but no leaves will have appeared.

One of the dangers of leaving pruning until spring is the possibility of wind-rock in the winter gales. Avoid this by cutting back long shoots in November.

RAMBLERS

Prune in late summer or autumn once flowering has finished.

Prune at or before the recommended pruning date for your part of the country

- **EARLY APRIL**
- **LATE MARCH**
- **MID MARCH**

Pruning too early may result in buds breaking prematurely in a mild spell, followed by frost injury if freezing weather returns.

Despite this possibility, some rose experts prune regularly during above-freezing weather in January or February and claim they obtain earlier flowering than with the more usual March pruning.

Pruning too late results in the plant being weakened. This is because the sap is flowing freely upwards once the buds are actively growing, and pruning at this stage is bound to cause considerable loss of sap.

How to prune the roses in your garden

	NEWLY-PLANTED ROSES (Planted in previous autumn/winter or due to be planted in spring)	ESTABLISHED ROSES (Planted at least 12 months ago)
HYBRID TEA BUSHES	**Hard pruning** is required to build up a strong root system and to stimulate the growth of sturdy fresh shoots from close to the base of the bush. Hybrid Teas should be pruned 4–6 in. from the ground, and Floribundas 6 in. In sandy soils, use moderate pruning at this stage and hard pruning the following year.	**Moderate pruning** is the best method for general garden display. For show blooms hard pruning is sometimes used. In poor sites and for very vigorous varieties light pruning is recommended.
FLORIBUNDA BUSHES		**Moderate pruning** is the basis for dealing with Floribundas, but some old stems are hard pruned to a few inches from the ground, whilst new shoots which arose from close to the base last year are only lightly pruned. In this way stems of varying lengths are retained which ensures a long period of continuous flowering.
HYBRID TEA & FLORIBUNDA STANDARDS	**Hard pruning** is recommended, but this should be less drastic than the treatment of newly planted bushes. Cut stems back to about 8 in. from the trunk.	**Moderate pruning** is used to form a properly balanced head which will produce plenty of flowers. Hard pruning should be avoided, otherwise over-vigorous shoot growth will spoil the tree. Make sure that the main branches are approximately equal length after pruning.
WEEPING STANDARDS	**Hard pruning** is necessary, leaving branches about 6 in. long at the top of the trunk.	As for Ramblers. In autumn cut out branches which have flowered, leaving the new vigorous shoots which will flower next year. Cut off the tips of these shoots in the following March.
MINIATURE & SHRUB ROSES	No pruning is required.	Very little pruning is required. Remove dead and sickly growth and trim to shape, if necessary. Remove and burn mildewed tips. Use scissors rather than secateurs for Miniatures.
RAMBLERS	These roses are often pruned before despatch. If this has not been done, cut stems to 12 in. from the ground.	The correct pruning method depends upon the variety — see pages 52–60. **Method 1** Ideally, all the stems which have flowered should be cut out at ground level in autumn and the new stems, which will flower next year, tied into the supports. If insufficient new stems are present, retain the best of the old main stems and trim their lateral branches to about 3 in. In practice, taking down the canes may not be possible. In this case just cut back the lateral branches to about 3 in. from the main stems. **Method 2** Ideally, all flowered growth should be cut away from the main stems in autumn at a point where a vigorous new shoot has appeared. Cut back one or two old stems to about 12 in. above the ground. In practice, taking down so much wood may not be possible. In this case just cut back the lateral branches to about 3 in. from the main stems. **Method 3** Prune very lightly — merely cut out old dead wood and tip back the laterals which have flowered.
CLIMBERS	Do not prune — merely remove any dead tips which may be present.	The correct pruning method depends upon the variety — see pages 52–60. **Method 1** Little pruning is required apart from the removal of dead and exhausted wood. Withered shoot tips should be removed, and lateral branches on wood which has flowered should be reduced to about 3 in. **Method 2** Little pruning is required apart from the removal of dead and exhausted wood. Withered shoot tips should be removed.

WATERING

One of the blessings of the rose is its deep-rooting habit of growth. This means that watering of established plants is not vital in some seasons.

Unfortunately, this ability of a rose bush to remain fresh and green in summer when shallow-rooted plants have started to wilt leads many people to neglect watering. Trials have shown that during a summer with several dry spells the failure to water leads to impaired growth, small blooms and an early end to flowering even though the leaves may stay firm and green.

Some roses may need watering after only a few days of dry weather — newly-planted roses, climbers growing against walls and bushes planted in sandy soil. All roses will need water, and plenty of it, during a period of drought in late spring or summer.

A watering can is the usual applicator — use about 1 gallon for each bush or standard and 3 gallons for a climber. Never water little and often. Hold the can close to the ground and water slowly through the spout, not through a rose. Follow the experts by adding a measure of soluble fertilizer to the water.

Trickle irrigation through a perforated hose-pipe laid close to the bushes is perhaps the best method of watering. A quick and easy technique popular in America is to build a ridge of soil around each bush and then fill the basin with a hose-pipe.

HOEING

The main purpose of hoeing is to keep down weeds, such as couch grass, which are not smothered by mulching. For this purpose hoeing must be carried out at regular and frequent intervals so that the underground parts of the weeds will be eventually starved.

Hoeing must not go deeper than an inch below the surface, or rose roots may be damaged. Do not bother to hoe to keep moisture in the soil — a "dust mulch" is of very little value.

The garden fork has little place in the established rose garden. A light pricking over in spring and again in autumn can be carried out but deep soil disturbance must always be avoided.

DISBUDDING

Many Hybrid Teas normally produce more than one flower bud at the end of each shoot. If you want large specimen blooms for exhibition, garden display or indoor flower arrangement, then disbudding will be necessary. This calls for removing side buds by nipping out with the thumb and finger as soon as they are visible. This allows the stronger terminal bud to develop to its maximum size.

CUTTING

The rose is perhaps the most attractive and widely used of all cut flowers for home decoration, and an abundant supply of blooms can be obtained from June onwards from even the smallest rose garden.

A certain amount of care is necessary to avoid weakening the bushes. Do not take more than one-third of the flowering stem with the flower and always cut just above an outward-facing bud.

If the bush is not growing strongly, the flower stems removed should not bear any leaves. Cutting blooms from newly-planted roses is not generally recommended during their first season in the garden, although removal of a few blooms without leaves will do little or no harm.

DEAD-HEADING

The regular removal of dead blooms from Floribundas and Hybrid Teas is an important task. When the flowers have faded remove the whole truss, cutting the stem just above the second or third leaf down. By doing this the plant's energy which would have been lost in forming hips is conserved, and a regular succession of new flowering shoots is ensured. Faded flowers on first year roses should be removed with very little stem.

Do not dead-head once flowering roses nor varieties grown for their decorative hips.

THINNING

Following pruning, it is often found that two or more shoots have developed from a single bud. Only one of these should be retained, the other weaker or inward-facing shoots being gently removed by rubbing out with the fingers.

FEEDING

Hunger Signs

premature petal fall

poor disease resistance

small, poor quality flowers

pale or discoloured leaves

small leaves

'scorched' leaf edges

stunted growth, weak stems

Roses, like most other garden plants, make heavy demands on the reserves of plant foods in the soil. If one or more of the vital elements run short, then hunger signs appear on the leaves or flowers and both vigour and display are affected. The answer is to feed your roses every year.

Mulching, as described on page 89, will provide humus and some nutrients. But extra plant foods will be required, and the basic way to provide them is to use a proprietary compound fertilizer containing nitrogen, phosphates and potash.

Powder or granular fertilizer is the usual form, sprinkled around the plants in spring and summer. The most famous powder mixture is Tonks Formula, devised about 100 years ago. A modern version is available as Toprose Fertilizer, which contains magnesium and iron plus gypsum as well as the three major plant foods.

Liquid fertilizers are available in bottles, such as Bio Plant Food, or as boxes of soluble powder, such as Instant Bio. An excellent choice for quick and inexpensive treatment — regular repeat treatments are necessary during the season.

Foliar feeding has aroused a great deal of interest and some argument in the rose world. The specially formulated fertilizers are used to supplement and not replace soil feeding, and have the unique advantage of getting into the sap stream only hours after being sprayed on to the leaves. A favourite with exhibitors, as trials have shown that the size of blooms is increased as well as the general health of the plant.

PLANT FOOD TYPE	PLANT FOOD	WHAT IT DOES
MAJOR (required in large amounts)	**NITROGEN (N)**	Nitrogen stimulates the growth of leaves and stems and increases the size of the plant.
	PHOSPHATES (P_2O_5)	Phosphates stimulate the growth of roots and stems and speed up flowering.
	POTASH (K_2O)	Potash stimulates the production of top quality blooms. It also improves drought- and disease-resistance.
INTERMEDIATE (required in moderate amounts)	**CALCIUM (Ca)**	Calcium, magnesium, iron, boron and manganese maintain the normal green colour of the foliage so that growth and appearance are not spoilt by leaf discoloration and premature fall. Boron prevents leaflet distortion, and calcium reduces the incidence of die-back of stems.
	MAGNESIUM (Mg)	
MINOR (required in trace amounts)	**IRON (Fe)**	
	BORON (B)	The minor plant foods, or trace elements, also contribute in some way to disease prevention and the general health of the plant.
	MANGANESE (Mn)	

The Feeding Programme

STANDARD PROGRAMME

Spring treatment before leaves are fully open

Apply 1 oz (approximately one small handful) of Toprose Fertilizer around each plant when the soil is moist. Hoe in lightly.

Summer treatment in June or July

Apply 1 oz (approximately one small handful) of Toprose Fertilizer around each plant. Do not feed after the end of July or soft, frost-sensitive growth may be produced.

QUICK PROGRAMME

Monthly, from April until the end of July

Useful where a large number of roses have to be fed and where economy is an important factor. Add 1 tablespoon of Instant Bio to 1 pint of water in a Bio Hoser — apply to 250 sq.ft of bed or border.

EXPERT PROGRAMME

Fortnightly, between the two treatments of the Standard Programme

Many exhibitors and keen rose growers enrich the Standard Programme (see above) by regular foliar feeding. Use Fillip in a sprayer, taking care to wet the leaves thoroughly. Do not spray in bright sunlight.

CHAPTER 7
ROSE TROUBLES

The rose, like any other living thing, is liable to attack by harmful organisms. As a general pattern, the insect pests of spring are followed by the diseases of summer and autumn. Good cultivation is not the whole answer. A well-grown bush is able to withstand the effects of an attack much more successfully than a neglected specimen, but there is no way of completely stopping rose troubles from entering your garden.

Don't immediately assume that every disfigurement is due to an insect pest or a fungus disease — many problems are caused by the weather, lack of nutrients, weedkiller drift and poor management. Fortunately, you are never likely to see more than a few rose troubles in your own garden, and the purpose of this chapter is to show you what the rest look like as well as to list the correct control measures.

Learning to identify the symptoms of rose troubles is, of course, less interesting than learning to recognize rose varieties but it is no less important. This is because most pests and diseases can be checked quite easily if treated promptly, but may be difficult or impossible to control if left to get out of hand due to ignorance or neglect.

How to reduce the risk of troubles in your garden

● **Buy good plants.** Abundant roots and sound stems are essential — see page 73. If you live in a disease-prone area choose varieties which are known to possess good disease resistance — see the A–Z guides on pages 9–46.

● **Never leave rubbish lying about.** Rake up and burn prunings and fallen diseased leaves. Pick off and destroy mildewed shoot tips.

● **Prepare the ground thoroughly.** A rose growing in poorly-drained soil is susceptible to a lot of troubles.

● **Avoid overcrowding.** Do not plant closer together than the recommended spacing — see page 88. Prune to produce an open-centred bush.

● **Feed the plants properly.** Potash is vital here, because it builds up disease resistance and accelerates the ripening of new wood. Phosphates promote a healthy root system.

● **Avoid overliming.** Too much lime in the soil will cause chlorosis — leaf yellowing due to iron and manganese shortage.

● **Plant in the proper place and in the proper way.** This will reduce the risk of problems due to drought, waterlogging, wind rock, frost damage, light deficiency, excessive suckering, etc.

● **Inspect plants regularly.** Catch problems early, when occasional insects can be picked off and diseases kept from spreading by using a fungicide.

Why roses fail to survive

A good quality rose bush planted in the manner described in this book should grow and flourish for many years. Failure to survive will almost certainly be due to one of the following causes:

Loose planting — see page 87. Test: Tug stem gently in spring after planting. If the plant moves easily, tread around the bush

Wind rock especially in exposed sites

Waterlogged soil around the roots because of poor drainage

Severe drought especially in poor soils

Severe frost — see page 96

Use of fresh manure at planting time

Hard pruning every year on Floribundas, and on Hybrid Teas in sandy soils

Dry roots at planting time

Too much lime in the soil

The fatal diseases: rust, canker and honey fungus — see pages 98 and 102

The underground pests: chafer grubs and ants — see page 99

Planting under trees can lead to death from the combined effect of root dryness, dense shade and toxic drip from the leaf canopy

Cultural Problems

NITROGEN SHORTAGE

Young leaves small and pale green. Red spots sometimes develop. Early leaf fall. Stems stunted and weak.

Apply a compound fertilizer.

PHOSPHATE SHORTAGE

Young leaves small and dark green, with purplish tints on underside. Early leaf fall. Stems stunted and weak.

Apply a compound fertilizer.

POTASH SHORTAGE

Young leaves reddish, mature leaves green with brown, brittle margins. Flowers small. Common on sandy soils.

Apply a compound fertilizer.

MAGNESIUM SHORTAGE

Leaves pale at centre, with dead areas close to midrib. Oldest leaves worst affected. Early leaf fall.

Apply a fertilizer containing magnesium (e.g. Toprose).

IRON SHORTAGE

Leaves with large yellow areas. Young leaves worst affected — almost entirely yellow.

Avoid overliming. Apply Toprose Fertilizer. On chalky soils use MultiTonic.

MANGANESE SHORTAGE

Leaves with yellow bands between veins. Oldest leaves worst affected.

Avoid overliming. On chalky soils use MultiTonic at the rate recommended on the box.

FROST DAMAGE

Affected leaves are crinkled and torn with brown markings. Yellow patches sometimes appear. In most areas of Britain this damage is not serious, and the damage to stem tips of even newly-planted roses is not likely to be a problem in an average British winter.

In northern areas where severe and prolonged frosts are frequent, some winter protection may be necessary. Cover the bush with straw and bracken, and then wrap sacking around the covered plant. Remove the protective coating after the worst of the winter frosts have passed and before the growth buds begin to open.

WATERLOGGING

Leaves with large yellow areas. Veins and central area turn yellow first. Prevent by ensuring good drainage and after heavy frosts or gales tread down all plants which have been loosened. No cure — replant in a better prepared site if growth is spindly and flowers are of poor quality.

BALLING

Buds develop normally, but the petals fail to open and then turn brown. It is usually due to the effect of wet weather on varieties with large, thin-petalled blooms. Balling is always worst in a shady spot where the buds are shielded from the drying rays of the sun. It can also be caused by a heavy greenfly attack.

LAWN WEEDKILLER DAMAGE

Leaf stalks twisted spirally, leaves narrow and twisted. Stems distorted and reddish. The cause is lawn weedkiller which has been allowed to drift on to the roses — never treat a lawn on a windy day, and never use a watering can for both weedkilling *and* watering roses. Cut off the affected stems — the bush will recover.

Pest and Disease Control

There are times when pests and diseases will attack, and a spray or dust will be necessary if mildew, black spot or greenfly threaten your roses.

Chemicals used to control garden troubles are called **pesticides** and are safer than the nicotine, arsenic and mercury compounds used in grandfather's day. But they still should be treated with respect and there are a few simple rules to follow.

SPRAYER TYPES

For a minor attack on a few bushes use a trigger sprayer. Ready-to-use ones are available but you pay more for the convenience. If an aerosol is used, keep the recommended distance away from the foliage. For larger quantities a compression sprayer will be required — choose a 1 gallon (5 litre) size for general use. Hose-end dilutors are an alternative way to apply pesticides and liquid feeds.

SPRAYING

BEFORE YOU START SPRAYING

● **CHOOSE THE RIGHT PRODUCT.** Insects and other small pests are controlled by **Insecticides** which are used at the first signs of attack. A **Systemic Insecticide** enters the sap stream — in this way new growth will be protected and insects hidden from the spray will be killed. **Fungicides** are designed to prevent (not cure) diseases and so spraying must start before the attack begins and repeat spraying is usually necessary. The **Systemic Fungicides,** such as Supercarb, go inside the plant and have some curative effect if a few disease spots have already appeared.

● **READ THE LABEL CAREFULLY.** Follow the instructions — do not make the mixture stronger than recommended. Never use equipment which has contained weedkillers.

Ready-to-use trigger sprayer   **Refillable trigger sprayer**   **Compression sprayer**   **Hose-end dilutor**

The weather must be neither sunny nor windy

During the flowering season spray in the evening, when bees will have stopped working

Leaves should be dry

Use a fine forceful spray. It is wise to keep all sprays off the skin. Wash off any splashes

Spray the top and underside of the foliage thoroughly until the liquid starts to run off the leaves

EXPERT ROSE CARE PROGRAMME

It is, of course, possible to keep a regular watch on your roses and then spray with the appropriate pesticide when each insect appears or each disease threatens. Some keen rose growers prefer to follow a routine programme each year, and just add extra treatments as the needs arise.

THE ROSE-AID KIT

Nobody wants a garage filled with a large collection of bottles, boxes and assorted brews. It is, however, a good idea to keep a small rose-aid kit for sudden emergencies — Long-last for greenfly and caterpillars and Supercarb for the common diseases. Alternatively you can buy Multirose for combined pest and disease control.

'COCKTAIL' SPRAYS

Because roses are attacked by a range of pests and diseases it is often necessary to apply a combined spray. Do not mix different chemicals together unless recommended by the manufacturer. Some sprays, such as Multirose, are already formulated to control both pests and diseases. More than one fungicide is included to improve the level of disease control. The inclusion of a foliar feed in the mixture helps recovery from pest and disease attack.

A single 'cocktail' spray in **MID MAY**

A single 'cocktail' spray in **MID JUNE**

A single 'cocktail' spray in **EARLY SEPTEMBER**

SUPERCARB when leaf buds are opening if black spot is a threat in your garden

Long-last + Supercarb + Fillip or Multirose

SUPERCARB if mildew continues to threaten

Long-last + Supercarb + Fillip or Multirose

SUPERCARB if mildew continues to threaten

Long-last + Supercarb or Multirose

AFTER YOU HAVE FINISHED SPRAYING

● **Wash out equipment thoroughly.** Wash your hands and face if the label tells you to do so.

● **Do not keep the spray solution.** Make up a fresh batch of spray each time you wish to treat your roses.

● **Store packs in a safe place.** Never transfer chemicals into a beer bottle or any unlabelled container and never keep old illegible boxes and bottles. Throw them in the dustbin after you have emptied the contents down an outside drain.

Diseases

The most serious fungal diseases are mildew, black spot and rust. Some varieties are described as "resistant to disease", which means that the bush will remain free from attack under ordinary conditions. But under epidemic conditions preventive spraying will be necessary, because these varieties are resistant, not immune.

MILDEW

The most widespread rose disease. White powdery mould on leaves and buds; leaf cockling and premature fall takes place. Usual time for attack — summer or early autumn.

It is encouraged by closed-in conditions, dryness at the roots, poor feeding and by hot days followed by cold nights.

Spray with Multirose or Supercarb at the first signs of disease. Repeat one week later and apply further sprays if the spots reappear.

RUST

Not common, but it is often fatal when it strikes. Rust-prone area is S.W. England. Orange swellings, which turn black in August, appear on underside of leaves. New shoots turn reddish and shrivel. Usual time for attack — July.

It is encouraged by potash shortage and by a cold spring following a dry summer and hard winter.

Spray with Dithane 945 every two weeks.

BLACK SPOT

S.W. England and S. Wales are worst affected areas. Less common in industrial areas. Black spots with yellow fringes spread rapidly, causing leaves to fall. Starts early; becomes clearly visible in July/August. Heavy infections spread to leaf buds and later to stems which die back. Severe defoliation may take place.

It is encouraged by potash shortage and warm, wet weather in summer.

Difficult to control. Always remove and burn fallen leaves which are diseased. Use two sprays of Multirose or Supercarb a week apart when leaf buds begin to open. Spray again in summer as soon as the first spots appear. Repeat as necessary.

PURPLE SPOTTING

Not to be confused with black spot. The markings are smaller, more irregular and without a fringe. It is caused by poor growing conditions, not a fungus. It can also be caused by using a copper-based spray. It is not nearly as serious as black spot.

Improve drainage. Apply a peat mulch and a compound fertilizer.

CANKER

Usually appears as a distinct brown and sunken area close to the base of a stem. The edge of the canker may be swollen and the bark cracked.

The canker fungus enters the stem through a wound caused by insect or disease attack or mechanical damage. Be careful when hoeing!

If the canker enlarges and encircles the stem, the whole of the growth above the diseased area will be killed.

Cut out and burn all of the diseased wood. Paint large cuts with Arbrex. Dip the secateur blades in methylated spirits after use. Apply a balanced compound fertilizer, such as Toprose.

DIE-BACK

Shoots may die back, beginning at the tip and progressing steadily downwards, for a number of reasons. Die-back is not a specific disease. It can be caused by frost damage, canker at the base of the stem, water-logging, mildew or black spot. Yellow and orange varieties are more susceptible than others.

A common cause is a deficiency in potash, calcium, phosphates and boron. Feeding is essential in spring if die-back is a problem.

Do not feed in the autumn as this leads to the production of unripe and frost-sensitive wood.

Cut off the affected shoot at a bud below the dead area.

Pests on the stem

Peach-potato aphid

Rose aphid

GREENFLY (Aphid)

The commonest and most serious of all rose pests. They can be orange, reddish and black as well as green. The first clusters of these insects can be found feeding on the sap of tender new shoots in the spring, and vigour is seriously reduced.

Growth may be stopped or distorted, and infested buds sometimes fail to open. A sticky substance (honeydew) produced by these pests is soon covered by a black fungus (sooty mould).

The best way to tackle aphids is to use Long-last, which contains dimethoate. This goes inside the plant, so foliage missed by the spray is protected, as are the leaves formed after treatment. Protection is not removed by rain.

Alternatively you can spray with a contact insecticide, which kills the aphids it touches. Choose from Malathion, Fenitrothion, Liquid Derris, Sprayday or Multirose.

FROGHOPPER (Cuckoo-spit)

White frothy spittle on shoots in May and June. Inside this froth lives the small yellow froghopper. Affected shoots are distorted and leaves may wilt.

If only a few shoots are affected, wipe off with finger and thumb. Froghopper is susceptible to Hexyl, but before using an insecticide, spray forcibly with water to clear away froth.

ROSE SCALE

Small scurfy scales form a crust on old and neglected stems. Unsightly, and growth is weakened.

Small outbreaks can be controlled by painting affected areas with methylated spirits. Large areas will require spraying — use Long-last or Malathion. Apply a forceful spray to drench the scales.

SHOOT BORER SAWFLY

A green maggot within the pith of the affected shoot. Outward symptom is withering of the tip.

Cut off and burn the branch bearing the maggot. A spray of Long-last or Fenitrothion in May will prevent this damage.

Underground Pests

ANTS

Soil around the roots is loosened and plants may wilt and die. A pest of sandy areas.

Sprinkle Anti-Ant dust along the runs, or use a few drops of Nippon.

CHAFER GRUB

Fat, curved grub, over 1 in. long. A serious root pest which can cause death or weakening of bushes.

Kill any found during soil preparation.

Apply Bromophos and rake into soil surface before planting.

Galls

"ROBIN'S PINCUSHION"

Spongy moss-covered gall on leaves, caused by the gall wasp.

It does no detectable harm, and can be retained as a curiosity. Otherwise cut off and burn.

CROWN GALL

Very large, brown and warty outgrowth close to the base of a stem. Causes little or no harm, but can be cut off and the wound painted with Arbrex in autumn.

Crown gall is a much more serious problem when it occurs on the roots.

Pests on the leaf

COCKCHAFER (May bug)
Irregular-shaped holes in leaves in May or June may be due to this large, reddish-brown beetle.

Pick off and destroy beetles. Spray with Long-last.

LEAF-MINER
White blisters on leaves, containing a grub.

Hand-pick affected leaves and burn. Hexyl and Malathion are the recommended sprays.

ROSE SLUGWORM
Skeletonised areas on leaves, as only internal tissues but not veins are eaten. Affected areas turn brown.

Greenish-yellow grub may be seen on surface. Spray with Long-last or Liquid Derris.

RED SPIDER
Bronzed patches on upper surface of leaves, minute yellowish 'insects' and fine webbing on underside.

Attacks occur in hot, dry weather. Spray with Long-last or Malathion.

CATERPILLAR
Irregular-shaped holes in leaves may be due to caterpillars —

Vapourer moth   Winter moth   Yellow tail moth   Buff-tip moth

Pick off by hand if not too numerous. All of these pests can be very simply controlled by spraying with Fenitrothion, Multirose or Long-last.

LEAFHOPPER
Pale mottled patches on leaves. Small yellowish insects or their empty white skins may be found on underside.

Growth is checked. Leaf fall occurs after a bad attack. Spray with Long-last or Sprayday.

LEAF-CUTTER BEE
Regular-shaped holes at sides of leaves.

Control measures are not usually necessary, but destroy nests if found.

Flower Pests

CHAFER BEETLE
Petals and anthers eaten. One-sided blooms sometimes result.

Rose chafer   Garden chafer

Pick off and destroy beetles. To prevent attack spray with Long-last.

TORTRIX MOTH
Buds holed; brown rose maggot may be found inside, or within a characteristically curled leaf (see page 101).

Spray with Fenitrothion, Long-last or Multirose.

THRIPS
Petal edges blackened, flowers and leaves mottled and malformed.

Minute 4-winged flies, known as thunderflies, may become serious in a hot summer.

Spray with Liquid Derris, Long-last or Malathion.

CAPSID
Young buds dead and withered. Small brown spots on young leaves, which become distorted. Bright green insects — which move rapidly when disturbed.

Spray plants and soil with Long-last, Fenitrothion or Hexyl.

Hide-away Leaf Pests

TORTRIX MOTH
Irregular-shaped holes in leaves. Leaflets spun together by fine silken threads. Brown or green caterpillars (rose maggots) may be found.

Pick and destroy rolled leaves. Spray with Fenitrothion, Long-last or Multirose in May.

LEAF-ROLLING SAWFLY
Leaflets tightly rolled. Greyish-green grub inside. Affected leaves may shrivel and die. Can be serious if roses are grown near trees.

Squeeze rolled leaflets tightly between thumb and finger and then pick off and burn. To prevent damage, spray with Fenitrothion or Long-last in May.

LACKEY MOTH
Irregular-shaped holes in leaves. The white, orange and grey caterpillars can cause complete defoliation.

Easy to recognize because of the 'tents' of fine white threads which they spin.

Destroy 'tents'. Spray with Fenitrothion, Long-last or Multirose.

Virus Diseases

Fortunately, virus diseases have not become a serious problem in Britain. No drastic measures are required, but infected plants should not be used for propagation.

VEIN BANDING ROSE MOSAIC
Pale yellow or cream veining, distinct in late spring but much less so in summer. No serious effect — some regard it as decorative. Feed generously, as recommended on page 94.

LINE PATTERN ROSE MOSAIC
Yellow lines on leaf surface, sometimes forming an oak leaf pattern. Distinct in late spring, much less so in summer. Effect much more serious than vein banding rose mosaic — feed generously.

Blindness

Empty wheat-like husk instead of a flower bud on top of a mature stem. Blind shoots can occur with nearly all varieties, but some are particularly prone — *Gold Crown, Peace, Red Devil* and *Bonsoir* are examples.

Causes are many and varied — frost damage, lack of food and short-age of light have been blamed. If you are sure the shoot is blind, and not merely slow in flowering, cut it back to half its length to a healthy bud. This will then produce a shoot which should flower normally.

Weeds

It is surprising that weed control is ignored by so many books on rose growing, because weeds are certainly a major problem for millions of gardeners.

There is no single miracle cure for the weed problem — there are a number of interlinked tasks you will have to carry out. You probably already know that some weeds are annuals, and these generally can be kept in check quite easily by hoeing, mulching and spraying. The real problems are the perennial weeds — couch grass, bindweed, docks, thistles, ground elder etc. which will come up year after year if left unchecked.

At soil preparation time remove all the roots of perennial weeds that you can find. If the site is a sea of couch grass then you have a real problem. The age-old way of preparing such soil is to treat with Sodium Chlorate, but this will mean waiting for up to two years before planting. A better way is to spray with glyphosate before planting — follow the instructions carefully.

To keep weeds down among growing plants there are several chemical techniques. You can use simazine or dichlobenil — if applied to weed-free soil in spring they will stop most annual weeds from germinating. Alternatively you can use Weedol later in the season as a chemical hoe to burn off all weed growth. Make sure you keep the weedkiller away from the rose leaves. If perennial broad-leaved weeds are present, paint the foliage with glyphosate. For grassy weeds use alloxydim-sodium.

Weedkillers, provided they carry a specific recommendation for roses, are valuable aids but the mainstay of weed control remains hand weeding and hoeing. Pull out or dig out perennial weeds, cut off annual weeds just below the surface, and apply an annual mulch as described on page 89.

Green slime and moss usually indicate poor drainage, surface compaction or fertilizer deficiency. Hoe regularly, and feed twice a year.

Suckers

Suckers are shoots which grow from the rootstock rather than from the named variety which has been grafted on to it. If nothing is done to check this growth then suckers may take over the plant completely and the bush will have reverted.

Suckering is encouraged by loose planting, severe frosts, root damage by hoeing, incorrect removal of previous suckers or the use of R. rugosa as a rootstock. You can easily recognize a sucker from a desirable stem by its origin below the bud union and by its different leaflet form and colour. Do not rely on the number of leaflets per leaf as your guide.

Tackle each sucker as soon as it is seen — removal is then a simple job. Trace it back to the point of origin on the root — some soil removal will be necessary. Then pull it off and replace the soil. With a recently planted rose, keep the plant firmly in place with your foot as you pull off the sucker. Snipping off suckers at ground level will only lead to an increase in sucker production.

With standards, rub off sucker growths on the stem as soon as they are seen.

Honey Fungus

A harmless-looking group of toadstools may appear next to a bush in autumn — in fact these toadstools are deadly to roses if they are the honey fungus (armillaria root rot) illustrated above.

On the roots of attacked plants you will find black "bootlaces" produced by the fungus. Remove and burn dead and dying plants with as much of their roots as possible in order to prevent the disease from spreading. Before replanting, using Armilla-tox might be a wise precaution.

Soil Sickness

So many books assume that you will always be planting your new bushes or standards in virgin soil which has never grown roses before. Unfortunately this is not always so, and if the site has grown roses for more than ten years then it is liable to be rose-sick.

This curious complaint has still not been completely explained. Exhaustion of trace elements and the build up of root diseases and rose-root poisons are all undoubtedly involved, but minute eelworms are probably the main culprits.

Oddly, the old roses growing on the site may have shown little or no ill-effect as they have adapted to the conditions. But planting a new rose in such soil can lead to poor growth ("replant disease") and for this reason the top soil should be changed (see page 86).

CHAPTER 8

GROWING ROSES AS A HOBBY

Most people who grow roses would not describe rose growing as their hobby. To them the queen of flowers is just a beautiful part of the overall garden picture.

For the rest rose growing is something more — the enjoyment of visiting rose shows and gardens, winning (or trying to win) prizes, propagating their own plants and keeping up with the latest trends and varieties. For them the study and practice of rose growing is an absorbing hobby.

Growing roses as a hobby dates from Victorian times, and one of its fascinating aspects is the way it has always cut across the various classes in our society. The workers of the Industrial Revolution were still farm hands at heart, and it was these people who set up the first flower shows. The legend is that it was a visit to a Nottingham miners' rose show which inspired Dean Hole to found the National Rose Society in 1876.

And so it is today, with people from all walks of life enjoying and succeeding in the hobby of rose growing. A rose in the buttonhole was once a badge of office for the man who was something in the City and for the man who looked after the local railway station. The ordinary gardener with a few roses has so much to learn from the hallowed names of the rose world, but it was still possible even in the 1970s for an engine driver with a tiny greenhouse to raise a new rose capable of winning the Gold Medal at Rome.

Learning more about roses

There is always something new happening in the rose world. Each year brings forth a crop of new varieties, and one or more of these may mark another step forward in the quest for perfection. *Peace, Super Star* and *Queen Elizabeth* stand out like milestones along the way, and no one can say what the next advance will be.

Will the Floribundas become more and more like Hybrid Teas in shape? Will the boom in Patio roses continue? Will there be a new way of feeding next year? Nobody can begin to know everything about roses, and even if one did then some of the information would be out of date in a year or two. There are seven basic ways of learning more about roses. Use them all and you will surely become an expert.

Read books and journals on roses

Books and journals perform different jobs. A text book sets out to give you a sound background to the basic facts about the history, cultivation and selection of roses. The articles in gardening magazines and newspapers are usually concerned with new developments — the latest varieties, advances in feeding and pest control as well as the experiences of the writer or readers which would be out of place in a text book.

Study the latest catalogues

The catalogues of our leading rose growers are mines of information. Here you will find coloured illustrations of new varieties as well as old favourites. Essential reading for the enthusiast, but do look at the section on Rose Catalogues on page 3.

Visit nurseries in summer

An excellent way of seeing a multitude of varieties in flower — a great aid in making the right selection. In many ways a nursery visit can give the opposite view to looking through catalogues. The catalogue may give a picture that you might never achieve in your garden — the roses in the nursery are young stock which will be taller and more showy after a few years in your rose bed.

Visit the great Rose Gardens

See pages 106–107

Join your local Horticultural Society

Here you will be able to attend talks and meet fellow rose growers. Undoubtedly the greatest benefit is that you will be able to compare experiences with people who have to contend with similar conditions to your own — the same soil type, weather and air pollution. The knowledge of the long-standing members is especially helpful if you are new to rose growing or to the district.

Visit the Shows

The shows are the highlights of the year. You can see for yourself the beauty of the new varieties, and what experts judge to be perfect form. At the trade stands you can discuss your particular problems with a variety of knowledgeable growers and suppliers. Leading shows include:

Spring Competition, London	May
Chelsea Show, London	May
British Rose Festival, Hertfordshire	July
Lakeland Rose Show, Cumbria	July
Shrewsbury Show, Shropshire	August
Southport Show, Merseyside	August
London Rose Festival, London	September

Join the Royal National Rose Society

See page 104

The Royal National Rose Society

In 1876 a group of rose enthusiasts met in London to consider "what could be done to advance the interest of the rose, for in truth the Queen of Flowers has fallen on evil days." The National Rose Society was born. Its first show was held a year later — there were no Hybrid Teas, no Floribundas and very little public interest.

From these modest beginnings, with a deficit of £300 after the first year, one of the world's most important Horticultural Societies developed. In 1961 the Society moved its headquarters to Chiswell Green near St Albans and the heyday of the RNRS was reached in the 1970s. Membership passed the 100,000 mark, making it the largest specialist Society in the world of horticulture, and the prefix 'Royal' was added by command of H.M. Queen Elizabeth II.

Its awards are eagerly sought by rose breeders everywhere and its publications are important reference books. The gardens are unrivalled in Britain (see page 106) and many overseas Rose Societies have based their organization and rules on the successful British model.

The Society caters for all rose growers — the gardener with a few roses as well as the dedicated rosarian. Unfortunately the 1980s has seen a decline in membership as the cost of subscription has risen, but even at these membership rates you receive many benefits and privileges for the price you would have to pay for just a few rose bushes. Application forms are available from The Secretary, The Royal National Rose Society, Chiswell Green, St Albans, Herts AL2 3NR.

Royal National Rose Society,
Chiswell Green,
St Albans,
Hertfordshire

Benefits of Membership

FREE PUBLICATIONS

● THE ROSE Sent to all members four times each year — the Society's magazine filled with down-to-earth articles and items of news from the world of roses.

● HOW TO GROW ROSES Sent to new members on joining — a non-technical handbook containing up-to-date information on planting, pruning, problems, etc.

● THE ROSE DIRECTORY Sent to new members on joining — a list of over 700 varieties available in Britain, together with basic details such as height, colour, fragrance, etc.

FREE SHOWS

Your membership card admits you to the British Rose Festival at the Society's gardens in July. This two day event has become a mecca for rose enthusiasts from all over the world. There are displays, living catalogues and trade exhibits. Your card will also admit you to the London Rose Festival in September and the Lakeland Rose Show, plus many other shows in various parts of the U.K.

FREE GARDEN VISITS

The Gardens of the Rose and Trial Ground at St Albans are yours to enjoy throughout the season — there is free admission for yourself and a friend. Here you can see one of the finest collections of roses in the world.

FREE ADVICE

As a member you are entitled to receive advice from the experts on all aspects of rose growing, so useful when you can't find the answer to an out-of-the-way problem. You can also use the reference library if you need more information than is available in your local library.

Rose Growers Association

This trade association publishes an excellent booklet (*Find that Rose!*) which is invaluable for locating sources of unusual varieties. Suppliers of more than 2000 varieties are listed — for details write with a stamped addressed envelope to The Editor, 303 Mile End Road, Colchester, Essex.

Awards

An award for a new variety is obviously highly desirable for both the raiser and the gardener. For the rose breeder who raised it there is valuable publicity and acclaim — for the gardener who chooses it there is the knowledge that the variety has proved its reliability for ordinary garden use to a panel of impartial experts. However, winning a high award is not a guarantee of public acceptance. Among the bi-colour Hybrid Tea group it was *Westminster* which won the Gold Medal, not *Piccadilly*. And *Whisky Mac*, one of the most popular of all Hybrid Teas, received no award at all.

The granting of an award is not an infallible guide to excellence and the absence of an award does not necessarily mean that the variety is a poor one. There are four reasons for this:

- There was no National Rose Society trials scheme before 1928, so an old variety could not possibly have received an NRS award.
- Not all new varieties are submitted for trials.
- An award-winning variety can deteriorate after a number of years.
- Foreign awards may be granted to a variety which might fail miserably under damp British conditions.

BRITISH AWARDS

A new variety sent to the Royal National Rose Society for testing is grown for three years in the Trial Ground at St Albans and it is assessed regularly throughout the summer by a panel of experts.

This group looks for something more than a pretty flower. They consider many qualities, including vigour, growth habit, freedom from disease, fragrance, and freedom and continuity of flowering. If the panel feel that it should do reasonably well under most garden conditions, then a **Trial Ground Certificate** (TGC) is awarded. This is an award for reliability, not excellence.

If in the view of the experts the variety has something more — "some novel or outstanding quality or supersedes a similar variety which has declined" then a **Gold Medal** (GM) may be awarded. This is indeed a rare honour — it is more usual for a **Certificate of Merit** (CM) to be awarded in recognition of outstanding quality.

At the top of the award ladder is the **President's International Trophy** (PIT), awarded to a variety which has received a Gold Medal and is judged to be the best new rose of the year. There is also a fragrance award — the **Edland Medal for Fragrance** (EM) which is granted to the best scented new seedling of the year. The **Torridge Award** (TA) is given to an outstanding variety raised by an amateur.

The **James Mason Memorial Gold Medal** (JM) is awarded annually to a variety which has given "particular pleasure to rose lovers over the past 15 years".

The Royal Horticultural Society can grant an **Award of Merit** (AM) to plants which show "a distinct advance on their predecessors".

 President's International Trophy

 Gold Medal

 Certificate of Merit

 Trial Ground Certificate

 Edland Medal for Fragrance

 Torridge Award

 Award of Merit

 Rose of the Year

 James Mason Award

A panel from the Rose Growers Association and the British Association of Rose Breeders select annually one or more roses which should be promoted as the **Rose of the Year** (ROTY).

The RNRS Rose Analysis

The RNRS Rose Analysis is a useful guide to performance in gardens rather than trial grounds, and is published each year in the May issue of the RNRS magazine *The Rose*.

OVERSEAS AWARDS

New roses are tested in trial grounds in many parts of the world and awards are granted on the basis of their reliability or excellence over two or more years. This method of testing roses, rather than judging them on a single day, began in the Bagatelle Gardens in Paris and was not adopted in Britain until many years later. Important European trial grounds are situated in Paris, Lyons, Geneva, Belfast, Rome, Madrid and The Hague.

In the vastness of the United States it would not be practical to rely on a single trial site — more than a score of test gardens are used to gain an overall view of the variety under widely differing climatic conditions. Roses must score highly on all features of performance for two years in order to gain the **All-American Rose Selection** (AARS) award.

 All-American Rose Selection

 Gold Medal, Belfast

 Fragrance Award, Belfast

 Gold Medal, Geneva

 Gold Medal, Lyons

 Gold Medal, The Hague

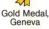 Golden Rose, The Hague

Fragrance Medal, The Hague

 Gold Medal, Rome

 Gold Medal, Madrid

 Gold Medal, Paris

 Gold Medal, Baden Baden

 Gold Medal, Roeulx

Great Rose Gardens of Britain

QUEEN MARY'S GARDEN, Regent's Park, London

Britain's favourite rose garden, as it is only a few minutes' walk from Baker Street tube station. The main circular garden is surrounded by a ring of pillars which are festooned with Ramblers and Climbers. There are large formal beds as well as small secluded beds to house the 40,000 plants grown here. Queen Mary's Garden is not to be missed by any rose lover, for here you will see all types and classes — Climbers scrambling through trees, enormous Shrubs in informal borders, formal beds of modern roses and many good examples of mixed plantings.

RNRS GARDENS OF THE ROSE, St Albans, Herts

From mid June until the end of September these 12 acres of gardens are open to the public for seven days a week. This display is one of the largest living catalogues in the world — you can admire the first Hybrid Tea or an old Shrub Rose and then move to the Trial Ground where you will see varieties still unnamed but which may become tomorrow's favourites. But the St Albans gardens are much more than just an impressive display of 30,000 plants covering 1,650 different species and varieties. Here you will find many separate gardens to show you how to use roses in your own garden — sunken beds of Miniatures, large beds cut in lawns, small pillars and stately pergolas ... and much, much more.

NEW ROSE GARDEN, Wisley, Surrey

In 1973 an area of the Royal Horticultural Society Gardens at Wisley was set aside as a New Rose Garden — a place where visitors could see how recently introduced varieties fared under ordinary garden conditions. Each year about 30 new varieties are planted. In the main gardens at Wisley there are many rose beds and borders of older varieties.

CITY OF BELFAST ROSE GARDEN, Belfast, N. Ireland

In 1964 the first roses were planted in the new Trial Grounds created in the beautiful Sir Thomas and Lady Dixon Park on the outskirts of Belfast. Since then it has become an impressive Display Garden containing over 20,000 roses.

SPRINGFIELDS, Spalding, Lincolnshire

The most famous bulb Display Garden in Britain recently joined the ranks of gardens for rose lovers. The British Association of Rose Breeders has donated an extensive collection of modern varieties to Springfields. The many thousands of plants represent a living catalogue of modern roses. Most but not all of the varieties are those holding Plant Breeders' Rights.

ROYAL BOTANIC GARDENS, Kew, London

Roses of all classes feature in our national botanical garden, but the collection is not particularly large and the displays are scattered throughout the gardens. The formal beds close to the Palm House are worth a visit, and there is also a comprehensive collection of Shrub Roses.

MOTTISFONT ABBEY, Romsey, Hampshire

Many of the gardens described on this page are designed to give the visitor an insight into newer varieties, so that he or she will not have to rely on catalogue photographs and descriptions. As a backcloth to these modern Hybrid Teas and Floribundas there are Shrubs, Ramblers and Climbers. Mottisfont Abbey is different — it houses the National Collection of Old (pre 1900) Roses.

PROVINCIAL DISPLAY GARDENS

Award-winning roses can be seen at the RNRS Display Gardens and Trial Ground at St Albans, but for many rose enthusiasts there is no way that they can make an annual pilgrimage to see these new varieties. To overcome this difficulty Display Gardens have been created in provincial parks so that local residents can see the award-winning varieties and information can be gained about their performance away from St Albans. Of course, these Provincial Display Gardens usually have impressive rose displays in addition to the RNRS award winners.

  SAUGHTON PARK, Edinburgh, Lothian
  QUEEN'S PARK, Colwyn Bay, Clwyd
  VIVARY PARK, Taunton, Somerset
  ROATH PARK, Cardiff, S. Glamorgan
  HARLOW CAR, Harrogate, N. Yorkshire
  THE ARBORETUM, Nottingham, Nottinghamshire
  HEIGHAM PARK, Norwich, Norfolk
  BOROUGH PARK, Redcar, Cleveland
  POLLOK PARK, Glasgow, Strathclyde
  CENTRAL TV GARDEN, Birmingham

STATELY HOMES AND GARDENS

Virtually all of the great gardens of Britain contain roses, but some have rose displays which are either impressive or unusual enough to make this feature well worth a visit by any rose lover. Good examples are:

  ANGLESEY ABBEY, Lode, Cambridgeshire
  BODNANT GARDENS, Conwy, Gwynedd
  CASTLE HOWARD, York, N. Yorkshire
  CLIVEDEN, Maidenhead, Berkshire
  CRATHES CASTLE, Aberdeen, Grampian
  HIDCOTE MANOR, Chipping Campden, Gloucestershire
  KIFTSGATE COURT, Chipping Campden, Gloucestershire
  NYMANS, Handcross, W. Sussex
  SAVILL GARDEN, Windsor, Berkshire
  SISSINGHURST CASTLE, Cranbrook, Kent
  THE ROSARIUM, Claydon, Suffolk

NURSERY DISPLAY GARDENS

Your local garden centre or nursery will have maiden plants in bloom during the summer months, and a few nurseries have special Display Gardens where beds and borders of mature roses can be seen.

Great Rose Gardens Overseas

FRANCE

LA ROSERAIE DE L'HAŸ LES ROSES, Paris
Not a vast collection of plants, but undoubtedly one of the most comprehensive outdoor rose museums in the world. Here you will find beds displaying the history of the rose, beds containing the varieties grown at Malmaison and even a Theatre of the Rose.

BAGATELLE, Paris
The Roseraie at the Bagatelle contains many thousands of rose plants, and one of its great attractions is the multitude of neat geometric beds bearing the latest varieties. The first International Rose Competition was held at the Bagatelle, and the Gold Medal of the Concours International des Roses Nouvelles is still one of the rose world's top honours.

PARC DE LA TETE D'OR, Lyons

One of the world's great rose gardens was opened in 1964 at the birthplace of the modern rose. There are 100,000 plants in 14 acres of Display Garden — Miniatures in rockeries, Climbers on pergolas, vast seas of bushes in beds, hundreds of Shrub varieties and the trial grounds for new French seedlings.

IRELAND

ST ANNE'S PARK, Dublin
The landscaped rose garden was created in the 1970s, and both the wide range of varieties and the beautiful aspect have received international acclaim. There is a trial ground here, and a recent addition is a Miniature Rose display garden — one of the first in Europe.

WEST GERMANY

WESTFALENPARK, Dortmund
The original German Rosarium was founded in 1903 at Sangerhausen, and it became the most comprehensive collection of roses in the world with more than 6,500 different varieties. But Sangerhausen is in East Germany, and so in 1969 a new German National Rosarium was started. The varieties are arranged geographically, and each recognized breeder has his own plot. Apart from these modern roses there is a large collection of old-fashioned varieties.

SWITZERLAND

PARC DE LA GRANGE, Geneva
Perhaps the loveliest rose garden of all, admired for its architecture as well as its roses. It consists of three terraces with pools and fountains. Each level is graced with many types of roses, and the whole area is floodlit during the summer months. Geneva Rose Week is the time of the International Rose Judging, and it is also the time when an open-air ballet is performed amid the 12,000 floodlit roses.

ITALY

MUNICIPAL ROSE GARDEN, Rome
This garden has the finest setting of all — a natural amphitheatre on the slopes of the Aventine Hill. In front of it are the ruins of the Palace of the Caesars. Around its edge runs a gallery of 200 climbing varieties and the central area contains Species Roses, early hybrids and popular modern varieties. An important International Rose Competition is held here each year.

DENMARK

VALBYPARKEN, Copenhagen
Opened in 1963, this large rose garden is only a few minutes away from the centre of Copenhagen. There is an extensive collection — about 20,000 plants representing 300 varieties. Danish rose breeders carry out their National Trials in Valbyparken.

HOLLAND

WESTBROEKPARK, The Hague
The rose garden in this public park was created after the war, and it has now become the largest and most important collection in the Benelux countries. More than 60,000 plants are set out in the large beds which make up the main display area of the rose garden.

SPAIN

PARQUE DEL OESTE, Madrid
A favourite argument amongst well-travelled rosarians is whether Geneva or Madrid boasts the loveliest rose garden in Europe. If variety is what you like — Miniature Roses hugging the ground near Climbers as tall as houses — statuary, fountains, cypress trees and flower-decked tunnels as well as an impressive collection of 30,000 roses then the Parque del Oeste would probably be your choice.

U.S.A.

HERSHEY ROSE GARDEN, Pennsylvania
If you had to pick just one of the countless American rose gardens to visit, then you would have to choose between the Hershey and the Park of Roses in Columbus. In the Hershey Rose Garden all rose tastes are catered for — there are thousands of modern Hybrid Teas and Floribundas as well as many hundreds of Shrub Rose varieties.

PARK OF ROSES, Columbus, Ohio
This 14 acre garden was once the home of the American Rose Society, and today it is a mecca for people who want to learn about as well as just enjoy roses. There are regular demonstrations throughout the year and the collection of over 50,000 roses covers all the various classes and types.

The New Classification

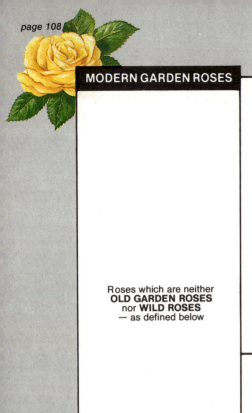

MODERN GARDEN ROSES

Roses which are neither **OLD GARDEN ROSES** nor **WILD ROSES** — as defined below

NON-CLIMBING MODERN GARDEN ROSE
A Modern Garden Rose with self-supporting stems

- **NON-RECURRENT GROUND COVER**
  See page 82
- **RECURRENT GROUND COVER**
  See page 82
- **NON-RECURRENT SHRUB**
  A plant, usually taller and wider than a bush, which normally flowers only once each year
- **RECURRENT SHRUB**
  A plant, usually taller and wider than a bush, which has an extended flowering season
- **RECURRENT BUSH**
  A plant of moderate height, particularly suitable for cultivation in groups, which has an extended flowering season
- **RECURRENT MINIATURE**
  A plant with miniature flowers, foliage and growth which has an extended flowering season

CLIMBING MODERN GARDEN ROSE
A Modern Garden Rose which is climbing or rambling with long spreading or arching stems normally needing support

- **NON-RECURRENT RAMBLER**
  A climbing plant, with lax stems, which normally flowers only once each year
- **NON-RECURRENT CLIMBER**
  A climbing plant, with stiffer stems than a Rambler, which normally flowers only once each year
- **NON-RECURRENT CLI. MINIATURE**
  A climbing plant, with miniature flowers and foliage, which normally flowers only once each year
- **RECURRENT RAMBLER**
  A climbing plant, with lax stems, which has an extended flowering season
- **RECURRENT CLIMBER**
  A climbing plant, with stiffer stems than a Rambler, which has an extended flowering season
- **RECURRENT CLI. MINIATURE**
  A climbing plant, with miniature flowers and foliage, which has an extended flowering season

OLD GARDEN ROSES

Roses which belong to a class in common use before the introduction of the Hybrid Tea Rose

NON-CLIMBING OLD GARDEN ROSE
An Old Garden Rose with self-supporting stems

- **ALBA**
- **BOURBON**
- **CHINA**
- **DAMASK**
- **GALLICA**
- **HYBRID PERPETUAL**
- **MOSS**
- **PORTLAND**
- **PROVENCE (CENTIFOLIA)**
- **SWEET BRIAR**
- **TEA**

CLIMBING OLD GARDEN ROSE
An Old Garden Rose which is climbing or rambling with long spreading or arching stems normally needing support

- **AYRSHIRE**
- **BOURSAULT**
- **CLIMBING TEA**
- **NOISETTE**
- **SEMPERVIRENS**

WILD ROSES

Roses which are original Species, or varieties and hybrids which bear a close resemblance to Species Roses

NON-CLIMBING WILD ROSE
A Wild Rose with self-supporting stems

Nearly all of the Species group of Shrub Roses (see page 78 and pages 61–72) are included in this new class — examples are *Rosa rubrifolia* and *Canary Bird*.

CLIMBING WILD ROSE
A Wild Rose which is climbing or rambling with long spreading or arching stems normally needing support

A few of the Rambler Roses (see pages 51–60) make up this small new class — an example is *Rosa filipes Kiftsgate*.

The terms Hybrid Tea and Floribunda have become household words. But the powers-that-be in the rose world have felt for many years that a more precise system is needed, and in 1971 the World Federation of Rose Societies accepted the British proposals. The New Classification has now arrived and in 1979 the RNRS began to use it in their show schedules, but it has not been universally accepted by the trade.

The Modern Shrub Roses plus the Rugosa Hybrids and the Hybrid Musks (see page 78 and pages 61–72) are included in these new classes of Recurrent and Non-recurrent Shrubs. Examples are *Fred Loads* and *Golden Wings*.

LARGE FLOWERED BUSH
A plant with shapely buds which develop into large or medium-sized flowers of traditional H.T. form — can usually be cut as an individual bloom on a long stem

The Hybrid Teas (see pages 8–29) make up this new class — examples are *Alec's Red*, *Peace* and *Super Star*.

CLUSTER FLOWERED BUSH
A plant with a mass of flowers in trusses, clusters or on many stems. The blooms may be single, semi-double or double

The Floribundas (see pages 30–46) make up this new class — examples are *Allgold*, *Iceberg* and *Masquerade*.

POLYANTHA
A plant with small flowers, rosette in shape and carried in large clusters. The leaflets are smaller than those on a Cluster Flowered Bush

The Polyantha group of Shrub Roses (see page 78 and pages 61–72) make up this new class within the Recurrent Bush Roses. An example is *The Fairy*.

The Miniature Roses (see pages 47–50) make up this new class — examples are *Starina* and *Little Flirt*.

Some of the Ramblers and most of the Climbers (see pages 51–60) make up this large new class. Examples of the Non-recurrent climbing varieties are *Albertine* and *Madame Grégoire Staechelin*. The Recurrent climbing varieties include the Kordesii Climbers (e.g. *Dortmund*), the Climbing Floribundas and Hybrid Teas (e.g. *Climbing Masquerade*), most of the Large-flowered Climbers (e.g. *Handel*) and the Climbing Miniatures (e.g. *Nozomi*).

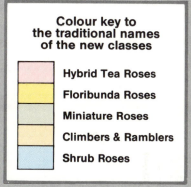

Colour key to the traditional names of the new classes

- Hybrid Tea Roses
- Floribunda Roses
- Miniature Roses
- Climbers & Ramblers
- Shrub Roses

Most of the Old-Fashioned group of Shrub Roses (see page 78 and pages 61–72) are included in this new class — the exceptions are the Rugosa Hybrids and the Hybrid Musks. Examples are *Frau Karl Druschki* and *Complicata*.

Many of the Ramblers and Climbers (see pages 51–60) are included in this new class — old favourites such as *Gloire de Dijon* and *Madame Alfred Carrière*.

Naming New Roses

A new rose may bear only a code number during the trials stage, but the time comes when it needs a name. This name may be descriptive (*Allgold*), poetic (*Peace*), or it may be a famous person (*Queen Elizabeth*), a member of the raiser's family (*Ena Harkness*), or the product of a sponsor (*Peaudouce*).

Unfortunately this original name sometimes has little meaning overseas, and so many roses have synonyms (alternative names) – *Red Gold* became *Rouge et Or* on the Continent and *Schneewittchen* became *Iceberg* when it came to Britain.

Avoiding foreign-sounding names is helpful for the purchaser but it can lead to confusion. Depending on which country you are in, *Frau Karl Druschki* can be *White American Beauty, Reines des Neiges* or *Snow Queen*, and so breeders have come up with an answer. They suggest that the 'official' variety name should always be printed in catalogues as well as the popular name, and this official name should be based on the breeder's name — *Meinatac* (*Susan Hampshire*) is a Meilland rose, *Mactru* (*Trumpeter*) is a McGredy rose and *Dicbar* (*Memento*) a Dickson rose.

The history of the rose

About 5000 years ago Mediterranean man created a new concept — Civilization. Very quickly such basic features as writing, cities, the use of metals and the wheel appeared... and so did an interest in the Rose.

In Ancient Crete in 1600 BC roses were being painted on palace walls, and in Egypt a thousand years later they were portrayed on tombs. It would be wrong, however, to pretend that all ancient civilizations were fascinated by this flower — there are only two mentions of roses in the whole of the Authorized Version of the Bible ... it may tell you to look at the Lilies of the Field, but it does not ask you to look at the roses!

The Greeks were perhaps the first to take the rose seriously. They had a good publicist — Sappho the poetess called it "The Queen of Flowers"; they also had a good technical adviser — Theophrastus wrote that roses should have their old wood removed to bear better flowers, that cuttings grow better than seeds and that success depends primarily on picking the right planting spot.

If the Greeks were the first to grow them in gardens and pots throughout the land, it was the Romans who first fell in love with them. They slept on the petals, carpeted their floors with them, imported early flowers from Egypt and raised their own blooms for winter in artificially-heated conservatories. They used them in food, wine, perfumes and medicines. The Legions took them to Britain and the other outposts of the Empire ... and then Rome fell. The rose, now unloved and neglected, declined so that only the hardy varieties survived.

The early Christian Church rejected this floral symbol of Roman depravity, but it was back in favour by about 400 AD. Rosaries were made from the hips, medicines were made from the petals and circular windows in churches were designed on the pattern of the blooms.

We can take stock of the British garden roses as they existed in 1500. There was the most ancient cultivated rose of all — the Red Rose, **Rosa gallica.** A survivor from Roman times or brought over by the Crusaders, we can leave it to the experts to argue about its origin in the gardens of the Middle Ages.

Next the White Rose, **Rosa alba** — another very ancient rose brought over by the Romans. The fragrant **Damask Roses** came to Britain much later — modern research dates this introduction to just before 1500 rather than in the luggage of a returning Crusader as stated in many textbooks.

The red one, the white one and the richly fragrant one were all in the Tudor garden in 1500. One of the varieties was the *Autumn Damask* which had an unusually long flowering season. Not important in the early garden, perhaps, but as a parent of future generations it was destined to become one of the most important of all roses.

By 1700 other varieties had arrived. The globular and fragrant **Centifolia** or Cabbage Rose appeared in about 1550 from the Continent. Others came from much further afield. The **Austrian Yellow** had come to Britain via Vienna from Persia in 1580 and the **Musk Rose** had come at the same time from the Himalayas.

A bouquet of ancient garden roses — once flowering, limited in colour, globular in bloom and spreading in growth habit — waiting for the introduction of the roses from the Orient a generation or two later. The marriage between these Western and Oriental roses led to a bewildering array of new varieties which culminated in the modern rose of our gardens.

Rose gardens existed in China when Western civilization was just beginning, and rose perfumes and petals were used for personal adornment and protection from evil spirits. The cultivation of roses in Japan also goes back into the mists of pre-history, but in neither country did the rose match the importance of the chrysanthemum, lotus or cherry blossom.

These ancient varieties are lost to us, but when the early 18th century traders from the East India Company arrived in China they found cultivated roses which were completely new to them. The flowers were small and without any distinct fragrance. The bushes were lanky and short of leaves, but the blooms appeared in flush after flush until the late autumn and there was a new colour — crimson. These were the **China Roses** — the first one to arrive in Europe was *Old Blush China* in 1752, followed by *Slater's Crimson China.*

The second wave of introductions from China occurred many years later. These were the **Tea Roses**, the first aristocrats of the rose world. Intolerant of frost and plagued with weak necks below the flowers, they still had outstanding properties — shapely buds, refined flowers, delicate fragrance and a repeat flowering habit. The first Tea Rose to arrive in Britain was *Hume's Blush Tea-Scented China* in 1810, followed by *Park's Yellow Tea-Scented China* in 1844.

Here were the ideal marriage partners for the western roses — the repeat flowering habit of the China Roses and the beautiful blooms of the Tea Roses to combine with the frost-hardiness and robustness of our own varieties.

The importance of these roses from China in the evolution of the modern rose is described in detail in every history of our favourite flower, and yet the role of the rose from Japan is often overlooked. In the 1860s **Rosa multiflora** was introduced from this relatively unknown country. The blooms of this wild Rambler would not win any prizes in a rose show — small and plain white flowers in large heads. Yet **R. multiflora** was the parent of some Ramblers and all our Floribundas.

THE MARRIAGE OF EAST AND WEST

The first east-west marriage was a chance cross in Italy between a red China Rose and *Autumn Damask*. The result was *Duchess of Portland* — the first **Portland Rose**. Between 1800 and 1850 this group became moderately popular, but its decline was rapid and very few Portland Roses are now available.

Another marriage took place across the Atlantic at about the same time — this time the partners were *Old Blush China* and the *Musk Rose*. Despite the fact that South Carolina was the site of this cross, the group was named after a French nurseryman — the **Noisettes**. Some Noisette hybrid Ramblers are still grown — *Madame Alfred Carrière* is described on page 57.

The big breakthrough came in 1818. A hybrid seedling was found at the base of a hedge containing *Old Blush China* and *Autumn Damask*. The place was Ile de Bourbon in the Indian Ocean and the tiny new rose was the first **Bourbon Rose**. Here at last was a truly successful east-west marriage — reasonably large flowers on a bush which flowered repeatedly. France was the centre of the Bourbon craze, and thousands of varieties appeared. Their popularity lasted through much of the Victorian era, and some are still listed in the catalogues.

In 1837 a new rose appeared — *Princess Hélène*. This cross between a Bourbon Rose and a Portland Rose heralded in the **Hybrid Perpetual**, and the Bourbon lost its crown as Queen of Roses. In both Europe and the U.S. rose breeders concentrated on producing more and more Hybrid Perpetuals until the end of the 19th century. Over 3,000 different varieties were introduced — in white, pink, mauve, red and purple. Some remain, led by *Frau Karl Druschki* which still keeps its place in the rose catalogues.

THE MODERN ROSE

The Victorian Queen of Roses, the Hybrid Perpetual, had its problems. The colour range was limited, repeat flowering was limited (a massive early flush was often followed by only sporadic summer or autumn blooming) and their garden use was limited — the bushes were large and rampant which meant that formal bedding in a small garden was not really practical. What was needed was the introduction of some of the elegance and delicacy of the Tea Rose. Many varieties of Tea Rose were available, but none was really winter-hardy. What was wanted was a cross between the hardy Hybrid Perpetual and the dainty Tea Rose.

There is some argument about the identity of this first **Hybrid Tea**, but the honour generally goes to *La France*, introduced in 1867. A momentous date, as this is accepted as the birth date of the modern rose. There

was no rush to buy this new rose, and the early Hybrid Teas crept in during the close of the 19th century. The acceptance of the group was accelerated by the appearance of some excellent varieties such as *Madame Caroline Testout* and *Lady Mary Fitzwilliam*, but the real breakthrough came in 1900. Pernet-Ducher in Lyons introduced *Soleil d'Or*, bred from a red Hybrid Perpetual and the *Persian Yellow* ... at last, a near-yellow flower on a bush with glossy leaves. Not truly a Hybrid Tea (it was called a Pernetiana at first), but it nevertheless enabled the Hybrid Teas to snatch the rose crown and keep it to this day.

The first pure yellow appeared in 1910 – *Rayon d'Or*. By this time the high-centred form of the Tea Rose was becoming dominant amongst Hybrid Teas — *Ophelia* (1912) was the first truly elegant pink. An impressive succession of trend-setting varieties were introduced up to the second World War — *Etoile de Hollande, Betty Uprichard, Shot Silk, Mrs Sam McGredy, Crimson Glory* and so on. Then just before the war a rose was bred in France which was to change the face of the Hybrid Tea. *Peace*, introduced into Britain in 1947, heralded in a new vigour and a new flower size. After the war, the steady stream of exciting advances continued. In 1960 *Super Star* came to Britain from Germany — the first of the vermilion roses. Then came *Fragrant Cloud, Alec's Red, Alexander, Silver Jubilee* ... and the quest for better Hybrid Teas goes on.

Hybrid Teas are not the only popular modern roses — the Floribundas are challenging them for the crown. Their story goes back to Guillot, the man who raised *La France*. In 1875 he introduced *Ma Paquerette*, which had *Rosa multiflora* and a China Rose as its parents. The small white blooms were borne in large clusters over a long flowering period on a small bush. This was the first **Polyantha Rose**, and the introduction of *Orléans Rose* in 1909 established the popularity of this group. *The Fairy* (page 72) survives in the catalogues.

But the Polyanthas needed something more — extra height and extra flower size, and here the Poulsen family in Denmark were the originators of the Polyantha x Hybrid Tea cross. These were the **Hybrid Polyanthas** or Poulsen Roses — *Else Poulsen* came first in 1924, followed by *Kirsten Poulsen* and *Anne Poulsen*. Many other varieties followed, bred in Denmark, Britain, United States, Germany and other countries, and the Hybrid Tea influence became stronger and stronger. A new name was obviously required, and the U.S. term **Floribunda** was accepted by the National Rose Society in 1952.

The milestones marking the history of the Floribundas are many, and any short list must omit numerous epoch-making roses. *Masquerade* and *Fashion* introduced new colours in the 1940s and *Queen Elizabeth* introduced a new size and elegance in the 1950s. New shapes and colours flooded in during the 1960s, and the 1970s were marked by the growing interest in dwarfs (*Topsi, Golden Slippers*, etc.) and new colours such as *Picasso* (1971) and *Double Delight* (1977). The 1980s saw the dwarfs (Patio Roses) come of age, and in the world of tall roses *Mountbatten* took away *Queen Elizabeth's* crown.

The next advance is just around the corner, but we cannot see it. The history of the rose is still being written.

Exhibiting your roses

You do not have to exhibit your blooms in order to be a rose lover or a rose expert. But the show-bench has a definite place in teaching you how to grow better roses, because it introduces the spirit of competition and makes you pay more attention to detail. Blooms which once were thought to be perfectly satisfactory may suddenly become second-rate when seen through the eyes of the exhibitor. The joy, of course, is in receiving an award rather than in the prize money . . . which is hardly likely to cover your expenses.

Start with your local horticultural show and don't go in for too many classes — you will soon learn that staging your exhibits takes far longer than you think. Begin by looking around this year's show — note the classes, write down the winning varieties and try to see why the winners received their awards. All of this will prepare you for your entry in next year's show. You may be puzzled by the poor standard of the First Prize display, but remember that you are seeing the exhibits *after* the judging — and judges make their awards for appearance at the time of their inspection.

If you want to take up rose showing seriously then you *must* become a member of the Royal National Rose Society. From them you will receive lists of varieties, judging standards etc., and also the right to exhibit in the RNRS classes at the shows.

Decorative Classes

The roses are judged on the basis of the overall effect of the blooms together with the leaves and stems in a bowl or vase. Artistry and peak condition are much more important here than flowers which are above average in size.

Specimen Classes

The roses are mainly judged as individual blooms. The usual container is the display box (see page 113) and the quest here is for blooms which are as near perfect as possible in shape and colour and which are significantly larger than average.

HOW ROSES ARE JUDGED

Points gained

Blooms: Decorative classes — good average size for the variety. Specimen classes — larger than average size for the variety. Hybrid Teas — half to three-quarters open with a circular outline and well-formed centre. Floribundas — fully open.

Petals: Bright, firm, clean and free from blemish.

Leaves: Clean and undamaged. Adequate in quantity and size.

Stems: Straight and in proportion to flower size.

Presentation: Graceful balance, artistically arranged. Flowers neither crushed together nor too widely spaced.

Points lost

Blooms: Fewer than the average number of petals for the variety. Size not typical. Immature or blown blooms. Hybrid Teas — blooms with split or confused centres. Obvious removal of petals or obvious overdressing (see page 113).

Petals: Faded, drooping, soiled or diseased.

Leaves: Diseased or damaged. Inadequate in quantity and size.

Stems: Weak, bent, diseased or twisted.

Presentation: Untidy or lop-sided. Poor colour arrangement or an excessive display of stems and/or leaves.

GROWING PRIZE ROSES

Pick your varieties carefully

The judges will be looking for large blooms with many petals and high centres. On page 75 there is a list of H.T. varieties which frequently win prizes at local and national rose shows. Some of these are not recommended for general garden display but others, such as *Alec's Red*, *Champion* and *Pink Favourite* will give you a fine garden display as well as prizes at the show.

Keep records

Most keen rose exhibitors keep a detailed diary. In this they note the time of pruning, feeding dates and other comments so that they will know for next year what they did, right . . . and wrong.

Get the timing right

One of the skills of successful showing is learning how to get a flush of blooms in peak condition just in time for the show. On average it takes about twelve weeks from pruning to the perfect bloom stage, but this can be as little as ten and as much as sixteen weeks. There is one basic way of making sure you don't miss having blooms on the vital day — try to grow as many plants as possible and prune them on different dates.

Follow the basic rules of rose care

Follow the principles of rose cultivation and soil preparation laid down in Chapters 5 and 6. Many rose exhibitors insist on hard pruning (see page 92) but this is not really necessary. Regular feeding is recommended — supplement the basic spring top-dressing with regular applications of liquid fertilizer or foliar feed (see page 94). Watering in dry weather and timely pest and disease control are vital.

GETTING READY FOR THE SHOW

About three or four days before the show you will start to get ready in earnest — at this stage you will look for blooms and stems which will be at their best on the big day. But there are several jobs, such as disbudding and covering, which will have taken place a week or two before selection, and even earlier you will have carried out one of the most important tasks of all — studying the show schedule.

Judges may mark you down or disqualify you for a minor breach of the rules — it does not have to be important. Select the class you wish to enter and make sure your exhibit will meet *all* the requirements. Does the specified number refer to blooms or stems? Is the old classification (page 7) or the new one (page 108) being used? Is wiring allowed? Are vases and bowls supplied? Clear up these and any other points well before the show.

DISBUDDING This should be carried out as soon as the side buds are big enough to handle — see page 93 for instructions. Stake the stem if the site is exposed or if the bloom is to be covered (see below).

In the case of Floribundas, some disbudding should be done about two weeks before the show. Remove the large central bud and one or two of the smallest ones from each truss, so that a large number of open and equal-sized blooms will be present on the day of the show.

COVERING A conical protector on a wooden stake above each bloom is a useful aid for the serious exhibitor. Rain is prevented from spotting delicate petals, which is vital in the more important classes.

Put the cover in position about ten to fourteen days before the show. It must be firm enough to avoid rocking against the bloom in windy weather, and it must be at the correct height to protect the bloom without shading it unduly. It must also be large enough to prevent rain from dripping down on to the petals.

TYING Many exhibitors loosely tie the centres of selected blooms with wool about three days before the show. The purpose is to lengthen the petals.

Choose half open (never fully open) blooms and use wool which is uncoloured, soft and thick. The petals must be dry at the time of tying. Secure the wool with a couple of twists and loosen slightly each day. This technique is best avoided by the novice as blooms can be damaged in unskilled hands.

CUTTING If you are exhibiting locally it is possible to cut in the early morning of the day of the show so that you can make a last-minute selection. If the selected stems have to travel some distance then cutting the night before will be necessary and many experienced exhibitors believe that cutting the previous night is the right time even for the local show. You will then have time to prepare and grade the stems properly — there will be very little time on the morning of the show.

As soon as the blooms are cut, remove the lower leaves and thorns and immerse in water to at least half the stem length. Keep in a cool and dark place.

ON THE DAY OF THE SHOW

Leave in good time and take everything you will need with you. Make a check-list — there may be a surprising number of items to carry. A typical list will contain pens, labels, scissors, secateurs, notebook, schedule, rushes, knife, camel-hair brush, house plant watering can, florist's wire and cotton wool.

TRAVELLING Cut and take double the number of blooms called for in the schedule. There are many methods of transporting them in a car, and each exhibitor has his or her favourite way. The rules are to keep the bottom of the stems wet, the blooms dry (wrap in soft paper) and the stems quite tightly packed together. If you use a bucket, put in a top layer of balls of newspaper to prevent undue splashing. If several buckets are to be carried, place them in a crate with packing material between each one.

LABELLING Do write the name of the rose or roses neatly on a card and place it alongside your display. If you do not know the name of the variety, state "variety unknown". A clearly-labelled exhibit does impress the judges.

DRESSING This is the final arrangement of the petals to secure maximum beauty. Use either your finger or a camel-hair brush to open the outside petals and partially open the second row. Never "overdress" or disturb the natural arrangement.

If an outer petal has been damaged, carefully remove it and gently press down the one above to take its place.

WIRING This is useful for roses to be arranged in vases, provided that it is not forbidden in the rules.

Push one end of the wire (obtainable from florists) into the swollen receptacle below the petals and twist the lower half around the stem. The flower can be easily broken off the stalk if this job is done clumsily, so practise on ordinary flowers from the garden before the big day.

STAGING THE EXHIBIT

3 bloom display

6 bloom display

Vases
Obtain vase from the Show Secretary on arrival. Pack with rushes before inserting the stems — make sure that lower leaves and thorns have been removed. Blooms should be close but not touching. Place the largest bloom at the base of the display. After arranging, fill the vase with water.

Bowls
Each bloom must be clear of its neighbour, but large bare gaps must be avoided. In a bowl of mixed varieties, do not have any two similarly coloured blooms next to each other. Use bright colours separated by pastel shades. If you have to supply your own bowl, make sure that it is simple in shape and neutral in colour.

Boxes
Box classes have declined in popularity. You will have to make or purchase your own specimen box for six or twelve blooms — they are not supplied by the organisers. Blooms should not touch — place the largest flowers in the back tubes which should be raised for extra display. Fill the space between the blooms with fresh green moss and label the display.

Increasing your stock

There are four ways of propagating roses — seed-sowing, layering, budding and taking cuttings. All of these methods are described in this section, but they are certainly not of equal importance. Seed-sowing and layering are rarely-used techniques for a limited number of varieties. Your basic choice, therefore, is between budding and taking cuttings.

Each of these two methods has its advantages and drawbacks. Most commercially-grown roses are raised by **budding**, which involves the insertion of a bud or "eye" of the selected variety into a T-shaped cut in the stem of a rootstock — close to the ground for a bush or some distance up the stem for a standard. It is suitable for all modern varieties, and the new plant has ready-made roots which results in quick development. But there are some disadvantages for the ordinary gardener — it calls for obtaining rootstocks and acquiring new skills.

Taking cuttings is the more popular method for the amateur — it really does mean getting new roses for nothing. The technique is child's play, but there are drawbacks. Not all roses can be propagated in this way and the new plants will take about three years before they are fully established in the garden.

BUDDING

1 Obtain rootstocks — for types available, see page 4. For suppliers — see advertisements in gardening magazines

Plant in November

Earth up stems after planting to keep the neck moist

12 in.

Neck should be barely covered, when planting

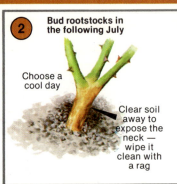

2 Bud rootstocks in the following July

Choose a cool day

Clear soil away to expose the neck — wipe it clean with a rag

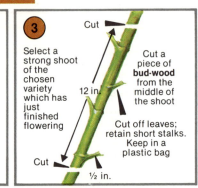

3 Select a strong shoot of the chosen variety which has just finished flowering

Cut

Cut a piece of **bud-wood** from the middle of the shoot

12 in.

Cut off leaves; retain short stalks. Keep in a plastic bag

Cut

½ in.

4 Use a budding knife to penetrate the bark of the rootstock, making a T-shaped cut

⅓ in.

¾ in.

Carefully ease back the two flaps, using the blunt end of the knife

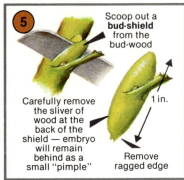

5 Scoop out a **bud-shield** from the bud-wood

Carefully remove the sliver of wood at the back of the shield — embryo will remain behind as a small "pimple"

1 in.

Remove ragged edge

6 Hold bud-shield by the leaf stalk. Slide gently into the T-cut. Make sure it goes to the bottom

7 Trim off the top of the bud-shield — the cut should be along the top of the T. Do not cut into the wood

Fold back the flaps

8 Secure (not *too* tightly) with damp raffia. Do not cover the bud

Knot on the opposite side to the bud-shield. Elastic ties are available

9 Leave ½ in., trim off later

By the following February a new shoot will have started to grow. Cut off growth of the rootstock which is above it

Secure the plant with a cane

TAKING CUTTINGS

This method is not recommended for many Hybrid Teas, especially the yellow varieties, as the root system may be too weak to transplant satisfactorily, but you can expect to succeed with Ramblers, vigorous Climbers, vigorous Floribundas and most Shrub Roses. An advantage of a rooted cutting compared to a budded rootstock is the absence of suckers — all shoots belong to the variety being grown.

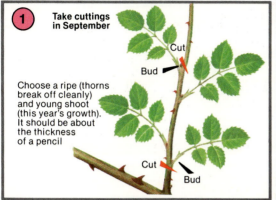

1 Take cuttings in September

Choose a ripe (thorns break off cleanly) and young shoot (this year's growth). It should be about the thickness of a pencil

Cut
Bud
Cut
Bud

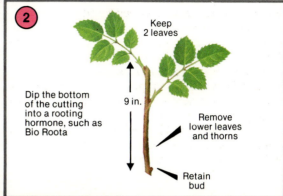

2

Keep 2 leaves

Dip the bottom of the cutting into a rooting hormone, such as Bio Roota

9 in.

Remove lower leaves and thorns

Retain bud

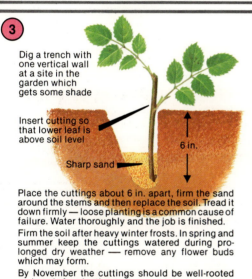

3

Dig a trench with one vertical wall at a site in the garden which gets some shade

Insert cutting so that lower leaf is above soil level

Sharp sand

6 in.

Place the cuttings about 6 in. apart, firm the sand around the stems and then replace the soil. Tread it down firmly — loose planting is a common cause of failure. Water thoroughly and the job is finished.

Firm the soil after heavy winter frosts. In spring and summer keep the cuttings watered during prolonged dry weather — remove any flower buds which may form.

By November the cuttings should be well-rooted and ready for planting.

Miniature Roses

Propagating Miniatures from cuttings has two advantages — you get more plants at very little cost and this new stock maintains its dwarf habit because it grows on its own roots.

The cuttings should be about 3 in. long — select shoots from this season's growth. Early autumn is the best time for this job — trim the cuttings to a leaf bud (see stage 2 above) and dip the bottom of each cutting in Bio Roota.

Plant firmly in pots containing Seed & Cutting Compost. A recent innovation which has proved successful for propagating Miniature Roses is the Rooting Bag — compost packed in a stout polythene bag. The method consists of cutting fourteen slits in the upper surface of the bag and then inserting a cutting through each slit.

Keep the cuttings out of direct sunlight. When new growth appears the rooted cuttings should be potted up separately into 3 in. pots. Keep indoors over winter and plant outdoors in spring or retain in pots for home decoration (see page 118).

SEED-SOWING

Raising roses from seed is usually dealt with briefly or not at all in the textbooks. There is no point in trying to raise a hybrid in this way — it will not breed true. The Species Roses will be true to type when grown from seed, but they will take years to reach a reasonable size and are much more easily raised from cuttings.

Miniature Roses are different — it is worthwhile growing them from seed and you can buy packets of various mixtures from several seedsmen. No long delays are involved — seeds sown in gentle heat in spring may be in flower by summer. Sow indoors in April in Seed & Cutting Compost. Germination is rather slow and erratic so try to sow a reasonable quantity of seeds. Prick out the best seedlings into small pots and make your selection in summer. Some of the young plants are bound to be poor and spindly — throw them away and just keep the most attractive. Repot as necessary and overwinter the plants in a cold greenhouse or on the windowsill of an unheated room.

LAYERING

Layering is an excellent method of propagating any rose which bears long and flexible stems. Of course, it is ideal for Ramblers but it can be used for many Shrub Roses as well.

In July or August work some peat into the area where the layering is to take place. Choose a stem which is mature but still flexible, and make a cut about 3 in. long on the side of the stem which will be buried in the prepared area. Place a twig in this cut and then bury this section in the ground. It should be pegged down with a forked stick.

The tip of the shoot should be secured in an upright position by tying it to a cane, and the ground should be kept watered in dry weather. Rooting will have taken place by the following March, and the new plant can be separated from the parent by cutting through the section of stem between them. Transplant the new Rambler or Shrub; do not allow it to flower during its first season.

SEED PARENT
The plant which serves as the female. It is fertilized to produce the seeds.

POLLEN PARENT
The plant which serves as the male. It is used to provide pollen for the seed parent.

Breeding a new rose

Breeding roses at home is like buying a national lottery ticket — it is easy to enter but almost impossible to come up with a winner. To raise a new rose is simple — you just transfer the pollen of one variety to the stigmas of another and then sow the seeds which result. Each seedling will be unique, but the chance of one being a significant advance in the rose world is almost nil.

Professional breeders often talk about the large element of luck in the discovery of a winner, but for them it is much more than a lottery. Great care goes into the selection of parents, hundreds of thousands of seedlings are raised and a high degree of skill goes into the detection of desirable characteristics at an early stage.

None of this need worry the novice. Home-bred plants need not be world-beaters — there is great satisfaction in having a variety, however flawed, which doesn't exist anywhere else!

1   Parent selection

You will need to select a seed parent and a pollen parent for the proposed cross. Try to choose two varieties which could combine desirable characteristics to produce a unique blend — a blood-red *Peace* is a much sought-after example. Crossing Floribundas is perhaps the easiest way to start but there are no strict rules — it is very much a matter of trial and error.

If you want to be a serious hybridist then you will have to study the family trees of candidate parents — *Roses* (Jack Harkness) is an excellent guide book. Pot up the selected plants in autumn in 10 in. pots and take them into a cold greenhouse in February.

2   Pollination

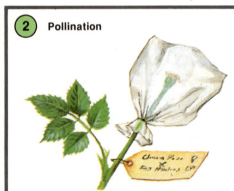

A sunny day in late May or early June is the ideal time for pollination. Prepare the seed parent. Choose a half-open flower and gently remove all the petals, taking care not to leave any bits behind. Next, pick off all the anthers with tweezers and finally place a paper bag over the emasculated flower.

Carry out pollination the following day. Snip off a flower of the pollen parent and remove or pull back the petals. Brush the anthers against the stigmas and then replace the paper bag over the seed parent. Tie a label to the stem, giving details of the parents, and continue to care for the seed parent plant as normal.

3   Seed preparation

Remove the paper bag after a couple of weeks and allow the hips to develop. Remove these swollen seed cases from the plant in autumn when they are ripe but not shrivelled. Bury them in wet peat in a flower pot, and let them stand outdoors throughout the winter — do not protect from frost. Remember to insert an identification label in the pot.

In February bring the hips indoors and squeeze out the seeds into a bowl of water. The floaters are infertile — sow the ones which have sunk to the bottom. Use Seed & Cutting Compost and when the first true rose leaves appear transplant the seedlings into small pots.

4   New rose selection

Some of these young plants will produce a bloom or two in May or June and this is the time for the first selection. One of the great skills of breeding is to spot desirable characteristics at this stage — you will have to rely on beginner's luck. Scrap all the worthless ones and transplant the promising ones into larger pots.

Carry out a second judging in August and grow as pot roses for a second season the few you wish to retain. If one shows promise you can plant it outdoors on its own roots or bud it on to a rootstock in July. You now have your very own rose variety growing in the garden.

CHAPTER 9
ROSES IN THE HOME

Half of this country's gardeners are women, and for them the rose has the added pleasure of having a place indoors. The use of cut roses for flower arranging is universal. Apart from countless garden blooms employed for this purpose, scores of millions of florist roses are sold every year.

There are many other uses for roses indoors, but the part they play in the home has declined in the sophisticated world of today. In the homes of Ancient Rome, in the refectories of mediaeval monasteries and in the kitchens of large Victorian villas you could find rose wine, rose perfumes, rose jams and so on. These are now rarities, but there is no reason why you should not try some of the old recipes which appear in this chapter.

THE ROSE AS A CUT FLOWER

It is not surprising that the favourite garden flower should be so popular for cutting. Unfortunately, as poets throughout the ages have pointed out, rose blooms are short-lived. Although you cannot expect cut roses to last as long as carnations, anemones or chrysanthemums, their life can be considerably extended if you follow a few simple rules when cutting, conditioning and arranging.

1 CUTTING

Choose a variety recommended for cutting. See list below and check in the A–Z guides (pages 9–46)

Blooms cut too early or too late will disappoint. Hybrid Teas: Sepals opened out; petals in the bud showing colour. Floribundas: Most of the flowers in the truss half-open

Cut in the evening if you can — otherwise cut in the morning

Cut just above a leaf. See page 93

Put cut blooms in a bucket of tepid water immediately

2 CONDITIONING

Remove lower leaves and thorns. Slit the bottom of each stem upwards for about 1 in. Stems should be stood up to their necks in water

Keep the bucket of roses in a cool dark place overnight

Bucket filled with water containing a dessertspoonful of sugar

If the leaves have wilted in the morning, stand ends of stems in 1 in. of very hot water for a few minutes before arranging

3 ARRANGING

Arrangement can be a single flower or a massed display. Roses can be grouped alone or mixed with other flowers

Keep the arrangement in good light but out of direct sunlight

Fill with tepid water — add Bio Flowerlife to extend life of blooms and keep roses fresh

If plastic foam is used as the base, soak thoroughly before use and fix in position before inserting stems

Drying Roses

Dried roses will last almost indefinitely if you handle and arrange them with care. Choose semi-double blooms — cut off the stems and when quite dry lay the flowers face upwards on a layer of oven-dry fine sand in a biscuit tin. Leave about 1 in. between the blooms. Slowly add more dry sand so that all parts of the flowers are covered — avoid air pockets. Finally, cover the blooms with a 1–2 in. layer of sand and replace the lid. Seal with adhesive tape.

Store in a warm dry place for three weeks. Remove blooms gently — they should be dry and crisp. Turn each one upside down and shake out the sand — remove any remaining grains with a fine brush. Insert a piece of stout florist wire in the base of each bloom and cover with green florist tape.

RECOMMENDED VARIETIES

Hybrid Teas	Floribundas
ACE OF HEARTS	ANISLEY DICKSON
ALEXANDER	ANNA FORD
ALPINE SUNSET	ANNE COCKER
APRICOT SILK	ANNE HARKNESS
BLESSINGS	ARTHUR BELL
BLUE MOON	CHANELLE
CHAMPION	CITY OF BELFAST
DIORAMA	COPPER POT
ELIZABETH HARKNESS	DEAREST
JULIA'S ROSE	ELIZABETH OF GLAMIS
LADY SYLVIA	ENGLISH MISS
MADAME BUTTERFLY	ESCAPADE
MISS HARP	GLENFIDDICH
NATIONAL TRUST	GREENSLEEVES
OPHELIA	ICEBERG
PASCALI	ICED GINGER
RUBY WEDDING	MARGARET MERRIL
SILVER LINING	MEMENTO
SILVER WEDDING	PADDY McGREDY
SUNBLEST	PINK PARFAIT
SUPER STAR	QUEEN ELIZABETH
SUTTER'S GOLD	RED GOLD
SWEET PROMISE	SEA PEARL
TROIKA	SOUTHAMPTON
VIRGO	SUNSILK

THE ROSE AS A HOUSE PLANT

The more books you read on growing roses indoors, the more confused you will become. At one end of the scale are the British authorities who claim that the Miniature Rose is not a house plant at all. It is a garden plant, to be brought indoors when the buds start to colour and then taken out again as soon as the flowers have faded.

At the other end of the scale there are the U.S. enthusiasts who scoff at such an idea — for them the Miniature Rose is a true indoor plant, providing regular flushes of blooms every two months throughout the year.

Surprisingly, both these opposed views are correct — it depends on the care provided. If all you want to do is put the pot on the sideboard and water it occasionally then it is right to keep the plant indoors for as short a time as possible. If however you can provide fluorescent lighting above the pots and a humid atmosphere around them, then it is perfectly feasible to achieve the American all-the-year-round result.

The best compromise for most rose growers is to use the Pebble Tray technique. By this method you can have Miniature Roses in bloom by early spring in the living room, and there they can stay, producing regular flushes of flowers until late summer or early autumn.

The secret is to ensure that the plants receive **maximum light** and **adequate humidity** whilst they are indoors — see the diagram below for details.

Use rooted cuttings rather than Miniatures which have been budded on to rootstocks. In autumn transfer the pots outdoors and bring them in again in January. Prune to about half their present height and stand the pots in an unheated room for about two weeks before placing them in the heated room where they are to bloom. Avoid temperatures above 70°F. Keep a careful watch for red spider mite.

South-facing window. Screen from midday sun in summer. If possible move the pots near a fluorescent light at night in spring and autumn

Water liberally. Allow the pot to dry out slightly between waterings. Feed with Baby Bio each time you water

Mist leaves frequently with a hand sprayer

Waterproof tray about 2 in. deep

1 in. layer of gravel. Keep the bottom of this layer wet at all times, but the water level must be kept below the top of the gravel

THE ROSE IN PERFUME-MAKING

Pot-pourri

Pot-pourri is a mixture of dried flower petals and sweet-smelling oils, spices and fixatives. When the mixture has matured, it is placed in open bowls or pomanders to scent the room or placed in sachets in drawers to scent the linen.

Choose fragrant roses when they are at their prime. Cut them when the petals are dry. Spread a thin layer of petals on newspaper and place in a warm, dry room — an airing cupboard is ideal. Stir occasionally and when the petals are cornflake crisp after one or two weeks, place them in a polythene bag. Add the following mixture to the bag:

For each quart of dried petals —

    1 oz dried orris root (to 'fix' the scents)

    ½ teaspoon allspice

    ½ teaspoon cinnamon

    A few drops of rose oil

Shake thoroughly and leave the bag closed for about three weeks — then place the pot-pourri in any attractive container.

This is the basic rose pot-pourri. To vary the scent add dried orange and lemon peel, or dried aromatic leaves such as scented geranium, mint, rosemary, etc.

Rose Water

You can buy rose water from your local chemist, but if you have a plentiful supply of fragrant blooms you can try to make your own in the following age-old way:

Clean rubber tube

Airtight joint

Large bowl of cold water

Large kettle (*not* electric) half-filled with compressed petals which are then covered with water. Allow to simmer; do *not* seal lid

Glass jar

Chair

Rose water

When the kettle is nearly (but not completely) dry, switch off the heat. Carefully drain the contents of the tube into the glass jar.

Rose Oil

You will not be able to obtain concentrated rose essence from your roses (it takes about 5 tons of fragrant petals to produce just one pound of attar of roses) but you can make a simple rose oil if you have an abundance of petals and time.

Place a pint of olive oil in a large bowl and add as many fragrant petals as the container will hold. Leave them to soak in the oil for two days and then squeeze through a fine strainer. Press the petals against the inside of the sieve to ensure that all the oils are squeezed out.

Repeat the process about ten times with fresh petals. Finally, decant the oil into a container with an airtight screw lid. Use the oil as a perfume or for making pot-pourri.

THE ROSE IN THE KITCHEN

The rose is not a vegetable — it is a plant to be admired for its beauty in the garden outdoors or in a vase or pot indoors. But there are recipes which call for roses, and one or two of them can be tried by the adventurous cook. If you intend to follow any of these recipes, make sure that the petals or hips are fresh and disease-free, and they should not have been recently sprayed or dusted. Petals and hips can be used in many ways, but never use rose leaves.

Rose Hip Jam

Wash and 'tail' the rose hips. Place in a large pan with an equal volume of water and cook until tender — about 15 minutes. Push the pulp through a fine strainer and to each cup of pulped hips add half a cup of sugar. Cook and stir until the mixture thickens to a jam-like consistency and then pour into sterilized jars and seal.

Rose Vinegar

Fill a large glass or glazed earthenware jar with red fragrant petals. Press them down and cover with wine vinegar. Cover the jar and leave for several weeks; then filter into screw-topped bottles.

Crystallised Rose Petals

Prepare a bowl containing beaten egg whites and another containing granulated sugar. Remove the petals gently from a dry bloom and using tweezers dip each one first into the frothy egg whites (avoid any excess on the petals) and then into the granulated sugar. Dry the crystallised petals on a lined baking tray in the airing cupboard. Store between layers of greaseproof paper in an airtight tin.

Rose Honey

Wash and 'tail' 4 oz of rose hips and boil in a cup of water in an enamel saucepan for about 15 minutes. Push the pulp through a fine strainer and add 1 lb of honey. Boil and stir the mixture until it thickens to a jam-like consistency and then pour into sterilized jars and seal.

Rose Wine

Rose wines have been made in Britain for centuries, but the methods used often led to failure. The modern techniques of home wine-making have taken the risks and guesswork out of this absorbing hobby, and both petals and hips can be used to make rose wine. You will need about 4 pints of petals or 2 pints of hips to make a gallon of wine.

There are more ingredients than just rose petals or hips plus sugar and water. The list is a long one, including yeast, nutrient tablets, Campden tablets, pectin-destroying enzyme and grape tannin. There is also special equipment — fermentation jars, airlocks, filters and the rest. Do not let this list put you off — if you have never tried your hand at wine-making you can begin with roses and a simple guide from your bookshop will give you step-by-step instructions.

If you do not wish to go to the trouble and expense of wine-making it is possible to make 'instant' rose wine. Just mix ½ lb of red fragrant petals with a pint of hot water and pulp them through a fine sieve. Add more petals until the liquor is a rich red colour and then stir in 1 lb of sugar and ½ pint of brandy.

THE ROSE AS A BUTTONHOLE FLOWER

Once the buttonhole rose was the badge of nearly every stationmaster and City gentleman, but its popularity has greatly declined. No more will you find it described in the rose books, but some men do still wear a rose in their lapel — the summer-long symbol of their hobby.

Any shapely and compact bloom will do — the ideal is a half-opened bud, pointed and high-centred with a good colour. There are varieties which have earned a high reputation as buttonhole roses (*Cécile Brunner*, *Madame Butterfly* and *Ophelia* are examples) but many other Hybrid Tea and Shrub Roses will do just as well.

Pick your buttonhole rose in the evening and stand its short stem immediately in tepid water. Leave it overnight and then prepare it for your jacket. The fashion in the early years of this century was to insert the stem into a water-filled metal tube worn at the back of the lapel, but these and the glass tubes which replaced them are now gone.

The modern way of preparing a buttonhole rose is shown on the right. As you can see, neither skill nor a special holder is called for.

Silver foil or green florist tape wrapped tightly around both the stem and the cotton wool covering the base

Cotton wool, soaked in water, placed around the cut end of the stem

CHAPTER 10
ROSE CALENDAR

JANUARY

Frosts are likely, so there is usually little to do in the rose garden this month.

Check roses growing on supports to make sure that the ties are strong enough to hold them. Inspect autumn-planted bushes and standards to see if they have been loosened by frosts. Firm if necessary.

Planting can take place if soil is free-draining and not heavy, and if weather is dry and not freezing. Beds to be planted in March should be prepared this month.

Heating of the greenhouse containing pot roses may be required to keep the temperature at 40°–45°F.

FEBRUARY

The soil will almost certainly be wet and cold, but planting can continue in light-soil areas if the temperature is above freezing. In mild districts the pruning of vigorous Floribundas can begin at the end of the month. Stocks budded last year can be cut back.

Pot roses will now be starting to grow, and a temperature of 50°–60°F should be maintained. Spray the shoots with water to create moist conditions. Greenfly and caterpillars can cause serious damage to the new and tender shoots, so keep careful watch for these pests and spray at the first sign of attack.

MARCH

Finish planting this month. In most areas March is the best time to prune bush and standard roses. Burn all prunings.

Fertilizer may be spread around the bushes immediately after pruning and lightly pricked into the surface, but it is generally better to wait until April.

Weed beds thoroughly; apply a simazine-based weedkiller if regular hoeing is not possible.

Pot roses in the greenhouse may now be in bud. A weekly liquid feed with Bio Plant Food will improve bloom quality. Continue spraying shoots with water. Increase house temperature to 60°–65°F.

APRIL

Pruning must be completed by the beginning of the month, as roses will now be starting to grow actively. Rub out any surplus young shoots.

Apply a fertilizer, such as Toprose, which contains the main and minor plant foods needed by the rose. Keep the powder off new growth, and lightly prick into the soil surface.

Neaten bed edges with a half-moon edging iron. In areas where bad attacks of black spot are common apply two carbendazim sprays a week apart as soon as leaf buds open.

Continue feeding and watering pot roses under glass, some of which will bloom this month. Spraying with water should now be directed at the paths, not on the roses. Keep watch for mildew, greenfly and caterpillar. Ideal house temperature 65°–75°F. Apply Coolglass to the panes if weather is sunny.

MAY

Garden roses will now be growing rapidly, and a mulch should be applied around the stems. Hoeing can be carried out to destroy weeds, but do not dig in the mulching material.

The first of the early-flowering Shrubs (e.g. Canary Bird) will now be in flower.

Greenfly attacks are likely, and a systemic insecticide which works internally is the best method of control (see page 99). A spray or dust for other insect pests or early disease outbreak may be necessary — watch for first attacks. If using a liquid fertilizer, such as Instant Bio, apply this month when soil is moist. Apply a foliar feed such as Fillip to backward plants.

Visit the Chelsea Flower Show in London.

Pot roses which have finished flowering should be moved outdoors and stood on concrete, ashes, etc., but not on earth. Water as necessary.

JUNE

Roses are now coming into flower. Hoeing, spraying and watering should continue as necessary.

Mulch with grass clippings if they are free from weedkiller. Cut flowers for indoor decoration from established plants, not from newly-planted bushes.

Disbudding of Hybrid Teas (see page 93) will ensure top-quality blooms. A summer fertilizer dressing with Toprose will keep the plants growing vigorously and help to produce a succession of flower buds. If you plan to enter your roses at a flower show, obtain show schedule as soon as possible. Continue foliar feeding for top-quality blooms.

Apply a mixed systemic insecticide/fungicide spray to keep pests and diseases at bay.

The last of the pot roses should now be moved out from the greenhouse to their outdoor quarters.

JULY

Bushes and standards should now be in full flower — July is usually the best month to enjoy your roses. Dead-head (see page 93) flower stalks when the blooms they carry have finished flowering. Apply a summer dressing of fertilizer if this was not done last month.

Hoe, disbud, mulch and water if necessary as described for June. Keep a special watch for the first signs of black spot and mildew. Spray immediately if seen.

If you are going away on holiday, remove all flowers which have begun to fade so that hips will not form during your absence.

Visit the British Rose Festival at St Albans or the Lakeland Rose Show in Cumbria. Many local rose shows are held during this month.

Bud rootstocks this month.

AUGUST

The cultural techniques described for July apply this month, with the exception of fertilizer application which should stop at the end of July.

Now is the time to start thinking ahead to next year's varieties for your garden. If you can, visit the nursery of a large specialist rose grower to see the new varieties in bloom. Your local garden centre is well worth a visit. Some nurseries have special Display Gardens (see page 106). Other displays worth visiting are the RNRS Gardens of the Rose at St Albans, the Provincial Display Gardens (see page 106) and the Southport Flower Show.

Send off your rose order as soon as possible, as new introductions and popular varieties are frequently sold out before planting time.

Begin the preparation of new rose beds as described in Chapter 5.

SEPTEMBER

Roses will generally still be flowering freely, and dead-heading now will help to ensure a fine late display.

Ramblers and weeping standards should have been pruned by now (see page 92). Never leave these plants for pruning in the spring.

Carry on preparing new beds for planting in November and despatch your order to the nursery if this was not done last month.

Continue hoeing and spraying against disease if necessary. September is a good month to take cuttings of Ramblers, vigorous Floribundas etc. See page 115 for instructions.

Visit the Rose Festival in London — many local autumn rose shows are held in September.

OCTOBER

This month is the start of the rose grower's year. Tidy up beds. Hoe in the mulching material and collect up and burn leaves.

Finish preparing new beds. Nurseries start sending out their plants in October and planting can start at the end of the month. Trim off leaves and unripe wood as described on page 86 before placing each plant in its new quarters.

Inspect pot roses this month, and repot if necessary. Buy and pot up new plants. Remove shading and clean out greenhouse. Begin bringing the plants inside at the end of October.

NOVEMBER

Get plants ready for winter. In exposed areas, long stems should be cut back a little to prevent wind rock during winter storms. In cold districts the stems should be earthed-up with about 4 inches of soil (remove in spring) or covered with straw (see page 96).

An excellent time for planting. If the bushes or standards arrive when the weather is unsuitable or before you are ready, leave package unopened or heel-in plants as described on page 86.

All pot roses should be placed in the greenhouse during this month.

DECEMBER

The soil will now generally be colder and wetter than last month so planting should be completed as soon as possible. Never try to plant when the soil is either hard with frost or waterlogged.

There is no work to do in the established rose garden, but work can begin on the preparation of rose beds which are to be planted up in March.

All pot roses will now be housed under glass and the temperature should be kept above freezing point if heat is available. Keep the pots fairly dry for a short time after housing, and prune at the end of the month.

CHAPTER 11
ROSE GROWER'S DICTIONARY

A

ACID SOIL A soil which contains no free lime and has a pH of less than 6.5.

ALLEN, E. F. Honorary Scientific Adviser of the RNRS since 1959, and a prolific contributor to its publications. Mr Allen is also a successful amateur breeder — his *Golden Chersonese* received a Certificate of Merit in 1970.

AMERICAN ROSE SOCIETY Started in 1899, the ARS has become one of the most active rose societies in the world. Its members receive a monthly magazine together with the American Rose Annual each year, which features the *Proof of the Pudding* survey. The headquarters are at the American Rose Center where an extensive rose garden is being created. Details of membership can be obtained from the Secretary, American Rose Society, Shreveport, Louisiana, USA.

ANTHER The part of the flower which produces pollen. It is the upper section of the *stamen*.

ARMED Bearing strong thorns.

ATTAR OF ROSES A yellowish oil distilled from rose petals which is used for making perfumes. Its production has been a major industry in the Balkans for centuries.

AXIL The angle between the upper surface of the leaf stalk and the stem that carries it.

B

BALLING The clinging together of petals in wet weather so that the bloom fails to open — see page 96.

BARE-ROOT A rose dug up at the nursery and sold with no soil around its roots — see page 73.

BASAL SHOOT A shoot arising from the neck or crown of the plant — see page 4.

BENNETT, HENRY The father of scientific rose breeding. He was a cattle breeder, and realized the need to control the pollination and keep a careful record of the crosses. In 1879 he introduced his Ten Pedigree Hybrids of the Tea Rose.

BLEEDING The loss of sap from plant tissues due to late pruning.

BLIND SHOOT A mature stem which fails to produce a flower.

BLOWN BLOOM A many-petalled bloom which has opened wide, revealing its stamens.

BLUE ROSE No true-blue rose exists, and it is extremely unlikely that one will ever be raised, because the blue flower pigment (delphinidin) is missing from the rose family. The so called "blue" roses, such as *Blue Moon, Mr Bluebird* etc. are really lavender, mauve or violet.

BLUEING The transformation of a red or deep pink bloom to mauve or purple as it ages.

BOSS The ring of stamens when it is prominent and decorative.

BOX A container which bears six or twelve tubes for the display of specimen blooms — see page 113.

BRACT A small leaf-like growth on the flower stalk — see page 4.

BREAKING BUD A bud which has started to open.

BRITISH ASSOCIATION OF ROSE BREEDERS The objects of BARB are to encourage, improve and extend the introduction and growing of new roses under *Plant Breeders' Rights*. Trials are conducted, and a large rose garden has been created at Springfields (see page 106). About 250 nurseries are registered with BARB, and there is a very simple method of licensing new varieties to these growers.

BUD A flower bud is the unopened bloom. A growth bud or *eye* is a condensed shoot found in the *axil* of a leafstalk.

BUD UNION The point where the bud and the rootstock are united.

BUDDING The grafting of a bud into the neck of a rootstock — see page 114. The standard commercial method of propagating roses.

BURNING The bleaching or scorching of the petals in bright sunshine.

BUSH A growth type — see page 4 for details.

BUTTON EYE A condition found in the centre of the blooms of some old varieties — the petals are folded inwards to form a 'button'.

C

CALLUS The scar tissue which forms over a pruning cut or at the base of a cutting.

CALYX The green protective cover of the flower bud, which opens into five sepals.

CANE A main stem or basal shoot — a term frequently used in the U.S.

CANKER A diseased and discoloured area on the stem — see page 98.

CANTS OF COLCHESTER This distinguished nursery was started by William Cant in 1765. Its best-known success was *Just Joey*, and other well-known introductions include *Goldstar* and *English Miss*.

CHLOROSIS An abnormal yellowing or blanching of the leaves due to lack of chlorophyll. See page 96 for possible causes.

CLIMBING SPORT A mutation of a bush variety which bears longer stems but identical flowers to the parent.

CLUSTER A number of flowers connected by their *footstalks* to a single stem — see page 4.

COCKER, ALEC Scottish breeder, who began to raise roses in 1963 and died in 1977 — shortly before his great achievement *Silver Jubilee* received Britain's highest award. Earlier successes from the Aberdeen nursery were *Alec's Red, Anne Cocker, Rob Roy* and *Rosy Mantle*.

COMPOST Two meanings — either decomposed vegetable or animal matter for incorporation in the soil or a potting/cutting mixture made from peat ('soilless compost') or sterilized soil ('loam compost') plus other materials such as sand, lime and fertilizer.

CONE A conical protector used by exhibitors to prevent rain and bright sunshine from spoiling their show blooms whilst they are still on the plant — see page 113.

CONFUSED CENTRE The centre of a bloom where the petals are disarranged, giving an asymmetrical appearance.

CROCK A piece of broken flower pot used at the bottom of a container to improve drainage.

CROSS The offspring arising from cross-pollination.

CROWN The point on the bush where the basal shoots sprout from the rootstock.

CULTIVAR Short for 'cultivated variety' — it is a variety which originated in cultivation and not in the wild. Strictly speaking, all modern varieties are cultivars, but the more familiar term *'variety'* is used in this book.

CUT-BACK A bush which is one or more seasons older than a *maiden*.

CUTTING A piece of stem cut from a plant and used for propagation.

D

DEAD-HEADING The removal of faded flowers — see page 93.

DE-SHOOTING The removal of small shoots to prevent overcrowding. Another term for 'thinning' — see page 93.

DICKSON & SONS LTD The Dickson nurseries in County Down have a long and distinguished history of rose breeding. There were Dickson roses before the 20th century and *Shot Silk* (1924) still appears in the catalogues. More recent successes have been *Grandpa Dickson, Red Devil, Red Gold, Beautiful Britain* and *Precious Platinum*.

DIE-BACK The progressive dying back of a shoot from the tip — see page 98.

DISBUDDING The removal of young flower buds to allow the maximum development of the remainder — see page 93.

DOG ROSE The common wild rose found in hedgerows — so called because the Romans used it as a cure for hydrophobia.

DORMANT PERIOD The time when the plant has naturally stopped growing due to low temperature and short day-length.

DOT, PEDRO Spain's greatest hybridist. His work spanned 50 years and although he raised many noteworthy Hybrid Teas he will always be remembered as one of the world's leading breeders of Miniatures. *Josephine Wheatcroft, Pour Toi, Coralin* and *Baby Gold Star* are examples of his introductions.

DOUBLE BLOOM A flower with more than twenty petals — see page 5.

DRESSING The manipulation of an exhibition bloom in order to improve its appearance on the day of the show — see page 113.

E

EARTHING-UP The drawing up of earth around the base of a bush to protect it during a period of abnormally cold weather.

EMASCULATION A technique used in hybridising — the removal of the anthers from the seed parent to prevent self-pollination. See page 116.

EYE Two unrelated meanings — a dormant growth bud or the centre of a single or semi-double bloom where the colour is distinctly different from the rest of the flower.

F

FERTILE HYBRID A hybrid which bears viable seed capable of producing new plants. A sterile hybrid does not produce viable seed.

FERTILIZATION The application of pollen to the stigma to induce the production of seed. An essential step in hybridisation — see page 116.

FILAMENT The supporting column of the *anther*. It is the lower part of the *stamen*.

FIXED A vital feature for a new variety — it means that the new colour or growth habit is stable.

FLORIFEROUS The scientific term for *free-flowering*.

FLOWER-SHY A vague term indicating that a variety bears a below-average number of blooms during the flowering season. The opposite condition is *free-flowering*.

FLUSH The period during which the plant bears its normal complement of blooms — there may be more than one such period during the season — see *repeat flowering*.

FOLIAR FEED A fertilizer capable of being sprayed on and absorbed by the leaves — see page 94.

FOOTSTALK The pedicel or flower stalk — see page 4.

FORCING The process of making a plant grow or flower before its natural season.

FOSSIL ROSES Fossilized rose leaves have been found in rocks in Europe, Asia and North America. They are thought to be 7–30 million years old.

FREE-FLOWERING A vague term indicating that a variety bears an above-average number of blooms during the flowering season. The opposite condition is *flower-shy*.

FUNGICIDE A chemical used to control diseases caused by fungi.

FUNGUS A primitive form of plant life which is the most common cause of infectious disease — mildew, black spot and rust are examples.

G

GARNETTE ROSE A red Floribunda, similar to the variety *Garnette*, grown commercially under glass for sale as a cut flower.

GRAFTING The process of joining a stem or bud of one plant on to the stem of another.

GREGORY, WALTER One of the group of great Nottinghamshire rose growers, who began breeding new varieties in 1952. In the span of nearly 30 years before his death in 1980, he introduced *Blessings, Pink Perpétue* and his crowning glory, *Wendy Cussons*.

GUARD PETALS The outermost ring of petals.

GUILLOT, JEAN-BAPTISTE The first of the great rose breeders from Lyons. His creation in 1867, *La France,* was the original Hybrid Tea and started the era of the modern rose. In the following decade he introduced *Ma Paquerette, Gloire des Polyantha* and *Mignonette* — the first of the dwarf Polyanthas which gave rise to the modern Floribundas.

H

HARDY A plant which will withstand overwintering without any protection.

HARKNESS, JACK The family firm was established in Yorkshire about 100 years ago, and in 1892 a branch was set up in Hertfordshire to specialise in roses. It was Jack Harkness who first turned to hybridising and his successes have been outstanding — *Alexander, Mountbatten, Escapade, Compassion* and *Amber Queen*. His collaboration with Alec Cocker was one of the great success stories in the world of rose breeding.

HEAD The framework of stems borne at the top of the stem of a standard.

HEADING-BACK The removal of the stems of the rootstock above the union after budding — see page 114.

HEELING IN The temporary planting of a new rose pending suitable weather conditions for permanent planting.

HEP See *hip*.

HILDESHEIM ROSE A specimen of *Dog Rose* growing at Hildesheim Cathedral in Germany. The legend is that it was planted by Charlemagne over 1,000 years ago, but it is probably 300–500 years old. Generally accepted as the oldest living rose.

HILLING U.S. term for *earthing-up*.

HIP The fruit of a rose, large and decorative in some varieties — see page 6.

HOLE, REV SAMUEL REYNOLDS Although an active churchman (he became Dean of Rochester), Reverend Hole was the dominant figure in the Victorian rose world. He amassed a collection of 5,000 varieties, arranged the first National Rose Show and was a leading figure in the formation of the National Rose Society in 1876. The Dean Hole Medal is the RNRS's highest award for distinguished service.

HONEYDEW Sticky, sugary secretion deposited on the leaves and stems by such insects as aphid and whitefly.

HURST, CHARLES C. Cambridge scientist who worked out the family history of the modern rose, as outlined on page 111.

HYBRID A rose with parents which are genetically distinct. The parent plants may be different *cultivars, varieties* or *species*.

I

INFLORESCENCE The arrangement of flowers on the stem.

INORGANIC A chemical or fertilizer which is not obtained from a source which is or has been alive.

INSECTICIDE A chemical used to control insect pests.

INTERNODE The part of the stem between one *node* and another.

J

JACKSON & PERKINS Claimed to be the largest rose nursery in the world. At their trial grounds in California many great roses have been raised, first by Eugene Boerner and more recently by William Warriner. Some are readily available in the U.K. — examples are *Pristine, Dorothy Perkins* and *Masquerade*.

JOSEPHINE Empress Josephine, wife of Napoleon I, bought *Malmaison* in 1799 and set out to stock it with every variety of rose grown anywhere in the world. Her passion created the world's first rose display ground, and it made the rose a fashionable flower for the wealthy to grow on their estates.

K

KNUCKLE U.S. term for *bud union*.

KORDES, WILHELM Wilhelm Kordes, until his death in 1977, ranked alongside *Tantau* as the greatest rose hybridist in Germany. The list of his introductions starts with *Crimson Glory* in 1935. Others include *Iceberg, Perfecta, Korp, Ernest H. Morse, Peer Gynt, Meteor* and *Simba*. One of his most outstanding achievements was the development of the Kordesii climbers, such as *Dortmund*.

L

LANCASTER ROSE The Red Rose of Lancaster is *Rosa gallica officinalis* (see page 69). The legend is that the first Earl of Lancaster brought it from France to England during the 13th century.

LANKY Spindly growth — a stem with a gaunt and sparse appearance.

LATERAL BRANCH A side branch which arises from a main stem.

LAWRANCE, MARY Authoress of the first book devoted entirely to roses — 'A Collection of Roses from Nature' (1799).

LEACHING The drawing away of chemicals from the soil, caused by rain or watering.

LE GRICE, EDWARD Norfolk breeder who was responsible for one of the best yellow Floribundas — *Allgold*. His career was a long one; in 1938 he received a Certificate of Merit for *Dainty Maid* — in 1970 he was awarded a Gold Medal for *News*. In between these two were *My Choice* and *Lilac Charm*.

LENS, LOUIS The Lens nurseries have been the most successful breeding establishment in Belgium for half a century. Louis entered the firm in 1945 and later succeeded his father, Victor. His most famous introduction was *Pascali*, which remains one of the best white Hybrid Teas.

M

MAIDEN A rose bush in its first year after budding.

MALMAISON A château with extensive grounds situated near Paris, famous as the first great rose garden. Empress *Josephine* stocked it with more than 200 different varieties from all over the world and new techniques for breeding and cultivation were developed. Her work at Malmaison began in 1799 — following her divorce in 1809 she moved there permanently.

McCARTHY, ROSEMARY Rosemary McCarthy is the daughter of Charles Walter Gregory, who named *Rosemary Rose* for her. She is Managing Director of Gregory's Roses — the first woman in the Gregory family to hold this office. In 1983 she started her own nursery in Nottingham — Rosemary Roses.

McGREDY, SAM Sam McGredy IV has a family tradition of rose breeding, and since taking over the nursery in 1952 in N. Ireland and then emigrating to New Zealand in 1972, he has joined the ranks of the world's great hybridists. Even his major achievements are too numerous to list in full — they include *Mischief, Piccadilly, City of Belfast, Arthur Bell, Evelyn Fison, Handel, Chanelle, Picasso* and *Elizabeth of Glamis*.

MEILLAND François Meilland raised *Peace* just before World War II and secured an everlasting place in the Gardening Hall of Fame. Other successes included *Baccara*, but perhaps one of his greatest achievements was to secure breeders' rights for new roses. Alain now carries on his father's work — *Papa Meilland, Susan Hampshire, Sweet Promise, Starina* and *Chorus* are a few of the products of the Antibes nursery.

MODERN ROSES The first edition of this rose variety 'bible' appeared in 1930. The ninth edition of Modern Roses, published in 1986, contains details of many thousands of varieties. It is produced by the *American Rose Society*, which is the international organization for the registration of rose names.

MOORE, RALPH S. Californian breeder who has revolutionised the world of Miniature Roses. He has developed Miniature Moss Roses and Miniature Climbers, and many of today's favourites are his creations — *New Penny, Easter Morning, Dresden Doll* and *Little Buckaroo*.

MULCH A layer of bulky organic material placed around the stems.

MUTATION A sudden change in the genetic make-up of a plant, leading to a new feature. This new feature can be inherited.

N

NECK The part of the plant above the roots and below the stems.

NEUTRAL Neither acid nor alkaline — pH 6.5–7.5.

NODE The point on the stem at which a leaf or bud is attached.

NORMAN, A. An amateur rosarian, famous as the raiser of two outstanding varieties — *Ena Harkness* and *Frensham*.

O

ORGANIC A chemical or fertilizer which is obtained from a source which is or has been alive.

OVARY The part of the flower which contains the *ovules*.

OVERDRESSED Petals which have been bent back to such an extent on the day of the show that the bloom has an unnatural appearance.

OVULE The part of the female organ of the flower which turns into a seed after fertilization.

OWN-ROOT A plant grown on its own roots — one that has not been budded.

P

PEACE Seedling No. 3-35-40 was raised by François Meilland at Lyons before the outbreak of World War II and a few plants were sent out on the last plane to America as France fell. He had named the plant *Mme Antoine Meilland* but it was taken to Germany as *Gloria Dei*. When the War ended the U.S. nursery which had raised his stock placed a bunch of the flowers at each seat at the Peace Conference — and the rose received its final name — Peace.

PEDICEL The flower stalk — see page 4.

PEGGING DOWN The bending over of long shoots and the retention of their tips at ground level by means of pegs.

PERGOLA An arched structure used to support climbing plants; a rose-covered tunnel.

PERNET-DUCHER, JOSEPH Born in 1858, he earned the title "Wizard of Lyons" by transforming the colour range of modern roses. His early successes included *Mme Caroline Testout*, but he is best remembered for *Soleil d'Or*, introduced in 1900, which brought yellow to bedding roses.

pH A measure of acidity and alkalinity. Below pH 6.5 is acid, above pH 7.5 is alkaline.

PISTIL The female organ of a flower, consisting of the *stigma, style* and *ovule*.

PITH The spongy material at the centre of the stem. An unripe stem is sometimes described as 'pithy'.

PLANT BREEDERS' RIGHTS Until the 1960s a U.K. breeder of a new rose received no royalties from the growers who propagated and sold it. The first plant patent was awarded in the U.S. — *New Dawn* in 1930. British protection dates from 1964 (the Plant Varieties & Seeds Act). Growers pay a small royalty to the breeder for each patented rose they propagate. The payment of a royalty does not apply if you progagate roses for your own pleasure and not for sale.

POLLEN The yellow dust produced by the *anthers*. It is the male element which fertilizes the *ovule*.

POLLINATION The application of *pollen* to the *stigma* of the flower.

POULSEN The Poulsen family of Denmark have produced many great roses during the past 60 years. Svend Poulsen raised the first Hybrid Polyantha (later called Floribundas) in 1924, and he was responsible for several famous varieties, such as *Else Poulsen*. The company has carried on the tradition with *Troika, White Bells* and *Chinatown*.

PROOF OF THE PUDDING The U.S. equivalent of the Royal National Rose Society Analysis (see page 105). The ratings are based on the experience of members of the *American Rose Society* who have grown the roses in question.

PROPAGATION The multiplication of plants — see page 114.

PRUNING The removal of parts of the plant in order to improve its performance.

R

RECURRENT FLOWERING Same as *repeat flowering*.

REDOUTE, PIERRE JOSEPH French artist commissioned by Empress *Josephine* in 1805 to make a pictorial record of every rose grown at *Malmaison*. The three volumes of Les Roses portray 170 of these roses, and reproductions of these paintings are still immensely popular.

REMONTANT/REMONTANCE Same as *repeat flowering*.

REPEAT FLOWERING The production of two or more *flushes* during the flowering season — see page 6.

REVERSE The side of the petal which faces away from the centre.

REVERSION Two meanings — either a *sport* which goes back to the colour or growth habit of its parent or a cultivated variety which is outgrown by suckers arising from the rootstock.

RIVERS, THOMAS & SON LTD The first nursery in Britain — founded 1725. Their 'Rose Amateurs Guide' first appeared in 1837 and listed 700 varieties for sale.

ROGUE A rose supplied which was not ordered, and which is not close enough to be regarded as a *substitute*.

ROOTSTOCK The host plant on to which a cultivated variety is budded — see page 4.

ROSA The genus to which all roses belong. There are about 140 different species.

ROSACEAE The family to which roses belong, together with other plants which have rose-like flowers, such as cherry, plum, hawthorn and strawberry.

ROSE GROWERS ASSOCIATION The RGA is an association of the leading rose growers who jointly produce more than three-quarters of the roses sold in this country. They seek publicity for roses and rose growing, and to improve standards they publish information. The RGA stages a major exhibit at the annual Rose Festival held at the Gardens of the Rose.

ROYAL NATIONAL ROSE SOCIETY See page 104.

S

SANGERHAUSEN Founded by the German Rose Society in 1903, this Rosarium in E. Germany has the most extensive collection of old roses in the world.

SCION The technical term for the bud which is grafted on to the rootstock.

SEEDLING A young plant raised from seed; in the rose world it also means a mature plant raised by sowing seed rather than by budding or taking cuttings.

SEPAL One of the five green divisions of the *calyx*.

SHOOT A stem or cane. Some rose experts prefer to be more precise — a shoot is used for young growth, a stem describes mature growth.

SHOT A surface which changes colour when viewed from different points.

SIDE SHOOT Same as *lateral branch*.

SNAG A section of stem left above a bud when pruning.

SPECIES Roses which are genetically similar and which reproduce exactly when self-fertilized. The popular meaning is a wild rose or one of its near relatives.

SPIT The depth of the spade blade — usually about 9 inches.

SPORT A plant which shows a marked and inheritable change from its parent; a *mutation*.

SPOTTING The appearance of spots and blemishes on the petals during wet weather.

STAMEN The male organ of a flower, consisting of the *anther* and *filament*.

STIGMA The part of the female organ of the flower which catches the pollen.

STIPULE The small outgrowth at the base of the leafstalk.

STOCK See *rootstock*.

STRATIFICATION The breaking of seed dormancy by placing hips in a refrigerator or overwintering them outdoors in damp peat before removing seeds for sowing — see page 116.

STRIKE The successful outcome of taking cuttings — cuttings 'strike' whereas grafts *'take'*.

STYLE The part of the female organ of the flower which connects the *stigma* to the *ovule*.

SUBSTITUTE A similar variety sent out by a nurseryman if the ordered variety is not available.

SUCKER A shoot growing from the rootstock — see page 102.

SWIM, HERBERT C. Californian hybridist who has produced more All-America Award winners than any other breeder. His successes include *Sutter's Gold, Summer Sunshine, Mojave, Pink Parfait, Royal Highness* and *Mister Lincoln.*

SYSTEMIC A pesticide which goes inside the plant and travels in the sap stream.

T

TAKE The successful outcome of budding — grafts 'take' whereas cuttings *'strike'*.

TANTAU The father and son partnership of Mathias Tantau and Mathias junior has produced such world-famous roses as *Super Star, Fragraht Cloud, Fountain* and *Topsi.* The first Tantau rose from the N. German nursery was *Beauty of Holstein* (1919). Since then the list has been outstanding — *Deep Secret, Duke of Windsor, Whisky Mac, Blue Moon, Prima Ballerina* and many more.

THORN A characteristic spine or prickle, usually found on the stems but occasionally on the backs of leaves and on hips.

TRANSPLANTING Movement of a plant from one site to another.

TREE ROSE U.S. term for a standard rose — see page 4.

TRUSS A number of flowers connected by their *footstalks* to a single stem — see page 4.

TUDOR ROSE The royal badge of England, combining the Red Rose of Lancaster with the White Rose of York. It was adopted as our national emblem when Henry Tudor (Henry VII) married Elizabeth of York in 1486.

U

UNDERSTOCK See *rootstock*.

UNION See *bud union*.

V

VARIETY Strictly speaking, a naturally occurring variation of a species (see *cultivar*). The popular meaning in the rose world is any distinct type of rose which bears one or more unique features.

W

WEEPING STANDARD A Rambler budded on to a tall standard stem — see page 4.

WHEATCROFT, HARRY Until his death in 1977, Harry Wheatcroft was 'Mr Rose' to millions of British gardeners. His nursery at Edwalton, Nottinghamshire, produced two million plants a year, but he will be best remembered for his personal appearances and his introduction to Britain of such great roses as *Super Star, Peace, Fragrant Cloud* and *Queen Elizabeth.*

WILD ROSES Rose species which are native to a particular country. The British wild roses include *R. arvensis (Field Rose), R. canina (Dog Rose), R. pimpinellifolia (Burnet Rose),* and *R. eglanteria (Sweet Briar).*

WILLMOTT, ELLEN Authoress of 'Genus Rosa' published between 1910 and 1914 with illustrations painted by Alfred Parsons. This book is regarded as one of the milestones in rose literature, rivalling the work of Redouté.

WORLD FEDERATION OF ROSE SOCIETIES The rose societies of 17 nations belong to this worldwide organization which held its first meeting in New Zealand in 1971. It meets every few years, and its objects include establishing common standards for judging and classification, granting international awards, avoiding confusion over the naming of new roses and encouraging research.

WORLD'S FAVOURITE ROSE Competition run by the *World Federation of Rose Societies* in which each member society votes. Winners have been *Peace, Queen Elizabeth, Fragrant Cloud, Iceberg* and *Double Delight.*

Y

YORK ROSE The identity of the White Rose of York is not known for certain. It was probably *Rosa alba semi-plena,* but it may have been *R. arvensis.*

CHAPTER 12

ROSE INDEX